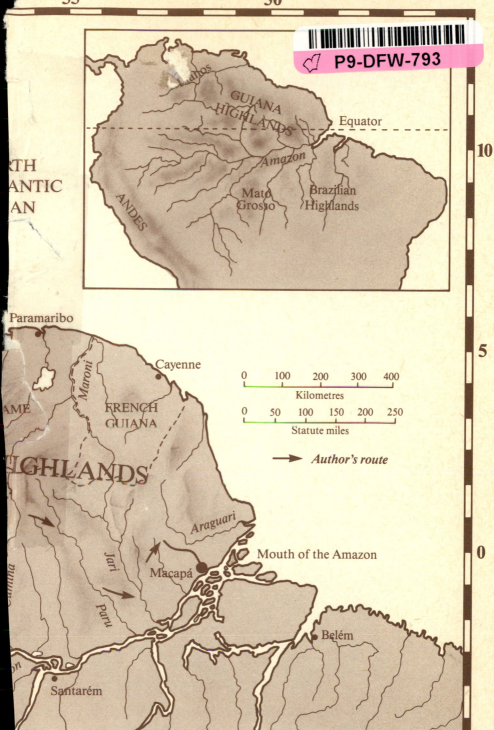

55

50

10

GUIANA
HIGHLANDS

Equator

Amazon

Mato
Grosso

Brazilian
Highlands

ANDES

RTH
ANTIC
AN

Paramaribo

Cayenne

5

FRENCH
GUIANA

Maroni

AME

HIGHLANDS

| 0 | 100 | 200 | 300 | 400 |

Kilometres

| 0 | 50 | 100 | 150 | 200 | 250 |

Statute miles

→ *Author's route*

Araguari

Jari

Mouth of the Amazon

0

Macapá

Paru

Guiana

Belém

Santarém

nd Amazon river mouths.

WHO GOES OUT
IN THE

WHO GOES OUT
IN THE
MIDDAY SUN?

BENEDICT ALLEN

An Englishman's Trek Through the Amazon Jungle

VIKING

VIKING
Viking Penguin Inc.
40 West 23rd Street,
New York, New York 10010, U.S.A.

First American Edition
Published in 1986
Copyright © Benedict Allen, 1985
All rights reserved

First published in Great Britain under the title *Mad White Giant*
by Macmillan London Limited.

Photographs from the author's collection.

LIBRARY OF CONGRESS CATALOGING IN PUBLICATION DATA
Allen, Benedict.
Who goes out in the midday sun?
1. Amazon River Valley — Description and travel.
2. Allen, Benedict — Journeys — Amazon River Valley.
I. Title.
F2546.A36   1986   918.1'10463   85-40778
ISBN 0-670-81032-0

Printed in the United States of America by
The Haddon Craftsmen, Scranton, Pennsylvania
Set in Plantin

*For my father, who is my inspiration,
and my mother, who is my 'prop, pillar and support'*

Contents

Part Three: The Test

Author's note

A great number of people steered me through the expedition's planning and execution. My gratitude to some, those mentioned in the text, should, I hope, be clear, but there are others whom I will always associate affectionately with the venture. Unfortunately space permits only a few of them to be included here.

Anna-Maria Pearson stoically tutored me in Spanish, over her kitchen table, for much of one winter. Roger Chapman, Robin Hanbury-Tenison, and Shane and Nigel Winser, amongst others, lent their precious expertise in the rooms of the Royal Geographical Society. Martin and Tanis Jordan, veterans of the jungle river also, were valued advisors during the bleak time of preparation – months blissfully ignored in the text.

Afterwards, it was Susan Locke who recuperated me in the peaceful hills above Rio. And when I was ready to return, my long-suffering immediate family and Charles Allen, Hilary Bradt and Bryan Hanson were all the most generous of stalwarts.

This book was eventually written between March and June 1984, and only then through the dedication, encouragement and tireless attention of my sister Kate Allen, who combed through it line by line, reviewing the drafts until they reached a measure of acceptability. I cannot thank her enough, nor my brother Stewart for putting up with it all. In addition, Vivien Green, my literary agent, has had patience beyond all reason during the evolution of the manuscript, and I am indebted to Alan Samson, my editor at Macmillan, for eyeing the result so sympathetically.

I have been at pains to omit more than fleeting anthropological, ecological and geographical references, but Nicholas Guppy, Dr John Hemming and Dr Peter Rivière, all champions of the Wai-wai and Tirió, have educated me in some aspects of my observations, which are written here only as *I* remember them, having travelled at great speed, lost many notes in the capsize, and become very ill near the end of the journey. Under these circumstances it would obviously be wrong to lend any serious interpretation to details I recall. My approach is exemplified by the lighthearted nature of the sketches that appear throughout the book.

These sketches have been lifted from my surviving notebooks, and those lost pages I remember. The 'survival diary' extracts presented in Chapters 17 and 18 were written during one sitting when I copied out the original text, elucidating when necessary as I went along.

I have wittingly disguised the identity of a handful of people and places, and contorted some dates and details to protect the more vulnerable characters in the book, and to uphold their privacy. This did *not* give me free rein to exaggerate: the journey across northeast Amazonia was perhaps achieved with greater hardship than is suggested in the text.

I have since contacted Gilberto Peña, the Madman, 'Fritz,' and am still in correspondence with the Sicilian cobbler of El Callao. I have plans to visit all those who will remember me, including a northern Englishman at Paraiso; the Carib Indians; the sole survivor of the goldmining gang attack; and the kind ladies of the hotel in Belém where I stayed while coping with malaria.

The book's only serious theme is the hope that the people of the forest will be allowed to live in the future they desire, and not the future desired for them by the outside world of *true* 'mad white giants.'

Part One

The Initiation

– 1 –

'No Need to Die'

When I first heard its name, Amazonia was a land of steaming jungle on the equator inhabited by naked savages. All the savages were headhunters and most would eat each other given half the chance. The fiercest of them were tribes of women warriors who cut off their right breasts to fire their arrows with greater ease. Their targets were mainly explorers, who roamed the forest in search of gold. But amongst these primitives were some Good Indians, and because explorers gave them presents of salt (hard to get in the jungle) they guided the white men through the wilderness. That was how it was to me at school, aged ten.

'The jungle is a mysterious world of darkness and insects,' the class mistress told us one day. 'Enormous snakes hang down from the creepers and wrap themselves around you, and squeeze you tighter and tighter until you suffocate.' The teacher, who was squeamish as well as romantic, stopped. Her face had gone ash white. We demanded to know more, but she said nothing. She stood motionless by the blackboard, with her hands gripped tight around her throat.

I imagined thick coils grappling with a moustached white man in a suit. I saw a struggle and then the snake being dispatched with repeated shots of a revolver, the bearded man straightening his pith helmet and tie, then walking away.

Months went by before I met anyone who had actually been to the Amazon. He was the father of Pinkerton-Smithe, a boy at school who had bragged that his father had just recently returned. I met him on Parents' Day.

He was easily recognizable as an explorer. He was tall and had a thick muscular neck. His beard was a black thicket. He had restless, intolerant eyes and looked much like the moustached white man who had executed the snake. I told him of the teacher's jungle and asked him the truth about the savages.

'The truth about the savages?' he said. 'The truth about the savages is that there aren't any.'

This was appalling, 'Aren't any?'

'Nope. Just people who have wars like us, and people whose lives aren't cluttered up by possessions, unlike ours.'

'The jungle is their larder. It's their home. What else do they need?' I wasn't sure. But Pinkerton-Smithe's father really seemed to know these people and their jungle. 'No, it's not the *Indians* who are the savages,' he said. Then, as if he thought that my teacher was as good an example as any of a savage: 'Teachers ought to know better than to fill children with garbage about which they know nothing.'

According to Pinkerton-Smithe's father, in the sixteenth century the jungle had been seething with Europeans 'all because a man called Cortez had made his name by conquering the Aztec Empire in Mexico, and become exceedingly rich on the spoils, like another man, Pizarro, who had plundered the Incas. And you can appreciate that all the adventurers of the day wanted to obtain the same wealth.' I said I could quite appreciate that. 'Well, straight away it looked as if they were in luck, because many Indians spoke of a lake in the jungle, the lake of El Dorado, the Gilded Man. Here was a tribe of such wealth, they said, that the chief used to anoint his body all over with gold dust, and wash it off with great ceremony in the lake water. Many explorers searched the jungle for this chiefdom. Sir Walter Raleigh from the Orinoco river, and the Dutch, Spanish, and even Irish from the Amazon.'

'Did anyone find El Dorado, then?' I asked.

'Nope. But explorers still go out to that jungle in search of it. They go, but some never come back.'

What Mr Pinkerton-Smithe had said, about the lost explorers more than the gold, excited me. Although my teacher had got it wrong – there were no breastless female savages – this was still a land of mystery. A place for the explorer.

If only I were older, I thought, then I could go there too.

Eight more school years drifted by, during which I developed a passion for fossils. Belemnites and ammonites mostly, they were dug up, dusted down and then maintained in orderly rows in the garden shed. To my parents it was a harmless enough hobby but, tramping mile upon mile of the rich blue lias cliffs of Lyme Regis, I unwittingly fostered the wanderlust that had seeded itself deep inside me. Once I was released from school, the fossils were no longer enough.

So I began to work on a plan. It was a simple one: to journey between the mouths of the Orinoco and the Amazon, through the heart of that El Dorado land. I found it was a route no one had attempted before; not even the explorers who had used the lower, slow-water stretches of both during the search for treasure. I bought some maps, inspected them closely, then saw why.

The mangrove forests of the Orinoco mouth looked straightforward enough. There was even what looked like a dirt track leading south through the jungle, out of the Orinoco system and up through hilly savannah. It was beyond this, at the end of the track, coming down again off the lip of the Amazon basin, that there would be difficulties. I would have to head east for seven hundred miles, across one of the remotest sections of Amazonian jungle, hopping the gaps between half a dozen different tributaries along the way. Only then would I reach the Amazon mouth. For someone who had never set eyes on the rain forest, and whose longest journey had been while backpacking in Greece, it certainly would be hard.

'Impossible' was the word chosen by specialists, when I broached the plan.

'What will happen if one of your expedition party gets a jungle fever? You wouldn't get to a village for months.'

'How do you think you'll get in all your food supplies? By helicopter or something? If so, where are you getting the money from? I can't imagine anyone *sponsoring* a scheme like this. You'll need the army at your disposal and God knows what else.'

'Are you stupid or something?'

I was beginning to admit that I was, when one day an idea came to me out of the blue. Why not write off to that explorer Pinkerton-Smithe, the man who had scorned my teacher's romantic jungle so long ago? *He* would offer advice and encouragement. What an inspiration he had been to me as a boy! He was sure to remember me.

He didn't, but that was the least of the shocks in store.

I had sent a note to him suggesting a rendezvous at the Royal Geographical Society, ten-thirtyish in the New Map Room. The man who came was a bent-over figure who had the look of a shrivelled-up prune. Mr Pinkerton-Smithe had transformed into an old man in those ten years. His beard was thin and like an old goat's. It hung like a hank of wool. I thought that a lifetime of exploration must finally have got to his health.

There was worse. He didn't like my expedition plans. He didn't even admire my optimism. At first he just stood shaking his head at the maps and tut-tutting.

'Do you realize how far you intend to go?' he said, after a while, sliding his thin fingers across the blank, green, unmapped spaces on the charts, tracing my intended route. He had observed that it took him four paces to cross the floor from one end of the maps to the other.

I said: 'One and a half thousand miles, as the crow flies.'

'As the vulture flies, you mean!' He chuckled loudly at his little joke. 'You can't plough straight through the jungle, you know.'

Pinkerton-Smithe wasn't talking like an explorer one bit. He seemed to have an almost cowardly fear of the jungle.

I said, 'Yes, I appreciate that.'

'Humph. Suppose you have *some* idea about what the jungle's like?'

'Of course I have.'

'Well?'

I paraphrased all I'd learnt. 'Well, the number of plants and animal species is very high in comparison to most temperate ecosystems. The soils are low in nutrients and heavily leached—'

Pinkerton-Smithe was breathing out heavily. 'No, no, no. That doesn't sound like the Amazon at all. You see, the Amazon is not like any ordinary jungle. For a start, everything there is bigger. I don't mean just your trees. I'm talking about spiders large enough to straddle a man's chest; killer snakes which people haven't yet got round to finding a name for; and—'

Was this man scared of snakes wrapping round his neck too? He was speaking just like my schoolmistress, and I couldn't believe my ears. I felt swindled.

'– and frogs that cluck like hens; and spiders that entice birds by rubbing their bristly legs like crickets. *That's* what the jungle is like.'

'But your expeditions. . . . You went off to the Amazon jungle.

Pinkerton-Smithe's jungle

You weren't bothered by the snakes, the crocodiles, the malaria
. . . were you?'

'Me go off to the Amazon jungle?' He looked again at the maps
and wagged his head. 'You're joking! I went on a pleasure cruise
up the main river.' He let the memories float through his head.
'Great ship . . . smashing bars . . . had a whale of a time. Two
weeks of bliss . . . they even gave us natural history lectures about
the jungle. I remember something I was told – what was it? Oh,
yes: the Indians aren't savages, they're just like us. Words to that
effect. Sounds funny, doesn't it? Load of nonsense. Just think of
them running around with bows and arrows – out there! Still, I
thought it was an interesting idea at the time.'

'You aren't an explorer, then?'

'Aah! Not me. But it's a hell hole, the jungle, believe me. Now
I'll excuse me, I've got to rush.' He was already on his way

I listened to his shoes squeaking along the corridor, then glanced down at the maps. What now?

This was the New Map Room. Perhaps more expeditions had been born here than in any other room in the world. To my right, across the floor on the far wall, was a portrait of Robert Falcon Scott. On the other wall, amongst others, hung H. M. Stanley. In front was a scale model of Everest, still commemorating the first successful bid for the summit, but dust now filled in the crevasses. Outside was a polished lump of black tree trunk. It bore a modest slip of cardboard, with the words in faded inktype: 'Section of the tree from the shores of Lake Bangweulu, Central Africa, under which the heart of Dr Livingstone was buried.'

'Damn!' I said aloud, and walked out.

In the next four years I passed through university, clocking up experience on expeditions to the world's last remote scraps along the way. In the virgin jungle of Costa Rica our party scooped up research samples of boiling mud from the cone of a volcano. joined an expedition of Gurkha soldiers to Brunei, and there netted bird-like moths, and bottled jungle wasps for science. Th I led fellow graduates to a distant glacier, where we meas pioneering plants, stared into crevasses and grew nur blizzards. It was all very interesting, but it was not enough

Not knowing what to do with myself, I hung on through one more academic year. Sometimes I dreamt once more of travelling the lands between the Orinoco and Amazon river mouths, but each time I dug out the maps and drew up plans, the experts, through weight of numbers, forced me into agreement. No, my expedition was just not practicable.

And that would have been that, had I not recalled something Pinkerton-Smithe had said ages ago. The memory came late one summer night, and sent me leaping out of bed. He had been talking about the Indians. He had probably picked up the phrase while sipping a gin and tonic on his Amazon cruiser. 'The jungle is their larder. What else do they need?'

The answer was 'nothing', and two thoughts fused together in my mind. The first was that taking an expedition anywhere using alien, Western technology and ignoring indigenous skills has little to do with true exploration. The second was that the Indians, not outsiders, should determine whether or not my journey through the land between the Orinoco and the Amazon was possible. If it was, then I must go alone, place my trust in them, and win their acceptance. I must learn to live much as one of them.

'The jungle is their home,' Pinkerton-Smithe had said. The Indians, if they wished, would guide me through it.

'Jungle Eddie' McGee, so people said, could survive in the starkest, most desolate place anyone could dream up. In any cold or hot desert, he could dine out on the land ('There's always food lying around somewhere') and simply thrive in the jungle ('Can't wait to get at those fat piranhas'). The wilderness gave him food, shelter and even medicine. He would treat wounds by binding up the gash with a cobweb. On top of the cobweb he would sprinkle the black spores of puffball toadstools, and the penicillin in the fungus would restore him to health. He was that sort of man.

When I first came across him he was standing on the lawn of the Royal Geographical Society. It was February 1982. There was a bitter wind. Snow was forecast. Eddie McGee was about to talk to a crowd of scientists who were planning modern-style expeditions to the rain forests. The title of the talk was 'No Need to Die'.

'All right. Gather round, please.'

The crowd shuffled forward. Some people were still nattering: 'You know that book called *The Jungle is Neutral*?'

'Yeah. The one by Spencer Chapman. True story, they say.'

'Well, if the jungle is neutral, why in God's name are we standing here in the perishing cold being taught how to survive in it?'

Eddie McGee said he'd appreciate it if he could have the group's attention. He was a short, compact man with a weathered face and alert eyes. He was sure to know something the Indians wouldn't.

'Now, I'm going to tell you a bit about how to cope if something goes wrong on your expedition. You'll all have your emergency arrangements, naturally – for rescue parties, evacuations and so on – but you can never be too cautious.'

Emergency arrangements. I wasn't going to have any *emergency arrangements*, and the words made me flinch.

'What do we mean by a "survivor"? Anyone?'

Silence fell. Someone sneezed.

'Well, I'll tell you. A survivor is a person who fights when others die.' He paused for effect, tweaking a button on the cuff of his army smock. It was sewn on with fishing line. 'And "survival". What is "survival"? It's fighting to live on when all hope has gone.'

Just then a crisp snowflake landed on the toe of one of his black boots. Everyone saw it and watched for it to melt. It did not.

'Now, if you remember only one thing today—' He waited for the attention of one man who was looking up at the white sky.

'Sorry.'

' – now if you remember only *one thing* today,' he repeated, 'let it be this: nothing counts more in a survival situation than our attitude. All right? Our *will to survive*.'

He had said this to set us thinking, but most people were trying to hide a smile, turning to each other as if taking partners for a dance. *They* wouldn't be in a survival situation. Not even a panic situation. Those were their thoughts, and their flippancy isolated me. I thought of them crowding the trees in the jungle with their 'emergency arrangements', and then thought of myself alone out there, living like an Indian. The vision in my head was of a gangling white man looking ridiculous in a loincloth. I wanted to forget the whole idea.

Eddie McGee took two paces backwards to a spot on the lawn between two wiry shrubs.

'Come this way, please. Now, the greatest killers in most survival situations are: one, the cold; two, wetness; three, the wind.' The audience shuffled as they made a show of turning their collars up and shivering. 'But in the jungle our main problem is wetness. So. We need to build a shelter, right? This is how we do it.'

He drew a string of fishing line from his clothing and strung some shrivelled leaves on it. Then he made a frame of twigs and covered it with the leaf chains. In a few minutes it was a tent, the leaves like roof tiles over it.

'Remember that in the jungle you've got leaves all around you to choose from.' By now every member of that audience was riveted. Eddie McGee had a habit of conjuring up things from nowhere. This man was a magician.

'One thing in passing. Don't camp near a river. In the tropics they swell and sweep over the banks, even after the shortest of downpours.' He remembered something else. 'Oh yes, and don't camp on a game trail. There was this man who went off to the jungle just last year. It was his own fault. Went by himself, the idiot. Got lost, of course. Lost everything. Followed the survival instructions. Managed to make a lovely tent from leaves as he'd been taught. At last things began to look up. He even found a nice bare patch of ground to camp on. Trouble was, it didn't belong to him, and at the crack of dawn he was flattened by a hippo. So *think* animal, *be* animal. OK? And that goes for tracking and snaring, which I'll talk about in a minute.

'Next most important thing: making a fire. Any boy scouts among you lot?' He showed how to rub two sticks together. 'You can't use any old sticks, mind you.' When he'd lit up some bark chips with the spark and blown up the flames, he spoke about cooking. 'I assume you all know how to skin a snake?' When the fire was dead he fished out a black splinter of charcoal from the ash and said, holding it up, 'One of nature's best medicines. Eat it and it will cure your stomach ache.'

I said: 'After eating that snake, you're going to need it.' My voice carried further than expected. Eddie McGee turned to face me and said:

'And what exactly are *you* going to be doing in a jungle?'

I told him.

'Pheweeee! How long a journey is that?'

I told him.

'Pheweeee!' He looked me up and down, so closely that I felt naked. 'Well, I hope you know what you're doing.'

★

During later months, while Eddie McGee was off on a chase after a
wanted murderer (the man was tracked step by step to a desolate
moorland hideout), I was working in a Hampshire warehouse. The
job was to pack books, which still smelt fresh from the printers,
into cardboard boxes for the dispatch department. It was a routine
that stretched my back and thickened my fingers, but the staff
were sympathetic, and allowed me to concentrate on my plan. At
the end of it all, I had financed the entire expedition as well as kept
up with the rent.

By February 1983 I was ready to depart for the Orinoco delta.

'Tell me,' said Eddie McGee, when I saw him for the last time,
and he had finished explaining how a wound could be wiped clean
with a feather, 'how old are you?'

'Twenty-two.'

'What do your parents think of the idea?'

'They say they're worried that I'm going alone.'

'Alone? You didn't tell me you were going *alone*.' Eddie McGee,
that tough, weather-beaten man who used cobwebs instead of
linen to bandage his cuts, appeared stunned. 'Look. Do you mind
me giving one more bit of advice?'

I said, 'No. Of course not.' But I was sure he was leading up to
say that I was an idiot to attempt this journey, like the man who
had been flattened by the hippo.

'Just remember this simple rule. *Never bluff. Always know your
stuff.* If you abide by that, I think you'll pull through.' He smiled.
'With luck, anyway.'

'Thanks,' I said. 'I'll bear that in mind.'

'Bye, then,' he said, clamping my hand in his.

'Bye.'

– 2 –

Tucupita
and its mystery

According to the maps, the town of Tucupita was perched on the very edge of the Orinoco delta. So when I arrived in Venezuela I headed there straight away. From Caracas I bussed through a series of messy towns, and when these ended I caught a lift in a car. We drove along straight red dust roads in the open heat, and through swampy grasses. Sometimes the swamps were more like lakes, and then there were cows daydreaming knee-deep in them between flocks of fishing birds.

Occasionally we swept through clumps of roadside houses, also messy. We stopped at one for a midday coffee. This was a town of tin sheeting and concrete blocks, banana palms and slumped men in doorways. Some of the houses were only huts. Their walls were grey and cracked and had lizards running up and down them. Inside there were only hammocks, fallen plaster and hens.

We moved on again. The road began to buck the car.

As we neared the delta I expected the air to become sticky and to hang heavily on my skin, but instead the swamps dried up into bald cracked earth patches. Some of the cows looked dead and I saw anthills for the first time, which were baked solid. As we passed through Tucupita's suburbs, the driver said that if it was the delta I had come to see, then I'd better take a look on the other side of town. There was no shortage of it there.

There was dust on the trees when I arrived. The Orinoco was low, judging by its banks, and the locals said that at this time of year the rain came only in light afternoon showers. Then it was directed into roadside troughs. Sometimes there was water on the streets, but that was when the troughs were clogged. Then fish-fry darted in the black water, picking clean the bones of dead dogs.

Life here centred on the town square, the Plaza Bolivar. It had trees with whitewashed trunks, sloths in the branches, concrete benches and courting couples. If there was a way through the forests to the sea, the real start of my journey, I'd find it there.

I took a stroll along the riverside and stared across the water to the forests. I practised my Spanish on a leaf sweeper and two teenage schoolgirls with blue jeans and exercise books under their arms. The one called Mereida wrote, 'Is very beautiful when we meet a friend', in my notebook.

Then I went for an early evening drink.

The bar was beside the plaza, and at the counter was a man in a tight suit with no front teeth and green eyes. He called for a beer and sat down opposite me. He was Señor Dolci, he said, and lived just down the road. He scratched a living by tinkering with broken-down transistor radios. After two more beers I learnt that Señor Dolci was from Uruguay. He was a writer, and had escaped during a military coup, leaving behind everything he loved. He showed me what he still possessed of his family – a creased photo of two shy children and a pretty woman. He called them his 'little ones'. He had jumped out of the bathroom window when the soldiers came for him, and hadn't had time to say goodbye. He wondered, drinking down the sixth beer, whether they were still alive.

Señor Dolci said I could sleep on his floor, and he led off into the dark back streets. He walked fast, as if I was chasing him. After a while we were at a yard strewn with empty non-returnable beer bottles. I could sleep anywhere I liked, he said. This empty yard (empty but for the refuse) was his home.

He barricaded us in from the street with a corrugated iron sheet. He said he thought we were quite safe tonight because there was moonshine. When there wasn't, Indians came out from the trees and went around robbing.

I stretched out a blanket on the earth, and lay down. Señor Dolci unfurled a mattress. Just as I was about to drop off to sleep he told me a story.

'Years back, when I first settled here, an Indian boy strolled into town and caused a sensation. He was straight from the jungle and stark naked. It happens like that sometimes. Indians see the bright lick of paint on the fishing boats out in the delta, and come nearer and nearer the town to see what's going on. They come close enough to smell the petrol fumes, which only fires their curiosity even more. Then they come right into the town hub, and scamper around the streets under cover of the dark. Then, just when they think they've had enough, and it's time to go back again into the forests to live with the monkeys, they find they can't. They're trapped, because now they've seen too much – snazzy dresses on the clothes lines, bars with men guzzling down spirits, children stomping to transistor music. They're hooked. And of course the only way they can satisfy their lust for these things is to rob for them.

'Well, anyway, one day this boy came into town as naked as the day he was born. Nothing much unusual about that, you're thinking, but immediately the townspeople saw there was something odd about this boy. His fingers were more like claws for a start.'

Señor Dolci was curling up the fingers of both hands so they looked like talons. He rasped the air under the moonlight, then went on.

'This boy was utterly bewildered by all the buildings and noise, of course, so all the people could get him to say was one string of Indian words. The *padre* of the mission kind of adopted the boy, and said he was saying, "My brother in *selva*. My brother in *selva*."

'The *selva* is what we call the jungle around here. Anyway, the *padre* put two and two together and decided that the boy was telling him that his brother had got himself into some sort of trouble in the *selva*. The obvious thing to do was to get a party of townspeople to go with the boy to look for him, and that was exactly what they did, on the morning after the boy first appeared. The *padre* dressed up the boy, washed him down, christened him and hacked his nails down to size. But try as he might he couldn't get shoes on to the Indian's feet. The toes pointed outwards. They'd never been near leather in their lives.

'So the rescue party canoed off out of sight, the boy in a brand-new suit but with bare feet.

'Days went by. They hadn't come back. They'd taken enough food for ten days. Those days passed, and more. Still no sign. People got worried. They sent out a rescue party to rescue the rescue party. But those townsfolk came back fagged out saying they had found nothing.

'All this might have been a mystery, except that one day a month or two later – I think it was in the wet season – who should come into town but the Indian boy? He was back to his own ways. He was naked except for a ribbon of bark around his hips. He had a fringe of black hair – right into his eyes it was – and his nails had grown back into claws. And yet he looked just a bit different.

'Of course the crowd swarmed around him like bees. As you can appreciate, these people wanted to know what he had done to the party of men who'd been with him. But he kept his mouth shut, tried to look as sweet as pie, and pointed out to the forests, where the party had last been seen.

'Now, this boy was in trouble, bad trouble. The police sensed dirty play and wouldn't let him go off again into the jungle. The women wailed at him, and almost managed a lynching. Twenty husbands had disappeared into the blue, and this boy had the only answer.

'The boy was sent off to the mission, and the *padre* set about making him presentable again: hair parting on the right, another new suit, and the shoes. But guess what? It wasn't the same boy! Yes, it was the long-lost brother. Would you believe it?'

On the whole, no, I thought.

'Do you know how they found out it wasn't the same boy? Well, when it was time for the *padre* to have a go at getting the shoes on to the boy – this time he was going to get them on whatever effort it cost him – he found the boy had an extra toe on either foot. Imagine that! Six toes!'

Señor Dolci kicked his sandals in the air, spread his toes and stared at them. 'Yes, *señor*, six toes.'

I said, 'What happened to the other brother?'

'I'm coming to that. Well, the *padre* tried his best to get the Indian boy to talk, but after two weeks he'd discovered absolutely nothing new about his brother. Or anything else for that matter. Then, one dawn, the *padre* climbed out of bed for mass, and found a pile of clothes there on the bedroom floor. They were the Indian's, and he'd gone.

'This time the *padre* organized the search party for himself. He took a bunch of Indians – mostly his converts – and went out into the delta in another canoe. By some extraordinary stroke of luck they managed to pick up the boy's trail. They tracked him day after day until one afternoon they came to a clearing. And there, sitting in the middle of the camp, were the Indian twins.

'No one else was to be seen.

'They were naked of course, except for the ring of bark around their waists, and they were busy cooking up a monkey to eat, turning it over on a spit in the flames of a fire. There was something funny about the clearing, and the *padre* and Indians could see exactly what it was. Around the edge of the camp was a circle of long sticks. They might have been acting as fence posts, except that sitting on the top of each one was a human skull. The skulls faced away from the camp towards the jungle around, and each one was grinning. The boys were surrounded by their ancestors.

'The *padre*'s Indians got the jitters and said they weren't going a step nearer. They said anyone who went into the camp would be cursed. So the only white man, the *padre*, stalked forward alone.

'Just before the boys caught sight of him he leapt on them. He held one down, but the other, the Indian with the extra toes, squirmed out of his grip, and got away. They dragged the first brother kicking and screaming back to the canoe. He died of fever before they got back to town. Very strange.

'At the Indian camp, the *padre* had knocked the skulls off the sticks. His party poked around for signs of the original search party. They found nothing. Not at the beginning, anyway.

'But before setting off again back to the town, the group decided to eat up the monkey the boys had been roasting. It was a little black and charred now, but it was a shame to waste it, and they had a long journey ahead of them. Anyway, they set about it with their machetes and took great bites from the monkey, when one of the men let out an almighty scream.'

Dolci sucked air through the gap in his front teeth. 'Then every man there spat out the meat he was chewing. Spat it out as fast as he could. One of them even puked up.'

'Why? Was the meat bad or something?'

'No.'

'Why did the man scream, then?'

'Because on the arm of the monkey was a silver bracelet.' Dolci's voice was shrill. 'A silver bracelet on a monkey's arm! Can you imagine such a thing?'

I caught a glint of his teeth in the moonshine, and knew he was smiling.

'No, of course you can't. Because what they were chewing wasn't monkey at all. It was a human baby! Then it struck them that the skulls around the camp weren't ancestors at all. They were the original search party. Yes, you've got it. These boys were cannibals!' Señor Dolci got to his feet and released a sequence of low chuckles.

'What a story the *padre* had to tell to the townsfolk of Tucupita! And – ' his voice went hushed ' – and all this might have been forgotten now, but for one thing. A few days ago, so I'm told, an Indian fisherman came in from the delta saying he'd seen human footprints in the sand. The toenails, he said, must have looked more like claws, because they left spikes in the sand. The prints were weird because they had six toes on each foot!' Dolci lay on his mattress and rolled over with a blanket. 'And you say you *want* to go out there, *señor*?'

Next morning, after no sleep, I went along to the mission to check the story. A clerk told me the *padre* was out administering the Gospel to some freshly arrived Indians. But my visit was not wasted. He'd left behind his Indian language dictionary: Spanish into Warao. I slid it from the shelf and thumbed it through, scribbling down the words for 'water', 'food', 'hello', 'goodbye', 'thank you', 'sorry', 'no', 'yes', 'me', 'you', 'understand', 'transport', 'friend', and 'danger'.

Next I sat in the shade of a tree in the plaza, and wondered how I was going to find a passage through the delta forests to the sea. I had read of only one Englishman who had passed through the midst of the forests, and that was Sir Walter Raleigh in 1595. The delta almost killed him. In the library of the Royal Geographical Society there was a book all about it, and I'd taken it home to Hampshire for a good read. Raleigh was on his way to find the elusive 'great and golden city' of El Dorado, and so far the expedition had proved promising. He'd captured a Portuguese ship full of wine on his Atlantic crossing, and had used it to ply the Spanish on Trinidad with it, obtaining what he thought were the secrets of El Dorado from them. He sped away – looking forward to his fortune – up the delta, and got lost in a complex of channels. Driven to despair, Raleigh nearly executed his incompetent guide. In the nick of time another guide came along. They might have wandered a whole year in that labyrinth, Raleigh said.

I spent days waiting in the plaza, asking how I should go about travelling through the delta. Old men ambling by used to press coins into the palm of my hand and say I should buy myself a drink.

The Indians had always seemed the best bet. I was sure they would know the delta, if anyone did. One of them was a boy who matched exactly Señor Dolci's description of the cannibal boys, except that instead of a bark strip around his waist he had a pair of tatty shorts on. He stared in awe at passers-by from behind the mango trees, ran when he crossed open spaces in the town, and jumped when car doors were slammed. One cool morning I left a bolivar coin at my side for him to take, and as I pretended to write my diary entry he sneaked up, took it, and ran for his life. That afternoon he was back and grabbed another one, without glancing at me.

This went on for two days, and in all that time he didn't say a word. He watched me dolefully from the other side of the plaza, waiting for me to put out another coin.

On the third day a sloth fell from a branch above my head, demolished the bench and almost concussed me. On the fourth I managed to get across to the boy what I wanted him to find out. And on the fifth, after a soft yellow sunrise, the boy came, and from a distance of about twenty yards beckoned me to follow.

He took me away from the paved roads, down a dusty track, along an alleyway of bruised-faced Indian women with children crying around their feet. This was a different Tucupita to the one I'd seen before. I felt embarrassed by it. The men pitched around drunk, and the concrete enclosure provided by a benefactor as a place where the Indians could hang up their hammocks had the stink of a horse's stable.

We were walking along the waterfront now. Nude Indian children with jaundiced skin and brown teeth were running out with their palms outstretched, pleading for money. Across a breeze-block wall was daubed: '*Cristo = miseria y hambre*' ('Christ = misery and hunger'). Further out, on the town's outskirts, we passed a roadside tree with a hand-painted sign high up the trunk: '*Cristo es tu amigo*'. It had been tacked up out of reach.

We dropped down to the riverside beach, into the shade of the acacia trees. There were plenty of Indians there, but no shacks to house them; just hammocks strung between trees above the river jetsam. These Indians were even sicker than the others. Flies walked over them. They were irritated by my intrusion, and I kept close behind the boy. They looked as if they wanted to get out of their hammocks to beat me up, but were too weak. The air fizzled with flies and stank of the putrid fish washed up along the shoreline.

Amongst all this was another white man. He was distinguishable from the Indians not because he was white but because he had no stoop and was strongly built. Nearer I saw his hands were large and thick. He was inspecting the hull of a dugout canoe. His trousers were rolled above the knees and his feet were in the surf. A fisherman, I thought.

The Indian boy nodded at the man, and ran off, kicking up the white sand and not looking back. In all the week I had known him, he had never said a word.

The man asked me in Spanish what I wanted, not taking his eyes off the canoe, where his fingers were smoothing over some cracks.

I told him that I needed a lift through the delta forests. He laughed and said we could talk about it over a meal, perhaps, but not out here in the stink and heat. He made a living trading with the Indians, he said. *They* caught the fish, with the help of his brother and his modern fishing tackle, and *he* kept a storehouse where the fish was salted and prepared for market.

He said his name was Juliano. He walked me to his storehouse, snatched a stiff dried fish from the top of a pile, and later, back at his hut, ordered his wife to prepare it for us. Juliano's hair was a snowy white. He looked about sixty and his teeth were few and far between, but large, like tusks. His wife had a face as scaly as the fish she was handling. She beat it soft over a log in the back yard.

Juliano listened to my plans while we gnawed at the fish, and said he would get some Indians to take me the very next day. He was sending some men out to collect some fish from a remote village by the sea.

I asked him to show me the village on the map.

'You make fun of me, *señor*. The village doesn't even have a name.' He said he would scribble a letter of introduction for me to give to his brother at the village. The Indians were uneasy about strangers, and it would pave my way considerably.

I was to come back at sunrise.

As I was leaving, he said, 'You know, it's a wonder that you got that boy to bring you to me at all. He's deaf and dumb. And he's an orphan. No one knows where he comes from, and I've tried my best to find out where he sleeps at night but can't. How he survives at all I just don't know. You're the first person to have communicated with him for years. That's why I'm helping you.'

– 3 –

Delta beauty

We slipped away from the riverbank before the sun was high. I had carefully added two baskets of bread rolls to my baggage, as presents to the village. Two of Juliano's Indian fishermen piloted the canoe. They were very different from the Indians I had seen clinging to the outskirts of Tucupita, who had had stick-like arms, and legs as thin as my wrists. These Indians had a good knowledge of Spanish, not just a smattering; their eyes were sharp and their bodies thick and muscular. Their skin was shiny, as if it had been polished.

One of the fishermen sat at the bow, trailing his legs in the spray; the other was at the helm, steering. The motor pushed us along in jerks, coughing up oily blue smoke, and leaving a streaky rainbow smear behind on the water. For a while we passed riverside huts, and banks of open grassland with crocodiles sprawling in the sun. Some lay with their mouths gaping open, and small birds with beaks like pliers hopped in and out picking food from their teeth.

As we went along, the Indian at the helm told the story of the Italian twin brothers, Juliano and Alfredo, and how they came to be with the Indians.

They had been brought up in Rome, where they had lived in a large, fashionable house, the two eldest offspring of a very religious family. The other children were girls, all eight of them. The mother of the family spoiled the children, but this was more than compensated for by their father, who was a stern, pious man and who ruled them, especially the boys, with a rod of iron. He would beat them mercilessly for the slightest wrongdoing, and as often as the fancy took him.

The boys were playing football together early one morning in the walled courtyard. Most of the neighbourhood was still asleep – it was a Sunday – but they played quietly so as not to wake anyone. There is nothing wrong with a quiet game of football, you might think. Their father had not expressed the wish that they shouldn't be playing. The mother was smiling, looking on as she had many times before. But when the father arrived on the scene and saw what his sons were doing, he began to scream blue murder. '*Ave Maria!*' he said. 'What do you think you're doing? This is the sabbath. The Lord's day. A day of rest. And here you are playing *football*! May you be forgiven!'

Well, the boys knew that their father, at least, wasn't about to forgive them. Knowing he had nothing to lose, Juliano spoke up. 'But, Papa, you've never before complained when we were playing football on the sabbath. Why now?'

The father did not reply. He was fuming with rage, and kept on walking in the direction of the cupboard where he kept his beating stick.

The mother leaned down and whispered, 'You're for it now! Why did you say that? You know that your father's a proud man. No one ever dares to question his authority.'

The family assembled for the caning, as if for a military parade. All eight sisters and the mother were lined up in a single rank to watch the delivery of the punishment.

'Let this be a lesson to you all,' the father said, addressing the entire family, including his wife. Then he ordered the sons to bend over, and flogged them.

To his friends, the father would justify this severity by saying a strict upbringing would prepare them for the worst rigours of life. 'The essence of my philosophy,' he would explain, 'is that you must be cruel to be kind. But, in case you think my children will bear a grudge against me and grow up to hate me for what I'm doing, I am setting them a test. On the day that they come of age, I will give both boys a letter addressed to my bank, instructing the cashier to pay out to my sons whatever sum of money they nominate. Now, you know that I'm a rich man, but I can tell you that when the day comes the boys will not wish to take a single coin from me.'

The day came. The twins had grown up and left school. The father summoned them to his study, and in front of one of his closest friends addressed his sons.

'You know that I've been hard on you, but you must know also that I love you dearly. I have given you more preparation for life than any other man in Rome. But now you are no longer boys, and for the first time I'm going to let you express your true feeling for me – your hatred or your love. In fact, you can demonstrate the exact price you put on your gratitude.' He waved the envelopes containing the instructions to the bank. 'Before you open them, I want to repeat that I think I have done more than my duty as father. I have sent you to the best schools in Rome, but I myself have taught you more than you learnt there. I have taught you how to survive. Sometimes I have not been fair, but that was for this reason: life is not fair either. It's tough and unpredictable. That's why, for instance, a long time ago I beat you for playing football on the sabbath. So think about your choice carefully, and tell me your answer in the morning.' He dismissed them, smiling confidently at his friend. Never in his life had he been disobeyed by his sons – or by his wife, for that matter.

Alfredo and Juliano considered their upbringing carefully. They talked it over all night, while their father slept soundly in the security of what he thought his sons would decide. Finally the sons reached what they felt was a fair decision.

Instead of waiting to go to their father's study at the arranged time, Alfredo and Juliano slipped away from the house at sunrise, kissing their eight sisters goodbye before they went. First thing that morning they presented the letters to the bank and cashed a sizeable chunk of their father's fortune. They withdrew all his money but put back just enought to keep a wife and family of eight children from starving in the gutter; no more, no less.

Freedom tasted sweet. They fled from Rome laden with cash, caught a boat overseas, and for the next few years drifted around the nightclubs of the world with a set of loose friends.

At each stop they whittled away their fortune; Paris, Monte Carlo, London, Rio and finally Caracas. By the time they sobered, ten years had slipped away. They had lost their wealth and their, shallow friends. They were thrown out of a back-street brothel in a wild frontier town, drunk on their last money. That night a bunch of Indians came across the brothers lying in a roadside gutter, with the vultures squabbling over them. The Indians carried them away on their shoulders, back to their huts in the forest, and restored them to health over several months. The brothers had lived with the Indians ever since. That frontier town was Tucupita, twenty years ago.

The river narrowed, the trees closed in, and there were no more riverside huts. We were alone.

The Indian at the bow yelled at intervals to divert us away from approaching snares: 'Rock to the left!' or 'Shallows to the right!' We continued weaving along like this, startling birds from branches, until darkness fell. Then, just as the fireflies rose, pricking the sky with darting lights, we turned up a narrow creek. The engine slowed, and I saw more fireflies. But these ones were bigger than the others and were not darting. They were stationary, hanging far up the riverbank. As I came nearer I saw that they were orange flames. About a dozen of them, each one standing alone. Just as I realized they were lanterns, dogs started barking at our approach. This was a village. Now some of the lights were jogging through the darkness towards us. I smelt the sooty reek of the oil flames before I heard the voices. A greeting was exchanged. The words were sung rather than spoken. Warao is a light, sweet language, and lends itself to lullabies.

We moored up by the roots of the bank, and a dozen voices jabbered by the side of the canoe in the darkness. Someone held an oil lamp high above the canoe to light me up. When they saw that my hair was fair there was some heated discussion. The language switched to Spanish.

Several male voices called out that they were glad to meet me.

It seemed unlikely. Mosquitoes were chewing at us, the night was growing cold and damp, and the female voices further into the darkness were appealing to the men to come back to their hammocks. The canoe lurched. Two heavy Indians clambered in, the motor started to judder again, and again I felt a wet draught on my face. We were moving, and soon we were once more in the forest groves with leaves slapping our cheeks. Later I understood that two new Indians had come on board to guide the canoe through this part of the maze of delta channels. The first two Indians had been left behind. During the night we stopped three times, and each time swopped two more Indians. Each pair knew every turn, every rock and every sandbank of their neighbourhood. Sometimes we had to get out and walk in only ankle-deep water and drag the canoe over shelves of soft mud. Other times we cut the motor dead to listen to the water flow.

That was how we managed to navigate the delta where Raleigh had almost failed. It pleased me, for we had done much of it in the dark, with not even a torch to guide us. Only twice did we strike the bottom unexpectedly and nearly spill out, and both times the sandbanks were newly spawned.

By daylight I could see the occasional Indian camps – palm shacks with waterfronts of brown mud; thin, silent children gaping at us from doorways; women, with melon breasts, bent double over tin cooking pots; men lolling in hammocks.

That night, as cold as the last, I was woken by a new, fresh tang in the breeze. I snapped off a leaf. It felt thick and shiny, not like the feathery ones of the day before. I licked my finger and dabbed it on the leaf, then smelt it: salt. We were in the mangrove swamps, and must be nearing the sea.

We arrived mid-morning the next day. Coming out from the trees, the water ruffled, and a seascape spread out before us. It was not a sea of clear green water as I'd hoped, but a thin brown soup of swirling choppy currents. And there in the middle of that sea was the Indian village: a line of huts, built on stilts. It must have been much the same view that the first Europeans had, coming along the South American coast for the first time: simple wooden scaffolded structures, shimmering above the waves. In a fit of nostalgia they saw in them a 'little Venice'. So they called the new land Venezuela.

Children sighted us first. They were naked, and against the sun their bodies looked black and dull. They stood still at first, uninterested, as if waiting at a bus stop. Then they spotted me, my pale skin, and they yelled and skipped the length of the village. In the wind I heard the creaking of the planks and poles that were strung along between the huts as walkways. The huts were open-sided and roofed with palm leaves. I could see inside some; no sign of adults, only empty hammocks, and untended cooking pots.

We came nearer. The children were surging to the front. The tide was low and so the village was perched high up out of the water. Flayed bark on the stilts quivered in the breeze. We looped a mooring line around a pole. A rope was let down from above and I attached its end to my baggage. A chain of boys hauled up the rope in a series of jerks, chanting as they heaved. Seeing no way up for myself, I took off my canvas shoes and shinned up one of the stilts. On the way I passed a section of green slime, and then at the tide line a crust of salt crystals, which scratched me and tore my trousers open. It took several attempts to reach the village platform; each time I failed, the children burst out laughing. Later I learnt that even the oldest members of the village had the strength to swing themselves up with their arms.

Once up, the two Indians in the canoe tossed up my shoes and yelled '*Adiós!*' They revved the motor and pulled away. By now the village children were fingering me, yanking my clothes, and pointing at my white feet. While I was fighting to keep my shirt I saw a girl on the edge of the mob examining my shoes. She peered inside them, giggled, tugged out the white laces, and spun the shoes out across the water. As they splashed down, she wrapped the laces around her forehead, sweeping back her raven-black hair. This girl was older than the others, and wore her hair longer. It was silky, and fell to her shoulders. Some of the children had smooth-shaven heads. Others had heads of prickly stubble, which tickled my stomach where the shirt had been ripped open. The girl with the white laces was one of the few to be wearing any clothing: an orange skirt, which was clean but threadbare at the back. Two other girls seemed envious of the laces; they pinched the girl's arm and attempted to swipe them. She kicked them fiercely.

When I tried to move to give myself space, the poles of the village floor pitched and rolled under me. I looked at the children and noticed they had a way of gripping the poles with their feet. Their toes were long and supple, like fingers.

In Spanish I asked where Alfredo was. The crowd hushed, but there was no reply. I repeated my question. Again there was silence – this time one so complete that I could hear the lapping of the water below us. The children stared dumbly into my face.

'*El blanco*? The white man?' I asked more loudly. The crowd edged back and looked threatened. I said 'sorry' in Warao, one of my dozen words in that language, and they stepped forward again. But they now looked confused. The truth was, they couldn't speak a word of Spanish.

I pushed through the crowd and gingerly walked through the village. The poles bucked, and the knots in the wood dug into my feet like barnacles on a rocky beach. The children followed at my heels, in a pack. Ahead I caught glimpses of women scattering. Most wore tight cotton dresses, slit at the sides up to their hips, which were wide and heavy. Some wore only skirts and ran with babies drooling at their bouncing bosoms. The children sometimes squeezed ahead and walled off certain shacks from me. The ones they allowed me to enter were dark and empty; they were floored with reeds and smelt dusty and sweet, like hay lofts.

I returned to my baggage, picked off some boys who had already shared out the two baskets of bread, and sat down. The crowd swarmed on to me again. I looked down at my feet and saw that the soles were red and raw; the white skin had come away in shredded layers. For the first time I noticed that when standing the children reached up for low roof beams and hung from them to take the weight off their feet. Their arms dangled like monkey limbs, elastic and elongated.

Looking down between the poles of the village platform, I saw that the tide was now well out. Instead of sea water, there was a grey, custardy mud, dotted about with animal tracks. In places the mud was bubbling, as if on the boil. Sometimes water spat out from the ooze and large hidden creatures churned around.

I wondered what they were. The children were waiting for me to speak, and so I pointed to the mud with my finger. Eels, maybe?

The children craned forward, stretching their necks, and peered down through the gaps between the poles. A crab scuttled by. The eyes of the nearest children widened. Their brows furrowed. Two pushy girls at the front looked startled. They spoke excitedly to the rest of the group, who became flustered like the birds we'd scared along the riverbanks earlier. What exactly had scared them? I didn't know, but it was too late to calm them. Many were shrieking. Some backed away, still staring down at the mud with gawping open mouths, but the younger children just ran. The girl with the shoelaces around her head was the last to vanish. She lingered, as if wanting to tell me something. For the first time she was not hidden by the crowd, and I saw her properly. She had a lithe figure, and dusky satin skin. Her skirt hung from narrow hips and reached down to her ankles. She wore the white laces tight around her head, covering her long fringe in thin bands. They gave her dark eyes a shine. I guessed her age to be twelve at the very most, and yet, wearing only that cotton skirt, it was obvious that she was almost fully grown up.

She swung round and left me alone.

The sun was white and burning. My mouth was dry and swollen from the salt and heat. I ambled over to a tin barrel which had been

placed in such a way as to catch the rainwater from the palm roof.
A green parrot sat dozing on its rim. When I came up to it, it flew
up, jerked and stiffened in mid-air, then fell to the ground and
limped away. I looked and saw it had a leather thong around one of
its scaly legs. I cupped my hands and drank. The water was warm
and smelt of the parrot, but it was sweet. I unbundled my
hammock, and hung it in the shade.

I lay there, gently swinging backwards and forwards, fanned by
the cool wind. I listened to the rush of the incoming tide against the
stilts below, and the water swishing and gurgling over the mud. I
heard a child humming dreamily. The softness of the sounds and
the rhythm of my swinging fused, and I sank into a deep sleep.

The humming had swelled into a chorus when I woke. The sun
was still high, the tide still rising. Not much time had passed;
maybe two hours. The men of the village would still not be back –
they'd be away for a full day's fishing. I might have ignored the
chorus, but as I lay in the hammock I was sure it was getting
louder. I got to my feet just in time to see a procession coming in
my direction. Some of the people were clothed, unlike the children
I had seen earlier, so at first I took them for a returned fishing
party. But no, as they came up I saw that they were the same village
children. They were walking along the poles and walkways in a
slow march, heading for me, goose-stepping forward, singing.
The column stretched far back, a gangling line of maybe fifty boys
and girls. The two pushy girls were now wearing blue cotton
dresses. They were busy herding the others, directing them on.

I saw now that it was not clothing that most of the children wore.
It was decoration: metal necklaces and bright beads hung from
their necks and waists. The procession came to a halt in front of
me.

A girl moved forward from the back. I recognized her immediately by the white laces in her hair. She stepped up lightly to stand
at the head of the line, pushing the others back. Whatever was
about to happen, I saw that she was insisting on playing the lead
part.

The singing subsided. I straightened up, not knowing where to
look. An arm's length away, the girl was staring into my face.
When I looked at hers she averted her eyes and ducked her head. I
glanced at her body. She had strung a chain of white beads around
her neck, and they flowed right the way down to her navel,

hanging out and swinging, suspended by her breasts. Her skin was wet, and she was breathing heavily, as if she'd been running.

Something was being passed down the line from the back. When the girl at last received it, I saw what it was: a wooden platter with some sort of roasted meat on it. She handed the platter forward to me, extending it on her upturned hands. Again, I had the feeling that she was taking care that our eyes didn't meet. I reached for the platter and took hold of the underside. Our fingertips touched. Then, as I pulled the platter away, she slipped one hand quickly over mine, and began stroking the skin, rubbing my hand softly. The feel of her warm fingers took me by surprise. I jerked my hand away, and almost dropped the meat.

The girl blanched, dipped her head, then scurried off.

The crowd didn't seem to notice her go. They saw I had the platter, and gathered around to watch me take the first mouthful.

I was still thinking about what the girl had done. Her touch had been a tender caress – almost a kiss. And because it was a sly, secret one, hidden from view, it felt like a forbidden act; a daring invitation.

The meat tasted rich and creamy. It was crabmeat; overcooked and dry but still good. I'd hardly eaten for three days and scoffed it down as fast as I could using my fingers. The crowd shuffled away, leaving me to think. The ceremony and the girl's emotions baffled me. What was it all about? I couldn't wait to ask Alfredo when he came back.

Alfredo came that evening. He looked much the same as his brother: skin tanned brown, blue eyes and strong white tusks for teeth. He stormed up angrily to me and in Spanish demanded to know why I had forced the children of the village to wade around in the mud. 'What?' I said, but he didn't hear me and continued to rant. All afternoon they had been chasing a crab just for me, he said, racing to capture it before the incoming tide swamped them. Alfredo was really raving now. Why had I done it? Why? Why had I put dozens of children's lives in danger? He poked me in the stomach and demanded to know the reason. I told Alfredo that I didn't know what he was talking about.

'If you *really* don't know, I'd better explain. Visitors to the village, by custom, are offered the food of their choice. Within reason of course. Usually it's a fish that's already been caught. *You* went way beyond the bounds of decency by ordering a crab. The prospect of having to catch it must have scared the living daylights out of them, as the tide was already on the turn. Why in Jesus' name didn't you stop them?'

'I was asleep.'

His face was a reddish blue, and trembling. 'Asleep? *Then*, not content with almost killing off an entire generation of the village, you capped your performance by accepting a present from that girl Zorola, who's just coming of age. She's not meant even to *see* a man, unless he's to marry her.' He whistled air through the gaps between his tusks. 'By the way, what are you doing here, anyway? You're the first white man I've seen in years.'

I handed him the note from his brother. 'He sends his best wishes,' I said.

'In that case, why does he send me an imbecile as a visitor?' He said it with a heavy sigh, but by his eyes I could tell he was smiling. He wore a scraggy shirt, with a broad chest of grey-tinged hair beneath, and a pair of jeans held up half-heartedly with creeper twine. He asked if I was by any chance English and when I nodded he broke into a chuckle, and rolled his eyes to the roof: 'Could have guessed!' Then he smiled and said, 'Sorry, I'm just not used to strangers, that's my problem.' He took my hand and gripped it tightly in his. 'How's Juliano? Has his hair all fallen out yet? *Hombre!* You look parched. Come and have a cup of coffee in my hut. No tea here for you, *inglés*,' he added, still squeezing my hand and grinning. 'Do they still play tennis at Wimbledon?'

While the coffee was brewing, Alfredo read the note to himself, mumbling over the words in Italian. Looking over Alfredo's shoulder, I could see the words of Juliano's letter for the first time; a flamboyant, smooth, tutored script. Juliano had sealed it without explanation. 'That will do the trick,' he had said, closing it up.

It did. Alfredo said that he'd better call a village meeting right away. '*Ave Maria!* That's a hell of a journey you're about to make!'

The whole village came, and they came at once, leaving pots of freshly caught fish on the boil, streaming from their huts like bees from a hive. The children ran ahead; then came the men, with hair still dripping from the sea. Some were hobbling with tangled rolls of fishing net. Afterwards came the women, silently. They tagged along behind, as if prisoners. They never looked up. All were assembled in Alfredo's hut.

I stood beside him while he made his speech. He said it first in Spanish, just for my sake, as a courtesy. Although the assembly listened patiently, lounging on the floor, hardly a soul understood. Occasionally a man or woman would cough or spit, but otherwise there was quiet.

'My brother,' Alfredo began, 'has sent us an important person. He is from a country many miles away, and my brother asks us to look after him. He asks something more besides. A very special favour. Your village has a long tradition of helping white people. Remember how you came to the rescue of Juliano and me, many years ago? Well, this white man is about to go on a long journey, starting here, then through the *selva*, the forests, to the mouth of another river far away. You can help him by teaching all you know about the forest: how you prepare meat, how you fish, paddle a dugout, and how you hunt. He knows nothing of these things. His land is cold and barren. The sun hardly rises at all sometimes; for half the year it is a white desert, and everything dies.'

I nudged Alfredo and whispered, 'That's laying it on a bit thick, isn't it?'

'I went to Britain once for two months, and that was exactly what it was like. I wouldn't want to return. Now, when we get to the end of the speech, in God's name look humble. Got it? Bow your head and look meek.'

'Why?'

'Something important has happened. I'll tell you later.' He turned to the crowd and spoke up again. 'As I was saying. I would like you to teach him, as you did Juliano and me. If you agree, we will be very pleased. But *you* must decide. He is weak and thin, and I doubt if he would spot a crocodile if it was breathing into his face. Besides, he was discourteous when he first arrived. But please remember that he does not understand our ways; he must learn them. He has told me he is truly sorry, and we are both pleased that none of your children were harmed.'

I bowed my head and looked meek. There were a few grunts from the crowd. The grunts told me who in the village could speak Spanish: a handful of men, who'd probably picked it up trading fish in the delta. One man in particular caught my attention. He stood at the back of the hut with his arms folded. He wore his hair in two long plaits, the only man in the village with it like this. The plaits were tied at the ends with two long shreds of green polythene, knotted in a bow. They rustled when he moved his head. He held himself stiffly, as if his spine was bruised, but this was just the way he expressed his dignity, for it was obvious that he was the headman.

The whole speech was said again, this time in Warao, punctuated with bickering as each point was clarified by the villagers. When the speech was over the bickering continued, and it grew wilder and wilder. One man began cuffing his wife. Another woman kicked out at her husband. The rest joined in, yelling and hissing at each other.

Alfredo nodded at the seething mass and said: 'You'd better sit down. This is going to go on for hours.'

As we sat cross-legged, waiting, the sun set. Alfredo told a boy to light an oil lamp. He sent another away to see what had happened to the fish that had been cooking earlier. The boy came back two minutes later, and Alfredo told me that all the food had been spoiled. 'But don't you worry yourself. They'd have gone back for it if they'd wanted. That's a good sign. Perhaps, despite everything, they've taken a liking to you. If they haven't you'll have to leave the village immediately.'

But how? Before I had a chance to ask, the headman spoke up.

He began in a slow stammering Spanish, ground to a halt, then slipped into Warao. I waited, watching Alfredo's face. When the end came, the audience cheered and roared. Alfredo's jaw fell open. Was it in relief or surprise? It could have been either. In all the speech, the only word I could recognize was 'Zorola'.

'You're in luck,' said Alfredo, as the villagers trooped out of the hut into the dark. Men who passed slapped me on the back. 'I don't know what you'd have done if they'd voted you out of the village. Can you swim?'

I didn't reply. I didn't know if he was joking or not. Instead I said: 'Tell me, what happened to that girl Zorola? She wasn't here tonight.'

'I said that something important had cropped up. The important something is about her. Remember I told you she is just coming of age, and is not supposed to see men? Well, she not only saw a man, but she formed a relationship.'

'That sounds bad,' I said. 'Who with?'

'You,' said Alfredo, pointing a finger in my face. His expression was grave, but underneath he was smirking. 'Taking those laces from you was tantamount to accepting a gift, as you didn't object to her having them at the time. And by being the person who presented the food at the welcoming ceremony, she got you to accept a gift from her. Those gifts are like bonds linking you together. Or so she hopes. Coming from the outside world she probably thinks you're immensely wealthy.' He stepped a pace back, looked me over, and added, 'Though I wouldn't bet on it myself.'

'Bonds?' I said. 'You mean she wants to *marry* me?'

'I don't imagine she's thinking of anything *that* bonding. Not yet.' He winked and grinned. 'But the nights can be cold hereabouts. Anyway you're too late now—'

'I wasn't thinking of—'

'— because she's been taken away from here. After all, these people can't have strangers popping into their village every now and then, pilfering their women, can they? Especially *that* beauty.' He closed his eyes and kissed the points of his fingers. '*Bella donna!*' He went on: 'Well, poor Zorola won't be allowed back until you're well on your way to the Amazon. That was what the headman was announcing to the village. "She's safe!" he said. It went down well with the men. Meanwhile she will be in disgrace for showing herself to you. She'll be left in isolation, somewhere in the forest. The women have probably already beaten her about a bit. You must not interfere. Don't even mention her name. The only reason why you were permitted to stay is because you accepted the gift in innocence. Tonight they might have pushed you off the platform into the sea if they hadn't been convinced of that. There would have been nothing I could have done about it. So watch your step.'

Alfredo hadn't been joking. He'd meant it when he asked if I could swim. Alfredo paced over to the edge of the hut and peeped out into the night. I heard him mumble, 'Wonder if you'd still be afloat out there?' He walked over to me and said: 'Oh, before I forget, the villagers asked me to say that they were sorry for the trouble the crab caused.'

'Trouble? It was no trouble at all.'

'You didn't eat it, then?' he said, raising his eyebrows into crescents.

'Of course I ate it. Every scrap. It was all right, that crab, wasn't it?'

'Fine, absolutely fine. Forget what I said.' Alfredo scratched his ear and let his eyebrows drop. Then he said suddenly: 'You ate *all* of it?'

'It would have been difficult not to – all those eager little faces watching.'

'Quite so,' he said with a nod and smile. Something was still bothering him. 'You know, they don't eat crab here,' he said slowly. 'Never ever. I'm sorry to say they won't have known how to prepare it properly.'

'It was a bit burnt and dried out, but absolutely fine. I really don't see why it's worrying you.'

'Basically because I reckon this crab would have had a poisonous sac in it.'

'Oh,' I said, 'I see.' My stomach lurched.

'Yes. I'm afraid they won't have removed it. I'm sorry – ' he winced '– but you're going to be very ill.'

And I was, all night, under the soft moonshine, while the villagers chattered around their camp fires, chewing the bread I'd brought.

They were dreamy, summer-like days, the ones I spent in the village; long, sweet and carefree. The hazy salt air was a balm. These people adopted and nurtured me. I was held closely under their wing. I was a child here and liberated from responsibility. During this time I learnt of their ways, and shared their life. These people lived gently. I knew that I would be sorry when the time came for me to leave.

The headman, Undo, was keen for every member of his village to play a part in coaching me. Not a moment was to be wasted. He buttoned the villagers down to it straight away. I was never to be left alone.

I was given my own space in the village, beneath the wooden racks used to dry out salted fish before their journey back to Tucupita. Palm leaves were spread in wads over the racks, and my quarters were the shade below.

My first task was to equip myself with a basic grasp of Warao. Four little girls, who spoke not a word of Spanish, were detailed to assist me in that. This was the day after my arrival, when I had recovered from the crab. They squatted naked on their haunches, pointing at objects round and about the village until there were no new ones left. I repeated the words after them like a parrot, trying to capture the way the words rolled off their tongues. I jotted the sounds as best I could into a notebook:

rope = *becatti*
hat = *yassi*
net = *tarria*
hut = *hanaco*

and we worked on into the midday sun, with the white pages dazzling us.

In the evening, still listing words, they took me for a ride in a dugout canoe – *whybacca* – and we paddled through the water – *hau* – into the forest. The girls were aged between only six and eight years, yet they headed deep into the delta without any fear of it. A yellow snake swam by, but they didn't fluster. They merely pointed it out and told me its Warao name.

Later, when it was getting late and I thought we ought to be getting back, I hinted at the time by indicating the yellowing sun. '*Ocohi*,' they said, and without breaking pace continued paddling further into the darkness of the mangrove trees. We went on until the moon was up. '*Wanicu*,' they said, mimicking my earlier gesture to the sun, and giggling with their hands in front of their faces. The moon was clear and bright that night, and it made the water glisten with white shadows.

I was a new playmate for these children. Earlier the youngest girl had unclipped the necklace she was wearing and placed it gently around my neck. It was a chain of a dozen hairclips and several jangling coins. They were bolivars, the type I had given to the Indian boy in the plaza to bring me here, and I laughed to myself because, unknowingly, that payment had now been returned.

At last the canoe was turned about, but the children were in no hurry to return. They thrust the paddle into my hands; to prove that I had been noting how they worked it in the water, I was made to paddle all the way through the moonlit forests, back home.

At dawn two boys of about the same age as the girls took me bird hunting. Their names were Narru and Camahu. Looking up those words in the notebook, I found they meant 'hand' and 'now'. Alfredo had said that Zorola was their older sister. I decided not to mention her unless they did. Had she thrown away the laces?

We took a dugout into the ash-grey mudlands at low tide. When we reached a bank of shrubby marshland we beached the canoe and stepped out on to the mud. It was like putty on the top, where the sun had baked it, but my feet dropped through that layer to another of sticky goo that squirmed between my toes as I sank deeper. Narru instructed me curtly to take off my clothes. Alfredo had already warned me that this was necessary. 'If you get yourself jammed in that mud, your garments will drag you under. A clumsy way to die.' I flung the clothes into the dugout, and stood on the mud as naked as they were.

Being stripped of Western trappings should have brought me closer to these people, but instead it distanced me. The children had never seen so much white skin at once. They gaped at my body with round open mouths. I felt awkward and embarrassed. Together the boys then smeared pats of mud over my back to protect my fair skin from the sun. As they spread it, using their palms, they seized the chance to study my skin close-up, dabbing and staring as they worked. The boys were less than half my age, but their skin was thicker than mine. At the elbows it was calloused, and their hands were wrinkled and scarred. Again I felt like a child, younger than these two, with their worn palms and horny fingers. While the sun cooked the mud on my back into a stiff cake, we each slapped some on to our fronts. This was a camouflage – so that, as predators, we should not be distinguished from the mudflats.

The boys were not yet old enough to be trusted with bows and arrows of any precision, so we were equipped with what the men regarded as playthings. Even so, they were armed with jagged metal tips; when I felt the sharpness of an arrow head I pricked my thumb and bled.

We slid across the mudflats on our stomachs, like alligators, closing in on the birds. Most were waders – scarlet ibis and white egrets – which pecked mudskipper fish from the shallows. It was a test of nerve, judging when to loose off the arrows, anticipating the moment before the flocks burst into the sky. Whenever pelicans were to be seen we headed for them first. They were white, round birds, like heavy seagulls but slower, and easy prey when they sat in the water, scooping their bills at it and pitching fish into the back of their baggy throat-pouches. That day we shot three pelicans and nothing else. We returned with one each dangling from a reed strap we had fastened around our middles. I had killed nothing, but Narru said it was important that we each had a trophy hanging from us to display to the village, and so each could return with pride.

Stalking in the delta

While I was attaching the bird around my loin I noticed my front was severely lacerated. The cuts were in streaky lines, from my knees right up to my chest, where I'd been slashed by sea shells as we crept along. I looked back and saw a trail of blood along my tracks. The Indians' tracks had none. Camahu, the younger brother, took my hand and led me to a pool where he instructed me to wash the cuts clean. While the sea water was still stinging, he sat me down and plastered mud along my body, delicately working the mud into the slits with the back of his fingernails to halt the bleeding.

The muds we were on that day were treacherous in patches, but to the Indians the only real fear seemed to be the muds immediately below the village, where I had sent the children looking for the crab. A collection of scavengers lived there, mainly carnivorous fish which had grown fat on the village debris. Very common were mudskipper fish – *patero*, the Indians called them. They had black glassy eyes on the crown of their heads which stared up like marbles from the mud. The *bagare* was another fish, a metre-long creature with trailing whiskers. A pet dog had fallen from the village once, and got caught up in the mud as the tide water raced in. But the dog did not drown: it was saved from that end by the scavengers which ate it before the tides arrived. It was gnawed to death, still howling. This was one of the bedtime stories circulated to the children to keep them from the slurry beneath the village. But there was some truth in the tale.

Later, after the day on the mudflats, I dressed my cuts under my shelter in the village, and some blood dripped down into the water. It drove the mud animals into a frenzy. The water simmered and splashed, and crabs scaled the stilts up to the village level and began to pick at my feet.

I spent the remaining days at the village with the men. Sometimes we were out fishing, dragging nets through the pools, wading with the birds, chasing with them for the shoals. Sometimes we harpooned the fish as they swept by with the tides, silver-flashing streaks in the murky water.

The nights were cool and mosquito-free. We often went out canoeing through the mangrove tree roots. I learned to tell many creatures just by the way they splashed through the swampy water; or by the distance between their eyes when a torch was shone to dazzle them; or by the way they frolicked, brushing through the trees. After our return to the village we would sit talking by the fireside. The women would seldom join in, but they would listen to our experiences, lying back in the gloom of the night, picking lice from their children's hair and eating them.

The Indians liked it best when Alfredo recounted his heady days in the gambling halls around the world. His stories of that glitter and material wealth thrilled them, and set their faces glowing. But nothing gave Undo more pleasure than to hear the words that Alfredo was always careful to include as an end-piece to each tale: in those days he had pined for many things, he would say, and now he pined for nothing.

Undo and Alfredo looked on each other as brothers. The night before my departure, Undo told me that it was he who had saved the two Italians, twenty years before. He had been just a boy. Beachcombing one night, he had come across them in the darkness, lying cold and scarcely breathing in a roadside gutter, with drainwater swilling over them.

I had been in the village, engulfed by the community, for two weeks. It was time to embark on the journey. These had been easy, magical days, and I knew they had to end. Undo and Alfredo arranged for me to slip away quietly, without a send-off, at dawn. They thought this would be best.

'After all,' said Undo in his best Spanish, 'you part of family, no longer guest. Come and go without fuss, like us Warao. Surely you come back soon anyway?'

Alfredo added: 'And when you return, you'll remember crab isn't on the menu, eh, *inglés?*'

I wondered what had happened to Zorola. Was she still out there in the forest?

Alfredo read my mind. 'If you come across her out there, give her a kiss for me!'

I settled into the canoe. We carried just one Indian pilot, plus Narru and Camahu, who had insisted on coming to see me off. Alfredo and Undo waved. Undo's eyes were red and streaming. He mopped his tears away using the ends of his plaits.

As we cast off, a white cloud of pelicans rose heavily into the sky ahead, beating a fine spray of salty mist into our faces.

The journey to the Amazon mouth had begun. That was my only thought as the pelicans swirled and gathered in the yellow dawn sky. I did not look back at the village on stilts. I kept my eyes forward, away from the open sea and into the forests. I was on the edge of my seat, excited. What would come next?

Into the forest the canoe went, the engine again wheezing a sweet, sickly smell of burnt oil. The sea waves sank out of sight behind, and we wound through the trees, which cramped us into alleyways of calm chocolate water.

What *would* come next? We four would cross the delta forests now, until we reached their southern edge. From there I would go on alone. I would find the road leading south out of the Orinoco jungle and up on to the dry grassland plateaux and then I would face Amazonia, the end of the road. I couldn't picture what the jungle wall would look like, but I could feel it well enough, waiting a thousand miles away, a looming black cloud. Maybe it would take two months to get there. That would mean April. I hoped it would be at least that, because, shrouded in its mystery still, I feared it.

The spray that drenched my face was no longer salty. It no longer hardened my hair, it softened it. We were in fresh water again, and the trees pressed in on us, their branches stretching above our heads and blackening the sky with leaves.

Up one of a thousand creeks we saw a lone hut on the riverbank. We steered towards it, passing brown thornbushes that spread along the water's edge like coils of rusty barbed wire.

No one appeared to welcome us, which meant, I thought, that

the hut was empty. As we came nearer I heard the sound of slow scuffing footsteps from within. An Indian girl came to the doorway, pulling a grubby cloth around her waist when she saw me. She looked sleepy, and her eyes were raw, as if she'd been crying. I recognized her. The girl's face was swollen with blue bruises, her fringe chopped away untidily, and the hair at the back hacked off so that it no longer hung down to her shoulders. It was Zorola.

I wanted to go up and apologize somehow for what had happened to her, but the canoe pilot held me down. We weren't meant to be here at all, he said. If Undo found out we would all be severely punished. Alfredo had secretly arranged for Narru and Camahu to come on the journey and smuggle in some food to their sister. After being beaten, she'd been left to fend for herself for the whole two weeks I'd been in the village.

I watched Narru and Camahu talk softly to Zorola. Both brothers stayed at arm's distance from her, and when she reached out to touch them they stepped back. She never turned to look at the canoe, where I was sitting.

The boys handed over a parcel of fish wrapped in fresh green leaves, then scampered back down to the river in tears. Both were breathing in gulps, whimpering. They crouched in the canoe with their heads down. Camahu, the younger, nuzzled the pet he had brought along – a white egret chick, a delicate little bird which was tied to the dugout by one of its bandy legs. Zorola went back indoors without waiting to see us go.

I asked the pilot in Spanish if Zorola had said anything to the boys.

'She say only one thing. She say she sorry for what she done.'

What *had* she done? Nothing much more than swop presents with a stranger.

'And she give you this.' The pilot prompted Narru, the older boy, giving him a prod.

'Take,' said Narru in Warao, and dropped a white shoelace into my hand. There was only one.

The pilot said, 'She mean to say she have nothing in common with you no more. She given up hope of marrying you. Now she allowed back into village.'

He didn't realize there'd been two laces. What had happened to the other?

As we returned up the creek, I watched to see if Zorola came back out of the hut. She did, but only when we were some distance away, and when the others weren't looking. This time there was no cloth draped around her. She stood stark naked, and though her head was turned away, she certainly knew I was looking at her, and certainly she meant me to see. Her body was as supple as before, but thinner, and darker than I remembered – the colour of warm cocoa. She stood with one foot resting on the other, her knees apart, her hands gripping the door frame above her head, and her hips forward. I wasn't sure at this distance, but I thought I saw a glimmer of white around her waist. The other shoelace? It was too late to tell. We had rounded the river bend and she was out of sight.

Our journey was to take us across the delta to the nearest southern mainland; an easy route, which would take less than a day.

Narru and Camahu cheered up as we came towards the mainland. They were going to see something new: the shining cars, the paved roads, the concrete. As we paddled along, they put on shirts, their first ever, and shorts. The material was clean, and the clothes fitted well, especially made up by the villagers for the occasion. But seeing them dressed up proudly in Western clothes saddened me. They looked ridiculous. Wearing clothes excited them but I knew their first glimpse of the town was going to thrill them even more – the steel boats along the dockside, the fruit stalls, the cranking cranes. Not wanting to see the bright-eyed look of admiration on their faces, I decided that we should part before we reached the town. I complained of a sudden bout of stomach trouble – 'Must be that crab still' – and they dropped me off at a quiet beach bordered by forest on the town's edge.

Narru and Camahu waved and smiled at me for a while, as the canoe carried on. As soon as the trees fell away and they were in sight of the houses they turned eagerly towards them. Once their eyes settled on the skyline of square buildings and telephone wires, they didn't look back; their heads were riveted, craning forward.

The canoe moved into the grey town smog. It wafted over them, and excitedly they breathed in the acrid fumes for the first time.

– 4 –

The rationals

The riverside town was sticky and hot. Next day I bought a new pair of shoes and stood by the roadside for a lift.

'Where are you heading?' a youth in a blue Ford asked, pulling up in front of me.

'South.'

'Then step in.' And away we went, the wheels spinning in the gutter water.

The driver's name was José. He had chestnut-brown, stringy hair down to his collar and a gold chain necklace. This had belonged to his father who had only freshly been laid to rest. 'Cancer,' he said, touching his hand to his stomach, 'completely riddled.' Now he was on his way to a farm in the hills. It was in the sticks, but he'd take me as far as he could.

My twenty-third birthday had come and gone in the delta. None of the Indians had known about it, but I still felt I had celebrated it with them. Now that I was away from the Warao family, I felt lonely and empty inside. It was the first week in March, and at home it would almost be spring. Here it looked like the autumn you get after a long, parched summer. The reddish soil had cracked into squares, the grass was tinder dry. The air shimmered like rippled glass in an old window and was sooty from bush fires.

Coming away from the river, the forest had been scrubbed out and the land worked into farmsteads. Where the forest of the Orinoco did remain, it was only way back from the road in messy degenerating patches. Goats trotted along the gutters, and pigs strayed in and out of the mud houses, grubbing in the earth yards, and in the shade of the mango trees. Some huts were roofed with rust-blistered iron, some were thatched with palm; all were crumbling.

For a time the road was smooth and flat. We didn't take lefts or rights, we drove straight on along the southbound road, with forests carpeting rounded hills in the distance.

José took one hand from the wheel and said: 'I speaking English.'

'You what?'

'I speaking English good.'

'You mean,' I said, 'you can speak English.'

'This is what I say.'

I said, slowly, 'Whereabouts is your family farm?'

'Yes.'

'I said, whereabouts is your family farm?'

'Yes,' he nodded. 'I am understanding you.'

'My birthday was just last week. When was yours?'

'Yes.'

We spoke Spanish the rest of the way.

He produced a half-bottle of rum from under his seat, and by the time the road was rising to the hills he had finished it.

The road twisted and turned. Boulders lay in the road like sleeping sheep. José's eyes became glazed and shiny, and he rolled in his seat. We rode straight over one of the boulders and lost the exhaust pipe.

'Why don't you let me take the wheel for a bit?' I said.

'No, no, *amigo*,' he said. 'Certainly not. These roads are dangerous. They need experience.'

The car horn was operated by a chain hanging from the roof. I reached for it and kept my hand ready to jerk.

Later we pulled up suddenly by the roadside, swerving as if we had hit a pedestrian. José ran to the bushes to be sick. He had to lie down after that, and so I took the wheel.

'Where's your farm?' I asked over my shoulder to the back seat. But he was snoring. We pottered along the only road leading to the south. The huts became more sporadic, the trees less frequent. Once we passed a road-gang of men in white cotton trousers, stripped to the waist, their backs sparkling with sweat. They were beating the roadside creepers with picks and clubs, swinging them heavily. As we went by they stopped, lowered them and held them like walking sticks. In the shadow of their straw hats their faces were black and featureless, but I could see that they were appealing to me to stop the car. They put their fingers to their tongues, extending them right out, and waggling them like turned-out pockets. They were begging for water. I looked at José's flask of water on the right-hand seat. Should I stop? These men looked lonely and helpless, as well as weary and dry. I felt pity for them, but I couldn't see their eyes, only their thick chests and bulging shoulders. I went on.

Off to the right was a smaller road. A sign read 'El Callao'. I turned up the road, just as José was coming round.

'Where are we?'

'A place called El Callao,' I said. 'Are you going on south?'

'Yes, just a bit more. Near to the prison at El Dorado.'

I looked in the cracked wing mirror and saw a blue-uniformed man with a bloated stomach thump one of his workmen in the ribs with a hoe.

'Convicts,' said José.

I looked again in the mirror and saw the hoe was a rifle. The man was barking orders, though I couldn't hear him. The men were cowering and slinking back from the road like scolded dogs. I got out of the car.

'Perhaps I'll see you around sometime, *inglés. Buena suerte!*' He accelerated away, grinding the gears.

I walked into El Callao. It was a sleepy town, snuggling in the forest of the hills, on the gold-rich alluvium of the Cuyuni river. There were mules in the streets, standing tied to wooden posts while their leather-skinned owners drank and spat in the bars before starting out for the goldfields. Much of the gold had been worked out. The huts had been gutted and the foundations of the town riddled with tunnels. People said that the restaurant had collapsed, undermined by them. The town was past its best, they said. The gold fever had gone, the bar men no longer raised their floorboards to sweep up spilled gold dust, and no one carried revolvers any more.

I spoke to a tall, lean man with a Groucho moustache. He had come to the town from Sicily, leaving his home on the lava slopes of Mount Etna as a boy. He'd arrived alone with two bolivars in his hand, and had found his fortune mending prospectors' boots. The miners came in from the hills after a month or two alone panning the river silts, and he used to run up to them as they rode into town on their mules, with toes showing through the soles of their shoes, while they were half-crazed for women and before they blew their money. Now he had a farm with a yard of twenty brown, coarse-haired pigs which he fed on mangoes. He also had a family: one son at university in Merida, two pretty and eligible daughters – he brought them out to display them – and a new baby, 'and one more *bambino* on its way'. The town had grown poor, the young were leaving and the Sicilian's crop had failed with the drought. He told me this in a worn, husky voice, wearing a leather apron, while tapping studs into an old man's shoe. I sat at his feet as he worked at the shoe on his lap. 'You see? I'm back to being a cobbler after twenty years.'

Over spaghetti he said the history of the town was written on the gravestones on the hill outside. I left the table after the meal and climbed the hill.

The light was a soft yellow. It was dusk.

The graveyard was maintained by a donkey. It idled away its life wandering untethered between the wooden and metal crosses, rasping at the palms, nettles and acacias and stamping to get rid of the flies. It had broken into one of the tomb chambers and used it as a stable. I'd already learnt that the original graveyard had been levelled into a football stadium, to keep the first prospectors, who were English, out of trouble. Venezuela's first ever football was played here, in this frontier town. The English flooded over the border from Guyana in the first rush for gold. Some stayed for ever, and their epitaphs were stencilled in English:

'In memory of Alexander Jefferson. Died April 24 1934.
Aged 53 years. RIP.'

Most of the inscriptions had rusted into obscurity, but the Sicilian had been right. The history of the town was here: Fernandez, Cortez, Hernandez, Marcano – none of the newer graves had English names. The English had departed as soon as most of the gold was exhausted. They had left in a hurry: on the way down the hill I passed the shell of a Vauxhall Velox one of them had left in the ditch. Other relics were the grey-haired Negroes who'd come as workers for the English from Guyana. They looked stunned, as if suddenly left in the lurch by a close friend. They sat on doorsteps and called out to me in an English I didn't understand. One showed me a wrinkled black-and-white snapshot of Prince Charles and asked me if I knew him. Another recalled the day the first motor-car arrived, and another said the town was founded in 1868 by a man who hadn't been able to hold his tongue on seeing the gold-lined rivers. One oldtimer said I'd missed the best carnival in the whole of South America. It had happened here in February. Yes, I said, I'd noticed the streets were still daubed with paint.

'Well, dere you are, den. Posoteve proof, coz dat dere carnival was a month or more back.'

Another Negro waved a stick from a window. 'Hey, son, precious few Englishman pass through dis way nowdays. You stop here and have yourself a cup of nice hot tea. I always keeps some.'

At dawn the next day the Sicilian took me up the road to El Dorado in his buckled red jeep. He said he couldn't give me any advice for the expedition. He wished he could, but there it was. He had seen much in his life; he'd panned gold with the miners, seen them die – 'mainly floods and tumbling rocks'. Most of all he had seen what gold had done to people, to his friends. His one bit of advice was to keep my wits about me when gold fever was around. 'Will you promise me that?'

'All right. I promise. If I can, I'll keep clear of anywhere with gold fever.' That seemed to please him. He asked how recently I'd fired a rifle. I told him a year or so ago.

'*Mamma mia!*' The jeep swerved into a ditch. We slumped forward to a stop, and the cloud of dust behind caught us up. 'Then *this* is where I can help out.'

We turned around, choking from the dust, and went back to a potholed track leading to some worked-out mines.

'Grab the Winchester. It's under your seat.' I tipped the seat back and saw a rifle. By now the Sicilian was lining up some Coca-cola bottles on a bank of dry yellow soil. The dark mouth of a mine yawned open in the hill behind. Down its throat I could see wooden props that looked like massive toothpicks. I powdered some soil in my hand.

'All the gold worked out here?'

'Maybe, maybe not. That's part of the fun. You never know. Now, *señor*, you mustn't leave until you can smash all six bottles in a row from thirty paces. That's further back than here.'

I couldn't even see the writing on them from this distance.

He said, 'I'll count the paces out for you,' and began goose-stepping. 'One . . . two . . . three. . . .'

He loaded the rifle up.

Crack! 'Squeeze the trigger, don't pull it.' *Crack!* 'That's better!' *Crack!* 'Now don't breathe out till you've fired off all six rounds.'

On the afternoon of the next day I did it. Six bottles lay splintered over the earth.

Preparation with the Sicilian

'Now I've got you used to these things –' he patted the rifle like a friend '– I'm going to tell you something. Never carry one of these unless you really have to. There isn't any law and order out there, but it's still best to stay clear of guns. Maybe you'll see what I mean, one day. But I hope not. Hop into the jeep. I'll take you to El Dorado.' He fused two dashboard wires together and the jeep engine turned over.

El Dorado was also on the bank of the Cuyuni, and in goldmining country. It was a far cry from the El Dorado that Raleigh had sought, but someone had had the idea of attracting trade to the town with the name; there was some gold in the soil and so it stuck. The town was assembled carelessly along the forest road, a string of mud and tin huts with flimsy children who moved like puppets, hanging about in the main road. There were skinny dogs, blotched with red sores. The town was in the shadow of the prison, the *cárcel*.

The Sicilian saw me off, squeezing half a dozen empty pasta bags into my luggage.

'You'll find a better use for them than I have where you're going. Send me a postcard to let me know you're all right. If I didn't have a family, I'd go with you further. But go to the *padre* in the church over there. He's a good man. *Ciao*.'

I went to the church and found it empty. I stared awhile at a plaster-cast model of Jesus: he'd been crucified already, a pale-skinned, black-bearded man lying back in a display case. He had a tender smile, but the image of the man was frightening, not beautiful. He was a life-sized doll and too real. I turned to go, and found myself face to face with an Indian girl in a blue silk dress with an ornate, solid silver cross pinned to her chest.

'Dazzling, isn't he?' she said, beaming at the display case. I asked where I could find the *padre* and she led me to him.

He was a Belgian. He had cropped silver-grey hair and blue eyes, and spoke a textbook Spanish. He'd been here for only three years. 'I am sorry. I am in a hurry. Soon it is time for holy mass and I must take down the washing of my children before it commences.'

He led me to an upper-floor room and began unpegging large men's clothes from the line. I said, 'These are your *children's*?' I joked that they looked more like convicts' togs.

'Yes. The convicts are my children. Two men are about to be released and will need something to wear.'

While folding up the clothes he told me more about the prison. There had been only two escapes ever. One man had been imprisoned for trafficking drugs. He was a Colombian, and fortunately his father was a rich and sympathetic general. One night he scrambled over the prison wall, made it through the bushes to the river, and sped away in a launch to the airport. While he was still changing out of his prison clothes, his father's plane came for him. He flew across the Orinoco jungle, landing in Puerto Ayacucho, on the upper river, where it borders with Colombia, within reach of his home.

The other escapee had committed murder. It was an accident – no one doubted that – but because the victim's family wanted vengeance, they plied the Venezuelan legal system for all they were worth and achieved a highly satisfactory sentence of twenty-seven years for the killer – a mild-mannered man who was afraid of spiders. It had been his nerves which had caused the gun to go off in his hand. After he'd clocked up ten years behind bars he had become part of the prison institution. Sometimes when the warders were occupied with a good round of poker, he did them the favour of locking up some of the inmates for the night. Meanwhile the governor had noted the prisoner's integrity and set him to work boosting his brother-in-law's business some miles away. The prisoner turned out to be a dab hand at the books and couldn't be spared. For a while two guards accompanied the prisoner to work, but this was reduced to one over the years.

One day the prisoner and guard arrived for work as usual and found nothing to do. They chatted a bit together and exchanged cigarettes. Before setting off back through the heat and dust to the prison, the guard told the prisoner to wait for five minutes while he had a shower. When the guard came out, fully refreshed, all he found was a note waiting for him. It was scrawled on a newspaper, which had been folded and propped up next to his rifle:

'*Many thanks for your hospitality. I am sorry but I must leave. Bye, friend. All the best.*'

He had served thirteen years, and had yet to reach the half-way mark of his sentence.

The Belgian said: 'Nice touch, eh? Leaving a note, I mean. You don't get prisoners like that any more.'

I said: 'Then, of course, there's the Frenchman.'

'Ah yes, the Frenchman. The Frenchie with his thirteen years as a prisoner; his nine escapes; his time in solitary cells; his undying spirit of freedom. He was finally released here in the 1940s, and started afresh in the goldmines of El Callao.'

'You've certainly studied the book.'

'Know it by heart. Part of my job. I read it to the convicts. It's the only thing which perks them up. All day it's Papillon, Papillon, Papillon.'

The *padre* helped me string my hammock between two beams, within sight of a wall poster. It showed a small Indian boy dressed in a brand-new suit with creases as sharp as a knife. He was looking up with a grateful, loving smile to a man off the edge of the picture. Only the man's large white hand was showing. It was a well-manicured one, with buffed fingernails, fondling the boy's dark hair. It's blue cuff was clerical. At the foot of the poster were the words: '*EVANGELIZAR ES ENSENAR A MIRAR A DIOS COMO PADRE*' ('Evangelism is teaching to look at God as a Father'). If I squinted, the Indian boy looked much like either Camahu or Narru.

The *padre* saw me read the message. 'That reminds me. I've got to go to Santo Antônio village tomorrow. I'm working to help the Indians there. They need medicines, but mostly just someone to listen to their problems. The rest of my duty is to the goldminers, who are mostly out digging in the forest; they come to mass only because it's the chief entertainment for miles around. That just leaves the convicts and the other Indians.' He pondered, then said: 'The convicts have less problems as a rule.'

The *padre* – a man I warmed to the closer I came to know him – drove me to an army checkpoint the following day. It was where the steel bridge crossed the river by the prison. The soldiers looked dopey in the early morning sun, leaning on their rifles as if they were brooms. The *padre* asked the captain of the guard whether he'd possibly stop a lorry to give me a lift. '*Sí, padre.* Of course we'll do that for you.' He smiled. 'Is your companion a man of God also?'

'Just a good friend passing through.'

The soldier nodded. 'Passing through, eh?' He offered his hand and said, 'See you soon, *padre*'; and to me, 'Pleased to meet you, *señor.*'

When the *padre*'s car was out of sight, the soldiers tucked their thumbs inside their belts. They surrounded me and stuck the barrels of their rifles into my face.

'OK, gringo. Tip your baggage out on to the road.' I did as they asked. 'Now step back against the wall.' They started rummaging. I had to act to stop it. Soon they would come across my jungle knives, and worse, the explosive flares I'd brought along as firearms for the jungle.

I took out a sealed envelope from my shirt pocket. I had hoped never to use it. 'Look, captain. I know you're doing your job – and very well if you don't mind my saying so – but you'd better read this.' I held the letter out and waved it casually just in front of his nose, but my hand was trembling.

When he saw the letter, the captain's face went red, but he didn't call his men off.

'Nothing so far, sir.'

He took the letter slowly, and felt it over with his fingertips. On the outside were rubber stamp marks and counterstamp marks; it was sealed with red sealing wax, and embossed with a crest. Inside was a message from 'R. C. Desmond', an 'official' of the British government of apparently considerable standing, with friends of even more considerable standing in Venezuela. The essence of the message was that the bearer was *una persona honesta* and should be allowed to pass freely. It had taken me hours to concoct.

The captain hadn't yet broken the seal. 'What is it?' he asked, looking at the paper's watermark in the light, and running his thumb over the sealing wax.

'It's from R. C. Desmond.'

'Arrsey Desmun?'

'That's right, the minister.' I indicated the rubber stamp.

'Hey, Chico! Stop what you're doing. You lot get back to your posts.'

But it was too late. 'Sir! Look at these. What could a gringo want with all these knives? Guess what! I think we've got ourselves a spy from Guyana. Must have sneaked across the frontier. Caught red-handed.' He handed them to another soldier and picked up his rifle. 'You, there! Put your hands against the wall!' I looked at the captain and the captain looked at the knives the other soldier was triumphantly whirling above his head. His eyes went back to the letter.

I saw him wavering, and whispered: 'If I were you, I'd open it.'

The youngest soldier and I waited on tenterhooks, leaning towards the captain on our toes, both daring him.

'Gringo! Get that stuff cleaned up off the road at once. There's a truck coming!' I pulled a face at the junior soldier as I bent over and stuffed my equipment away.

The captain slowed the pickup truck just enough for me to climb aboard, then waved it on. In the distance I saw him slap the young soldier across the cheek.

Beyond El Dorado, the forest squashed up against the road. Ground creepers edged out across the dust. The forest was advancing on the road, not retreating from it any more. On my map the road faded to a weak dotted line as we went south, meandering alone, without junctions or settlements. Butterflies were swept up behind us in the truck's gust, like autumn leaves, and the branches swayed with small quarrelling grey birds. I sat on the back of the truck trying to spot snakes hanging from the trees.

As we climbed, the soil was turning gritty and white.

The only snakes I saw were those lying in the road, some flattened and dried crisp in the sun, some freshly killed and bloody, run over by the occasional car. Then there were usually ants dragging red lumps away in black lumbering columns. When we passed by, black swarms of flies left the snakes and tailed behind the truck instead.

The slope steepened and the truck jogged and swung, manoeuvring through the ruts and water channels. Slowly we were coming out of the Orinoco water basin, but there was still a long way to go. The engine screamed as we pulled up higher. The air became chilly; the bird calls sounded choked and strangled. The flies turned back. My nose went numb and my hair became wet. We went up into a white sky of mist which thickened and the world became white and dead. This was the escarpment. We were climbing out of the Orinoco forest and up, on to the savannah by La Escalera, the Staircase. The truck tipped back further still.

We levelled out, and the air cleared in patches. What I saw through the swabs of white was a new world – one of grassland; no insects; no birds. It was like prairie farmland after harvest, fenceless and stark.

The breeze became warmer. It smelt of cattle. We dropped down off a ridge, seeing the Gran Sabana plateau before us. Now we were down there, crossing it in the truck. The soil was red – even redder, I thought, than at El Dorado – and it speckled the grasses, which were coarse sharp-bladed oceans of spikes.

The grass ocean rolled and dipped. The road was hilly and the wind licked waves into the grasses. We crossed rickety wooden bridges, and while the planks creaked and split we heard tinkling brooks dribbling beneath us. Here there were palm trees. These were little oases of parrots and monkeys in a landscape which was a desert. This was the *verano*, the dry season. Cows clustered in the shade – the only shade – and stood rolling their dull black eyes dreamily, with their hooves in the water. They were white cows with a hummock of fat; they had large bony hips with rib cages like barrels, and shrunken stomachs. They ignored the grass as if it were poisonous, and rasped at the stunted thorny shrubs. Birds hopped on their mud-capped haunches, and eased insects from their hides.

I hadn't yet spoken to the driver. It was possible that he didn't know I was aboard. At the checkpoint I'd just jumped up into the back amongst some reeking petrol drums. There was only one road and one destination, so I'd had no questions to ask. But now I had seen something: a name scribbled in the red dust on the window between myself and the driver.

'Peña'. The name rang a bell. Lucas Fernándex Peña, soldier of fortune, had set out in the early 1920s from Valencia, a thousand miles away, near the coast by the capital. He walked to the end of the last paved road and continued on through the jungle, up La Escalera, into unexplored terrain, on and on across this Gran Sabana plateau. He had no mule and lived off this land which had hardly a fish in the streams. The Taulipáng Indians sheltered him and taught him, and he lived from day to day with their succour. A few seasons later, in 1924, he arrived at the lip of the Orinoco basin, the end of the savannah, the beginning of the Amazon jungle basin, and the beginning of Brazil. There he stopped.

The Indians helped him build a house; he took an Indian for a wife, and then settled down, having noted a glint of yellow metal in the streams. He fathered twenty-seven children, with the help of a second wife. The first child was called Elena, and so that is what he called the place, which already consisted of a sprinkling of huts. Six years later, he had explored much of the Caroní, an Orinoco tributary. Then he found diamonds as well. He hit the jackpot on the river Surukúm. Before long the rest of the world knew about it; 1933 was the year of *la fiebre del diamente*, diamond fever. With increased usage it was shortened to *diamantina*, but soon the fever was a *plaga*, because a sparkling lump of 154 carats was unearthed. Some stories say it was 170 carats, others more. It came from Peña's El Polaco mine in 1942; whatever its size it was certainly the biggest in Venezuela, and for a short time made its finder, Jaime Hudson, a national hero. Hudson was a burly man, with dark skin and a stubbled chin. He wore a green stetson hat. He was known to his friends as Barabbas. Barabbas sold the diamond for hundreds of thousands of bolivars, the story went, and drank the lot away in three months.

This was the stream of thoughts the name Peña generated. I looked through the glass and saw a clean-cut man with greying thick black hair and middle-age spread. The old Peña, I thought, must be well decayed by now. For the moment I assumed this man was one of the thirty-odd offspring.

We drove on, the red dust clogging my throat. The backdrop to the grasses was the Tepuys, the jutting peaks which lay along the horizon in blocks. They had yellow walls in the setting sun, and

streaky silver quartz veins – 'green mansions', with rich herba-
ceous borders of dark, dank vegetation. One mountain, to the left,
the east, looked much like a thumb, and was named accordingly.
Another to the west was the grandest, a soaring peak in the dust of
the setting sun. Off its other, hidden, side spilled the world's
highest waterfall. It was named after a man called Jimmy Angel
who flew a plane too low over the savannah, hoping to take his
share of the diamonds, and discovered the waterfall moments
before the crash. To the east was a range of vertical tower-block
plateaux, the Roraima range. Their walls were straighter and
sharper than the rest, and their tops were crowned in cloud.

La Gran Sabana

The truck came to Santa Elena in the dark, with the flickering
white lights of the town ahead. I gave two raps on the metal of the
cab roof. The truck stopped, but the driver did not turn his head.

'*Señor Peña?*'

'*Sí. Qué tal?*'

We began talking about his father there in the road in the
darkness. He could not see my face, and I could not see him. His
voice was smooth, groomed. He asked me what I was doing here
and I told him.

'Well, certainly you're giving yourself a task.' I caught a
glimmer on his face, and guessed he wore spectacles. 'Come to the
house tomorrow and eat with me. I can give you advice.'

'Where's your house?'

'Ask anyone. Till then, *adiós*.' I saluted but he couldn't have
seen. He drove away towards the street lights, and I walked back
into the night to find some trees from which to hang my hammock.

The house was a large white barn-like structure, capped with a steep roof of decaying *moriche* palm. It lay mid-way between the gold dealers – whose sign read: '*Alex y Floyd compra oro aquí*' – and the mission.

Gilberto Peña said that the road by which I had come had been hammered from the dust by Colonel Llabanera and a unit of his men, the only road to have made it across the savannah. By the time it was complete, so much of the red dust had worked its way into his system that he couldn't be parted from it. Finishing the road off at Santa Elena, he dismissed his men, and set up house in a pleasant spot overlooking the shaded town plaza. Like so many people before him, he had remained here ever since. He had become an expert on flying saucers, which frequently appeared over the savannah.

'Believe me, this Gran Sabana gets in people's bones. Maybe it's just the gold and diamonds in the dust that they breathe in.' Señor Peña had an intelligent face with a pair of heavy spectacles mounted on his nose. He said his father was still alive, but with one foot in the grave, deaf and living in another village which he had founded nearby. It was named Santa Teresa after another daughter, who had welcomed me at the door. Teresa was a tired woman, whose black half-Indian eyes were fading, but who still had thick strong hair.

'Just how old was your father when he left Valencia for here?' I asked Gilberto Peña.

He tapped his spectacles, thinking, and said, 'Seventeen, maybe less.' I asked how he had survived in a land with scarcely a fish in the river. 'He did the journey *poco a poco*, living with the Indians and eating monkeys. Not bad for a teenager, eh? Along the way he discovered he had the knack of tipping over rocks and finding gold nuggets lying like pebbles underneath. Now, let's hear more about your journey, then I'll give you the advice you need. My father has told me enough for me to know.'

I told Gilberto how I would journey on down the road and then face the Amazon jungle, and how I would have to cut east through it, I did not know how. I was sure there was a way, but I hadn't yet found it. The Indians would be the ones to help.

'That's it, *señor*. You must use the Indians as my father did. You must journey light, with a pack on your back and nothing more, and journey *poco a poco*, like him. You must not look back. Papa always told me that. I remember sitting on his knee. "Keep moving," he said, "and look ahead to the horizon. On the horizon, somewhere out there, you will find your gold waiting for you."' He looked me straight in the eyes. 'For you, *señor*, the gold will be the mouth of the Amazon.'

'A nice thought, Gilberto,' I said.

'It's got to be more than that. It's got to be a conviction. *Poco a poco* you will be there. It may take time, but what is time? In the jungle it means nothing. The Indians don't count the years as they go by.'

'Thank you,' I said. 'Who would not be inspired by what you've just said? Any suggestions as to how I'm going to start?'

'Fritz. You must seek out Fritz. Ask for him in the town of Icabarú – it's two or three days' walk from there – in the Pacaraima hills. I'll ask the *padre* at the mission to give you a lift to Icabarú. He's travelling out for the Easter service.'

'*Fruta típica de Venezuela.*' Teresa put a wicker basket into my hand, and I smelt the sweet smell of a summer orchard. 'Take them to eat on your way to Fritz.'

Gilberto said the journey from Icabarú would be three days. Fritz lived the life of a hermit, panning for diamonds in the jungle. There was no one who could help me more.

The *padre*, who had red shiny cheeks and thinning grey hair, drove in his heavy brown cassock, forcing the jeep over the ruts and potholes and spouting phrases of Taulipáng for me to digest. We slipped into the jungle bordering the Amazon basin. Being perched on its very edge gave me a warm feeling of excitement and apprehension. Once again I could not wait to get started, but I knew I couldn't afford to rush things.

Icabarú was gentler now than it had been, the *padre* said. Founded in times of gold and diamond fever, it had once been a town consisting only of men, who panned the creeks and jungle rivers by day and night. Then someone had the idea of carting in women from Brazil for their entertainment, so they came by the hundred. With their earnings from all the miners' money, they gained respect and an independence unknown in any other population in Venezuela. Prostitution liberated them. The older girls, now worn out and wrinkled, held the most prestigious jobs in the town: owners of the bars. So said the *padre*.

The town was indeed quiet as we drove up. The schoolteacher was dizzy from cocaine, just out of prison for peddling, and little girls with scarcely bulbous breasts strutted the back streets at night, and stopped me to ask if I needed a good time, fingering my trousers. The *padre* drooled with excitement over the Easter cockfight, and the men cheered and spun their hats into the pit when two knives were drawn. The Indian policeman watched the men lunging at each other with a simpleton's grin: he tilted drunkenly against a tree with his arms folded and his pistol snug in its leather holster. Interest in the cockfight gave way to the fighting men, and the crowd egged them on.

'I like Icabarú,' said Ernst, looking on at the pitching mob. He had a thick golden beard and strong white teeth. The German had sold up his business to seek his fortune. 'I like it because there's a real sense of order here.' The brawl was getting worse and a man's hair was being tugged out. We moved back. 'All right, these people fight, but they don't steal. Well, not much. This – ' he held his hands out to the billowing crowd '– to me is real civilization. Caracas? It's a joke. A bad joke. You should see how the men worship the women here! They don't even bother with make-up to lure them.'

We had another beer together. Ernst said that his fellow countryman Fritz hadn't come out of the jungle for a year, and so must be running 'kinda short of supplies'. He gave me directions for the first leg of the journey.

'What happens if I get through the forest and he isn't in?'

He spoke in English for the first time. 'Zen,' he laughed, 'you are coming all ze way back again. *Ja?*' And we had two more beers.

I walked a day from the town through scrubby savannah and white sand, greeting broad-shouldered men along the track as they dug sand for gold as happily as children at the seaside. One man shovelled sand into a tray, another added a bucket of water, another swished the water round in the tray, and another leant on his spade as if by a cabbage-patch allotment, watching the brown water make its way through a framework of pipes and trays. The pipes were hollowed-out trees, and the filter which trapped the gold grit was a hemp sack. The ancient Greeks, I was taught at school, used sheepskin instead of a hemp sack, and the resulting golden fleece was the object of Jason's quest. So the technique had not advanced in all these centuries.

A miner with a blue parrot feather in his sombrero and a cutlass in his hand stopped me to sketch a flying saucer into my notebook. He said he'd seen it circling the moon in a silent cloud, then gather above Icabarú, and shoot like a rocket to the horizon. It was last November sometime, at eight o'clock in the evening, and not a drop of rum had passed his lips.

I went on. By nightfall I was by the side of the Los Caribes river and on the true edge of the forest. There I met a Frenchman. 'How is old Ernst, then?' he said. 'Does he still think Icabarú is the peak of civilization?'

'He's fine, but one of his mines has flooded and he needs a pump badly.'

'*Mon Dieu!* Don't talk to me about flooding! See that tree right up there on the other riverbank?' He stretched out his arm to it. 'That was where the water rose to once. Someone braved the water in a canoe and nailed a marker to the tree. See it? Up in the crown.' I saw a plank with gin bottles hanging from it by strings.

The Frenchman lived with his wife by the riverside and ran an operation sieving the Icabarú river. Any day now they were going to strike it rich, he said. I'd noticed that Ernst had said the same. 'Any day now. Just you wait and see.'

His wife boiled up some rice and beans for me, and watched me eat it. '*Bon appétit!*' She had a pet squirrel-like monkey that lived on her bosom and shoulder. I hung my hammock in a shack of theirs, which housed diving equipment and a parrot. The bird chatted to me all night, and stopped me sleeping.

The Frenchman directed two of his brawny Indian divers to take me down the Icabarú river to the Hacha tributary, where I could ask for further directions. We sped along in a large canoe, a *curiara*, whose tail had been amputated to fit a Japanese outboard motor.

The Icabarú river had sparked the dreams of thousands. It had been the centre of the diamond rush, and its gravels and silts had been worked and reworked by pumps and spades to the point where it dribbled and choked along in confusion. After Peña had attracted interest in the area of the Surukúm, the fever had spread here. The Taulipáng Indian children used to play with diamonds like marbles, they told me in Icabarú town. An Italian, Sadio Garavini di Turno, born in 1904 in the province of Forli, had had his farm in the Andes swept away in a hurricane, and so he came with nothing to lose. He set out up the Icabarú with nothing more than a crumpled sketch map, and headed off into the unknown, up the river Hacha, where his Indian guides left him. Taulipáng Indians took him in; he learned to love them, one in particular, and fished for the diamond stones at the bottom of pools. The news of the 'diamond river' broke, and a stampede of miners began. The Indians were caught in its path, and were trampled out of recognition. The Indian women were seduced by the miners, the Indian men by their bottles; and the Indians took to calling the white men *racionales*, the rationals, because they thought their own life in the jungle had been so backward.

We ploughed on through the water, along the jungle walls. I had forgotten the rich smell of the leaf-trapped air, its musky warmth and stillness, and how it clings to the skin and stifles, smelling all the time of mature compost.

Our approach flipped dinner-plate turtles off their branch perches and into the water. Ahead we saw a forest hen, pecking its way along a riverbank. One of the Indians took a potshot at it and, without slowing the engine, we swung the *curiara* towards it and scooped it up. We plucked it on the way. The feathers flew behind, curling in our slipstream, then settling on the water without a ripple. They were gobbled up, then spat out, by fish that looked like brown trout, but which had clean white teeth. Occasionally we passed Indian families slaving for gold dust in the shallows, panning with large wooden conical bowls, the Brazilian *bateas*. The Indians slopped about with buckets and spades, giggling and cross-eyed from *cachire*, a purple mush of distilled cassava and sugarcane, which they sipped from nutshell cups. These people were clothed in rags and nothing more. They were skinny scarecrow people, cast-offs from the gold rush.

A girl sat minding a tin pot which contained the collected gold; in her lap she cradled a bird's nest she had taken from a tree. It was filled with black chicks with extended necks, downy fur and yellow open mouths. She fed them white termite larvae, plucking them from a hulk of earth at her feet and dropping them with her fingers into the squeaking birds' throats. Another woman pulled a flabby breast from out of her shirt and fed a screaming baby. A youth with watery, limpid eyes stumbled by, a gin bottle swinging loosely in his hand. He wore shredded blue Levis and tipped over the gold dust pot without noticing.

We came to the Hacha settlement and found the inhabitants much the same. They had just stepped out of the river from work, and they shuffled forward to greet us in black rubber wellington boots. As soon as I was ashore, my transport turned back.

The headman of the village, an Indian with skin as tightly stretched over his frame as a drum, welcomed me. Some frail children hung from the arms of two women behind him. Neither of the women was dressed with any pride. Though mainly of Indian stock, one woman had blue Scandinavian eyes.

'Here we one happy family,' the headman said, gesturing at the group. 'We find gold in day, and drink at night. So guess what?' His face glowed. 'We no longer servants of forest.'

I said that, no, I didn't suppose they were, and remembered how like slaves the Indians had looked, digging for the gold. 'How far is Fritz?'

'Two day up Hacha river.' He drew a map in the sand. 'That get you to Loco Man for sure.'

'The Madman will know the way to Fritz?'

'For sure, he know.' He took me by the arm. 'Now we drink. You like some whisky? *Vamos!*' He led me to a thatched hut, but stopped half-way. 'Hey, dog!' he said. 'What you got there?' I looked down and saw a mongrel dropping a round object at my feet. The Indian bent down.

'What is it?' I asked.

He shrieked, 'Holy Mary Mother of God!' and sprang up into the air.

'Let's see,' I said, bending to examine it.

It was black and round, spongy like a deflated football. It was also hairy. I kicked it and it rolled over. As it turned, sprinkling specks of blood on the sand, I saw it was a head. White worms were scattered behind, wriggling. Before I could look away it came to rest face upwards; both eyes were open, staring at the sky. They were black, but lacked lustre. The nose of the face was black, like tyre rubber. It was surely an Indian child's face. The sight made my stomach turn, and it set the Indian screaming.

'Get it out of here! Get it out of here! Get it *out!*' He was pointing to the river, wheezing, his face stretched and white. Then he bent over and touched his toes, retching. The stench of the head reached me, and I thought I could hear the maggots inside. I gave the head a punt with my boot. It slopped through the air into the river and then bobbed in the water, spinning. A pack of dogs surged into the water after it. Behind, the Indian was still coughing and spitting, swilling out his mouth. He had his head between his knees, and without looking up he said:

'That sure means bad luck for you, *racional*.'

'*Cómo?*'

'I say,' he lifted his head up, 'that sure means bad luck is coming to you.' The man's eyes were almost out of their sockets, white and wide open, like a trapped rabbit's. Looking me in the face with those threatened eyes, he made the sign of the cross over his T-shirt. 'I do not know where that child's head is from, and I don't care to know. Ever seen anything so unnatural?'

'Can't say I have.'

'Exactly. So I want you out of here this very minute.'

'You can't mean that.'

'This minute.' He turned his back on me, and whisked into one of the huts. I stood alone outside. The man crossing himself in front of me like that was almost worse than the stink of the head. What had he said about it? *Bad luck coming to you.* Stupid buffer! What was he talking about?

Just then he poked his head out of the hut. 'I said get yourself out of here, didn't I?'

I wasn't about to get myself anywhere this late in the day. The sun was below the treeline, and the air cooling.

Down by the river I chased the dogs until they gave up the head, dropping it among the riverside reeds in a creamy froth of their spittle. With my boot toecap I flicked it into the water again to rinse it clean. The head of a child? Before I looked properly I closed my eyes and put the image of a bloody face into my mind's eye, as disfigured and corroded as I could make it – something like a gorgon's head – so that what I saw wouldn't shock me. Then I held my breath and took a good look.

A head, certainly, gashed open and punctured by the dogs' teeth. But this was the head of an animal, not a human. It was a sloth's. I toyed with telling the Indian. Did it matter anyway? This was a stupid superstition. I would ask Fritz about it, casually, but only if the chance arose.

I prodded the head out to midstream with a twig. The trout fish with porcelain-white teeth began nibbling at it, setting it revolving, the eyes leering each time the face flashed round.

– 5 –

The hermit

Wrapped up in bed one winter's evening at home, I had read all about Sadio Garavini di Turno's 'diamond river', and the unexplored Hacha. In a few decades it hadn't changed. It was still a 'miserable little stream, full of dead leaves and silted up with mud'. He had taken a *curiara* and pushed up the stream with four Indian guides – Antonio, José, Francisco and Angelito – eating sardines from the can and flat cakes of cassava as they went. I ate the same, but the Hacha was less navigable; this was the dry season, and the Indians at the mouth of the river weren't going to lead me anywhere. I'd spent the night in the forest, my hammock between two palm trees, near the huts but out of sight. Only the dogs had known I was there.

This was the darkest jungle I had seen yet. The banks were thickets of dead canes, and the sky showed only through the leaves above, in white freckles. Walking up the stream was like walking through a mountain tunnel, with no light at the other end.

I sloshed along in water the colour of nicotine, not able to see my boots on the brown boulders of the stream bed. Spiders' webs bridged the stream, and peeled away like lint in my face. Where the water flowed slowly, small dead leaves floated by like corn-flakes; I was submerged up to my chest and had to heave my pack on to my head. It kept snagging in the overhanging branches and bringing nests of ants down my back.

I rested where the water was only a trickle, and rubbed soap into my trousers to drive waterbugs out. Toucans clacked up in the higher branches, and slender fishing birds dive-bombed the stream to extract brown prickly-skinned fish which I'd flushed from the muds. Some fish skated over the water surface to escape the jaws of other fish; the leaves of the riverbank rustled in the waves of surf I was creating. Once, my wet boots slipped as I crossed over a deep stream channel on a fallen tree. I clung with my hands from the trunk, digging my fingers into the chinks in the bark, my feet dragging in the peat water. A rat the size of a guinea-pig ran over my hands, scratching them with its toenails. That was how I met most animals, when they scampered by in bursts of panic.

After two or more miles of journey like this, I came to Loco Man. He lived alone in a ghost settlement of miners' huts, in a glade by the stream.

I slopped out of the water, shaking off like a wet dog, and stood for a while baking dry in the warm sunlight. As I walked into the settlement, there he was, marching across a yard of foot-smoothed earth, singing loudly. There were no words to the tune; it was just, 'La la, la di la, la la la.' He wasn't startled to see me; he didn't even turn his head. He said, in a rough, screeching voice, 'It's the quietness I can't stand', and kept walking. 'La la, la di la.' His eyes were black and protruding and wild, his hair was in mats to his shoulders, and his teeth glittered with gold. He wore a pair of brown trousers made of sacking which had grey mud packs on the knees. He was bare-chested and his thin ribs stuck out like the bars of a bird cage. 'La la, di di la.'

'*What* quietness?' I said. The jungle was screaming.

'That's what I mean. There's nothing to hear. That's why I'm pleased to meet an old friend. Someone to talk to.'

I said, 'But I've never met you before in my life.'

'Never too late.' He said that his dog companion had left him for the dog packs at the mouth of the Hacha. I told him that was where I'd spent the night. He had marched right past me, but now he reversed and, when he was close, revolved to face me; he cocked his head to one side and said, 'Sex.'

'Sex?'

'The dog. That was why it went to join the others. They think of nothing else. Do you?'

'Do I what?'

'Do you,' he said, breathing into my face, 'do you think of anything other than sex?'

'Can you tell me where Fritz lives?' I asked.

He grinned, still standing too close for comfort. 'La la, la di la.

No.' He beckoned me into a hut. 'You're lucky, my friend,' he said, as we ducked our heads and entered.

The hut smelt like a cave. It dripped cold water, and a layer of algae flourished on most surfaces.

'Why am I lucky?'

'Didn't you see a woman in Icabarú?'

'Plenty. So what?'

'Do you know the last time I saw a woman?'

He pointed at a log. I sat down. The log was the height of a stool; the green mould on the wood made it slimy. He sat the other side of a table that was a tree trunk split in two with the splintered inside uppermost. A green snail with a shell the size of a golfball was gliding silently over one of the beams, leaving behind a silver smear.

The man slapped the flat of his hand down on to the tabletop. 'When was the last time I saw a woman, do you think?'

'Can you tell me where Fritz lives?'

'I'll tell you. The last time I saw a woman . . . I'll give you one more chance to guess.' Suddenly he leant forward, gripped both my arms, digging his fingers into my skin. His grip was hard, and his fingers bony. His hands were shaking; he was gritting his teeth, breathing huskily through them. I unpicked his hands from my arms, and he fell back into his seat. 'You don't want to guess?'

I was not the least bit interested. I said, 'Now, please. I want to know where I can find Fritz.'

His shoulders drooped; he looked hurt. 'Tomorrow, friend. I will tell you tomorrow.' Then he sat up. He looked as if he was about to grab hold of me again, so I put up my hands. 'Today,' he said, 'I will tell you about the last time I saw a woman.'

'Now! Tell me now.'

'All right. It was in 1962.'

'No, I meant tell me where *Fritz* is.'

'Bet you were thinking it was more recently, eh?'

I stood up, sliding the log back. 'Where is Fritz?'

He began drumming on the table like a spoilt child. 'Tomorrow, tomorrow, tomorrow!' He dropped his head and rested his chin on the tabletop. He pouted his lips. He was going to sulk.

'All right,' I said. 'You tell me tomorrow.'

'Maybe,' he said. He sat up and started singing again. 'La la, la di di. . . .'

Loco Man had strolled alone up and down the rivers of this forest for a couple of decades, in his search for gold. In all that time he'd found no more than a pinch of it a day – enough to feed him, and no more.

If this had been a cold country he'd have died by now, he said. He took me along with him to scatter some maize to the hens he kept. They were Rhode Island reds, a dozen of them, chasing cockroaches.

When I mentioned Fritz, he told me I should stay well clear of him if I knew what was good for me. I asked why.

'He's quite mad.'

'Mad?'

'It's in his blood.' He ran his index finger along the veins of both his arms. The veins were swollen and blue, and looked like earthworms. 'Don't go there,' he went on. 'Stay with me. He doesn't take kindly to strangers.'

Loco Man had calmed down now, but his screeching voice still jarred my nerves. He talked in riddles, and had tantrums when I glossed over them.

I produced a tin of sardines, and we shared them. He licked every drop of oil from the can, working his tongue into the crevices, like a cat. Darkness came; he took a match and lit a dozen oil lamps to hang in the tree where the hens roosted at night. We hoisted the lanterns up into the branches on the end of a long pole. I asked him what the nightlights were for, thinking they were to keep the night chill off the hens.

'*Vampires*,' he said. 'The lights scare the bats off.' I laughed. I had thought it a joke, but later Loco Man gave me a lamp for myself. 'Wrap yourself up well tonight. Especially your toes.' I went out into the darkness to the hens' tree to see the truth for myself.

The bats had already got there. They swirled through the tree branches, pestering the hens. Their wings caused a draught on the oil lamps, and set the orange glow flickering on the leaves. I watched as the bats came in closer, then a hen would give a screech like a child awakening from a nightmare, each time it felt a nip. Their cries and flustering wing-beats spooked the night and kept me from sleep. In the morning there were dribbles of dark clotted blood on the branches.

'You see?' said Loco Man. His mood was as calm and predictable as it had been the previous night, so I guessed the time right to put the question to him again.

'Can you direct me to Fritz, please, as you promised?'

'No, my friend. Today let's talk about the last woman I saw. When did you last see a woman? Let's talk about it.'

That night I hid the vampire oil lamps in a clump of bushes. The darkness fell, the bats began pivoting through the air as they had the night before, and Loco Man went down on bended knee, swearing by almighty God to tell me the way to Fritz the next day.

'Not good enough,' I said. 'Here's some paper.' I held up a candle for light. 'Start sketching.' He laughed and turned away.

'Suits me,' I said, and lit up the bedside lamp I'd kept for myself. 'Sweet dreams!' He stood on the threshold of my hut, waiting; his eyes were shrunken and frightened. 'Oh,' I said. 'I thought you'd gone. Noisy tonight, isn't it? What with the whirring and whistling of those bats, I mean.'

He came back in, dragging his feet, and sketched the map.

At sunrise, as I lifted my pack on to my shoulders, adjusted the weight and humped off up the path, the Madman shrieked at me:

'The map is wrong. Don't you see? I lied! You *must* stay with me. I promise you the map's wrong. You'll die out there.' Now far in the distance behind me, I could hear only a soft whimpering: 'Please stay. Please. Please. *Please.*' I didn't turn my head.

The track was thin and obscure. After an hour I thought that the madman had been telling the truth. His map *was* a lie. I wanted to wring his neck. I thought I'd have to retreat again and face his stale breath, the slimy hut with the green snails, and the vampires. But then I recognized a landmark: the carcass of a light aeroplane that had crashed, a monument to the diamond rush. It was scattered over the ground in tatty chunks; silver metal drooling a spaghetti of wires, a propeller bent as if rubber, and windscreen glass fragments amongst the leaves like the diamonds the passengers had come for.

The path swerved, dived, then climbed through dark, dripping leaves and midges that floated in the air like dandelion seeds. Then the leaves against my skin were dry. The air cleared. I was out of the jungle swelter. My skin could breathe again, and I was in grassland. Locusts kicked into the sky from the tufts ahead.

He doesn't take kindly to strangers, Loco Man had said. There was sure to be some truth in that. Fritz had chosen to live like a hermit. How would he react to a guest? I walked on, clearing spiders' webs with the tip of my machete.

Seeing a footprint in the white sand, I stopped and bent down. It was fresh. Today's, I thought, because there'd been a rain shower the day before, and the mark was still unsplattered by raindrops. It wasn't an Indian's – the foot was too long and narrow. It had been trained and stunted by shoes, and yet was hardened. I saw other prints now. This person was heavy and fast, and had a long stride. He would be tall, and walking with a dog.

'Unt vere do you sink you are going?'

The voice made me jump. Then the dog yapped. The tall white man was up ahead on the path. He spoke in clipped English, keeping his lips taut and tight against his front teeth. The man had a thick beard of frizzy brown hair, which almost hid his strong jaw. His eyes were sharp and hazel. The dog was a stocky white mongrel; it scuttled around the man's legs. The man was naked but for some clean yellow underpants. I had grown so used to only Indians being naked that I expected to see smooth peat-coloured skin, but his was a muddy white and carpeted with hair. His arms were folded, and poking from them was a single-barrelled shotgun, aimed at my feet.

'I said, unt vere do you sink you are going?'

'You are Fritz?'

'Maybe I am Fritz. Maybe I am not.' His eyes were shifting over me, noting details. I looked at the gun. Its barrel was scrupulously clean, cleaner than those of the soldiers at the checkpoint. I could smell its fresh oil, a garage smell of grease and metal.

'If you are Fritz, I've come to see you.'

'You have brought some rum or some visky?'

'Nope.'

'But novone comes here visout bringing ze alcohol. Who told you I am living here?'

'Gilberto Peña.'

'Unt he did not say zat I like a little drop to drink?'

'Didn't mention it. Sorry.'

'Vhy do you vant to see me?'

'Peña said you'd be able to teach me a few tricks about the jungle. I'm heading for the mouth of the Amazon.'

'Ze Amazon jungle?' said Fritz, furrowing his eyebrows. 'Sure. Come along unt have a talk about zis in my hut.' Before we moved off, he said, nodding to himself, 'You valked vell coming here along ze footpath. Like a deer almost, as if you are knowing ze jungle vell already. You know, Chico did not even hear you approaching.'

I followed his eyes to the dog. It was sitting on its tail, panting, with its tongue trailing from its mouth. 'Zat is goot, very goot, because sometimes he is hearing ze Indians valking along vit ze bare feet even furzer back.'

I asked him how he knew I spoke English.

'For ze first sink, you are obviously European or North American. Your fair hair unt blue eyes tells me zis. Unt ze next sink I vas noticing as you were valking along—'

'You've been watching me? How long for?'

Fritz winced at my interruption. 'Ze next sink I vas observing vas you vor ze German paratrooper boots. So I am sinking maybe you are German. But zen I am noticing your vatch is not German. Or Sviss eizer.'

'Timex.' I clicked the glass face with my fingernail. 'British.'

'Zen I vas looking real close unt I vas knowing you vere British. You guess how I know zis?'

'How did you know?'

'Your machete is made off Sheffield steel,' he said.

I ran a finger along the blade. 'Handy little knife, this,' I said.

He said, 'Hopeless. Get yourself a real von made out off ze proper German steel.'

'You always notice such details?'

'Do you sink I am crazy or somesink? I am alone here, and I am a diamont miner. Do you sink I can have folks strolling about in my jungle, snooping into my house vit all my diamonts lying about ze place? No, of course not.'

All this time he had been standing with his meaty white arms crossed, leaning backwards. Now he let his arms hang loosely. 'Right. Stick close behind me. Ve shall go to my hut. You vill stay for only as long as I sink necessary for you. Zis is not ze holiday camp.' He walked with gangly strides, but he was light-footed and stepped with his weight on his toes. That annoyed me. I'd missed that detail in his footprints. The dog trotted at his heels, with its head upturned towards Fritz's eyes.

'Dump your stuff zere, unt put avay zat knife. I do not feel comfortable vith veapons in range of me.'

We were standing in the porch of a small shack. It was a neat home, built with skill and precision. It was snuggled amongst a garden of vegetables – swelling melons, yuccas and avocados – which were in beds of leaf compost, fortified from the insect battalions by trenches of poisoned water. The trees in the clearing were hung with fat mangoes, decorated with orchids which spilled down the trunks. Amidst all this, the hut looked like a large doll's house. It had all the permanent features that had been lacking in the Indian huts I'd seen. The Indians had lived in throw-away shelters which dissolved into the jungle a few seasons on, but this one was roofed with a blend of aluminium and leaf palm. It had window frames, checked curtains, a bedstead, sills, shelves, and by the bedside a book: a German volume on the principles and practice of medicine. Later I looked and found it was his only one.

Fritz rapped a beam with his knuckles. 'See zis? Made out off ze extra special hardwood. Ze termites cannot get zere teeth into it. Now, if I had chosen to use ze normal junky forest vood, zis house vould have been a heap off sawdust by now. But look. Sixteen years olt unt as goot as new. But you are dying to ask me somesink, *ja?*'

'Not really.'

'Yes you are. You are struck by ze cleanliness of zis place. Look at ze sand round and about your feet. Not a leaf to be seen! All ze nasty weeds rooted out. Eliminated! Unt ze house?'

'The house? Very tidy too.'

'*Very tidy?* No. You are kidding me! It is spotless. You are vondering ze reason, *ja?*'

I shook my head, but he was still talking.

'Ze reason is zat if I have ze intruder in ze night I know ver everysink is. I reach out from ze bed, unt I have my torch in my hand, unt my gun in ze other.' He spun round. He said that if you ever wanted to describe a person's soul you only had to describe their surroundings. Then he turned towards the pristine clearing, and looked with pride.

'And another sink: no insects. None off ze creepy-crawlies. I sveep them clear off my hut, unt off all ze paths in sight. I flush out all ze vermins. Nosink can hide from me. All is being sterilized. You know off course zat ze Indians are no better zan animals. Zey live in ze dirt along vith ze beetles, unt ze scorpions, unt ze cockroaches. Each time zey come spying on me here, zey bring some of zese pests. Unt zey are lazy as vell as dirty. Ze vild animals of ze forest eat unt hunt all day. But vat do ze Indians do? Zey lie back in ze hammocks unt get drunk silly on ze visky.'

Fritz didn't talk; he lectured. If I spoke he didn't seem to hear. Unused to the strength of his own voice, he boomed it into my face, making me cringe. This wasn't conversation. These were his thoughts turning over out loud. He addressed the dog as much as me. Chico sat staring into his face, with his brown felt ears pricked and his brow wrinkled, picking up each word. The dog seemed to understand and sympathize.

We were still standing beside my luggage in the porch. A looping caterpillar, the shade of a lichen-sprawled twig, swung down on an invisible thread from above. It settled on Fritz's wrist. He squashed it flat with his thumb, smearing the blood on the hair of his forearm. 'You see zis?' he said, pointing at the wrinkled, juiceless body of the caterpillar. 'If I vas an Indian I vould most likely haf eaten it by now.' He flicked it into the bushes. 'Ze Indians are animals. Unt vat happens ven von of zem dies? Nosink! Zat is vat happens. Funerals? Zey do not even bury zem!'

I diverted one of his speeches to the subject of diamonds. I wanted to know why people got so feverish about them.

'Stay here,' he said. He dipped into the hut entrance, and came back with his right fist clenched, as though he was about to punch me. But he opened his palm and there they were, diamonds the size of peas. 'You see how stupid your question vas now? Feast your eyes on zese beauties. Each von is like a naked lady.' He jiggled them like dice. 'Look at zem dancing. Now imagine seeing just von glittering in ze stream vater for ze first time. Zere is only von vord for it: fire. Zese stones have fire. Unt so all ze people come rushing into ze forest for zem.

'You know vat zey say? "Ze *mosquitero*, the mosquito net, protects against malaria, but not against ze diamont fever." So folks come in hordes to ze jungle, unt ze stupid vons, zey die. "*La selva es su gloria, la selva sera su tumba.*" Zat is vat zey say about ze victims. "The jungle is their glory, the jungle will be their grave." Unt I sink,' he said, drumming his fingers on the barrel of the gun, which was still slung over one arm, 'I sink zat you ought to remember zose vords for yourself as vell.'

'Thanks.'

He clamped his teeth together and laughed through them. 'I am only taking ze micky,' he said. If it was a joke it was the only one he cracked during my visit. He cuddled the dog. 'It is a funny joke, *ja*, Chico? Glory unt grave!' Chico wagged his tail, yapping. They chatted together for a while. 'Chico, Chico, *Chico*,' said Fritz, pulling the dog's ear. 'Now, I vas talking earlier about ze Indians. Zat was before you made me lose ze thread of my soughts. I vas saying zat ze Indians are savages. Vell, here's an example. Vonce, I had a dog which had ten puppies. Vell, I could look after only von of zem, so I strangulated ze others with my bare hants. I exterminated zem all, so zat I could give von dog a goot life. Zat is goot policy, *ja*? Vell, ze Indians do not sink of zis. Zey let zem breed and breed, unt zey are all getting ill, unt are having ze starvation. Vere are ze people's dignities? Ze answer is zat zey are having none. "*Noble* savages"? Vere are zey?'

'Fritz,' I said slowly, wondering whether I could risk fitting in a request to sit down, 'on the way here a very strange thing happened.'

'Unt vat vas zat?'

'A mangy dog ran up to me, and dropped a sloth's head at my feet. An Indian saw it, and thought it was a child's head. He went berserk, told me it was a bad omen, then said I had to get out of the village. What do you make of that?'

'You are proving my point exactly. Zese people are simple. Zere lives are crammed full up with zese superstitions. Vat to make off it? I don't know.' He scratched his beard with the gun's nozzle. 'Vas he caring about who ze child vas?'

'Not as far as I could see. Just told me to get the head out of sight, so I kicked it into the river.'

'Zis is not surprising me von bit. Zey are just not caring. Unt on top, he vas probably on ze alcohol.' For the first time he let the gun out of his hands. 'I am hungry. Brought any food vith you? Empty out your baggage, unt ve vill see.'

Fritz showed me his kitchen and said he would now make some dumplings. 'You vill observe how every implement here has its proper home. You may not touch anysink, vile you are stayink. Othervise everysink vill be in a mess.' I looked around. The tin pots were lined up in ranks, in height order. Next to an array of meat knives, spread out like a fan, and with blades buffed to give the reflection of a spotless mirror, was his place set at a table. One knife, one fork, one spoon, one Dresden mug, one Dresden bowl, one rolled napkin.

'Don't you ever feel lonely?' I asked, as the sun and the green shadows of the trees stretched over the hut clearing.

'Only in crowds,' he said, pummelling the flour with his knuckles. 'Go down to ze stream unt get some vater at vonce.'

A spiral of stone flags led down through a bank of moss and tree ferns to the stream. The flow had been dammed to collect just enough water for a pool the size of a bathtub. Snails with brick-red shells squatted on the gravel like whirls of ice cream. Others tumbled in the bubbles at the inflow to the pool, and at the water's edge was a football-sized tortoise, with an outstretched scrawny neck. It was lapping water, gurgling it down through an outstretched beaky mouth, and was secured to a tree root by a dog chain, which ran to a hole in its shell. The tortoise had a small cave in the bank as a house and a slipway channel in the mud, like a lifeboat's, leading to the water.

'My larder,' said Fritz, when I asked about the tortoise. 'Ven ze emergency is coming I vill yank it up by ze chain.'

When the dumplings were ready he dusted down an unopened pot of jam, and we sat down at the table. 'Ever seen such craftsmanship?' Fritz was looking at the tabletop, caressing it with both hands. 'Smooth as ze baby's bottom. But guess vat? I hacked zis from a tree in less zan a week. Unt look at ze fluting on ze legs!'

He divided the dumplings into three portions: two larger ones, which were for us I thought, and a small one for the dog. He spread jam over each dumpling, and spun a bowl to the dog, then one across to me. Mine was the small portion. 'Unt do you know vhy you have been saying you admire my table so much?' I hadn't said anything. 'It is because zis is ze real German craftsmanship. Can you imagine ze dumb Indians sitting down to zis meal around it? Off course you cannot. Tell me how it goes vith ze other miners. Ernst has struck it rich perhaps?'

I said that he hoped to any day now.

'Unt ze Frenchman?'

'The same.'

'Vhy do zey delude zemselves so? Vhy don't zey pack up ze bags unt go home? Zen I could move in, unt do ze job properly.'

Fritz interrogated me until every scrap of information I had was transferred to his memory. Was such-and-such a part of the river being worked? Had such-and-such a person looked especially happy? What about the people in the bars – was anyone in particular splashing their money around, or wearing spanking new clothes? But more important than anything else, had anyone asked me to see how his own mining was coming along – 'zose prowling Indian savages from back down ze river, for example?'

Each time I mentioned anyone I'd heard about, he would mutter, 'I told zat imbecile months ago zat he is crazy to keep on digging in zat grotty river, unt now look vat is befalling him! He will be dead vizin a veek, I shouldn't vonder.' Or, 'Ah, goot. If he is drinking heavily, zat means zere is flooding in his mines vonce again. He alvays drinks ven his mines are deep under ze vater. Ha ha!'

Eventually he said, 'You haf done vell. You are observant, and have noticed many sinks. Now, eat up your dumplings before zey are cold.' They were cold already, fixed solid to the plate by a layer of congealed white grease. I cut through a dumpling, and was about to load a first mouthful on to my spoon, when he said, 'Now go through everysink you have told me vonce more. You may have missed out somesink important to me.'

In the night chill, I sat there bleary eyed under the beam of the carbide lamp, batting away night wasps that were drawn and dazzled by the white light. Outside there was no moonlight, and so the insects of the night were bolder and screeched louder. Every now and again, Fritz would throw me a question to test how observant I was. The only reason he did this, I thought, was because it was the best way to judge how much I would take in about his activities and report to the outside world.

'How many electricity lines are hung betveen ze poles in Icabarú?' he would ask, out of the blue.

'Two.'

'Zat is correct. Two. Unt zey turn ze power off at ten in ze evening. Ven it is staying on all ze night, it means eiser ze man in charge is drunk, or somevon in ze town is dying. Ven zere are dyings, zey alvays leave ze lights on.'

Mostly, though, it was just one speech after another. He was unbottling himself. He wanted an audience. 'You see I sink up all zese ideas, vile I am digging up ze diamonts. I have novone here to interrupt my brainvaves.'

He went on, deeper and deeper into the night, while a heap of half-roasted moths, flying ants and wasps lay kicking at the foot of the carbide lamp.

When at last I slumped over asleep, he kicked me in the shin. 'Are you not interested in vat I haf to say or somesink? Vhy haf you come all zis vay to see me, if you are not paying ze full attention? If you are not interested I do not care. *You* are ze von needing ze help, not me.' Then he started a fresh spiel, about how he examined the path each day for new footprints, to see if any savages had been near, spying in the night.

'Zey vatch me and zey vatch me, but novone is knowing vere I am keeping ze diamonds.' After that he said, 'Vell, it is getting cold now. I am off to bed.'

I slept in my hammock, under the night sky, but for only a couple of hours.

'*Guten Morgen!* I am surprised you are not up already.'

'But it isn't even first light yet.'

'Zat is vat I mean. Take zis gun unt go unt shoot an animal for us to eat. By ze time ze sun is vaking up, it vill be too late. Remember: ze early bird is catching ze vorm.'

I walked through the mists of dawn, and came back to the hut only when the grey damp air had lifted, and the sun was out of the trees.

'Vat? Only a lousy parrot? Unt I do not sink I have seen such a miserable specimen in all my life. How many cartridges did you vaste?' He held out his forearm for the gun. 'I was hearing two shots at ze very least.' He tutted. 'Tomorrow I vill come vith you unt show you how to shoot properly.'

Fritz spent the day sifting river deposits in a narrow gully, and I watched him bully the pebbles through different grades of sieve. Once, holding the sieve below water, he said, 'You see zis? Zese are all quartz shingles. Zey are rubbish. Zey have no fire, so zere are no diamonts here.' He discarded the stones in heaps on the riverbank. 'Out of ze vay, Chico, here comes another load!' He hurled a cloud of shingle through the air.

'What do you do when you get ill?' I asked that evening.

'I have been ill vonce only. Zat vas ven I vas down vith ze fever. It hung around my head for two days, nosink vorse zan ze influenza. But zen ze zirt day, I vas very ill. I could not get out of ze bed. I lay sinking I vas doomed, my head spinning like I had been hit vith ze mallet. Two days later, unt I knew my end vas near for certain, I could not even crawl down to ze stream for ze mopping off ze brow. I had to make von last effort, othervise it vas curtains for me. So I got out ze rifle, unt valked over zere, by zat tree. I vas desperately requiring fresh nutrition. Vitamins. But vere from? Zat vas ze question. How vas I going to hunt down ze morsel in my condition? (Zis vas before I had ze tortoise.) I vas standing vondering about zis problem, my head crazy vis ze fever. Zen, can you imagine vat I see? Zere before my eyes is a deer! An enormous, fat, juicy deer for me to eat. I shot at ze animal. *Pow!* Unt got it through ze neck. Chico herded ze dying animal tovards me. Zen it is dropping dead at my feet. How about zat! Ve must alvays believe in ze miracles. Does God exist? Before zis I vas sinking not. But somesink or somevone vas kind to me zat day. So anyvay, I slit ze deer open, unt I took all ze most nutritious parts. Unt you know vat zey are? Zey are ze kidneys unt ze liver; I ate zem immediately. Unt zat is vhy I am still living today.'

'How did you come to be here?'

'Are you stupid or somesink? I have just told you.'

'No, I mean why did you choose this life?'

'As a boy I vas living ze outdoor life in ze Schwartzwald, ze Black Forest, hunting rabbits and deer vith my family. Later, I had ze itchy feet, and decided to see ze vorld a little bit. I came to ze Gran Sabana by chance. Zat vas in 1962. Somehow zat barren vaste got engrained in my system, unt I got hooked on ze place.' Fritz strolled over to his bedside, and came back with a photo.

'See zat man? Zat is Lucas Fernándex Peña. He must be ninety-two years olt, zis year.' It was a black-and-white print, fading to grey, taken in front of the family house. In the centre stood a thin man with white hair and a thick brush of a moustache. He wore a dapper suit, and was perched on the bonnet of a Daimler, which shone white in the sun. Black shadows splashed the house from the overhanging eves. The sun was high and strong. The photo must have been taken roundabout midday. The man's eyes were receded well into their sockets, but were the strongest features of his face. His hands were on two women, who wore tailored skirts of identical pattern and cut. 'Elena on ze left, Teresa on ze right,' Fritz said, snatching the photo back. 'Ven I first came, Peña vanted me married off to Elena. But I vas only tventy-eight, unt she vas forty-four, unt looked a goot deal more. So I gave it a miss, unt settled quietly here, bringing a prostitute from Icabarú instead. She did not last long.'

Fritz took me hunting. We stalked up a winding forest trail with myself and the dog at his heels. He showed me the spot where he had been charged by a boar. He had shot it squarely between the eyes as it tore through the undergrowth at him, gnashing its yellow tusks. It was not the shot that stopped the pig, it was the tree. 'I vas crouching behind it at ze time, praying for kingdom come.' He made me bend to inspect the buckled tree trunk.

Further up the track, we stopped for a drink. Fritz sliced open a liana creeper which looked like the iron cable used for mooring a ship, and sugary juice trickled out.

On another day we walked through a grove of banana trees, their green rubbery leaves tattered and waving like battle flags. Fritz showed me how to take water from their stems as well.

'See zat dopey bird up zere like a crow?' he said another day. 'Vell, never vaste a shot on it. Tastes like vale blubber.'

On the way back from hunts, when it was midday and most of the animals were curled up and snoozing, Fritz would tell stories. 'Did I ever say how Chico's mozer died? Vell, she vas killed by a vild boar. Pigs are ze only sink zat you need to be scared off in ze jungle. Apart from ze jaguar, off course. If you are bitten by a snake or spider, it is your own stupid fault. You have been clumpsy or somesink. Anyvay, vere vas I? Ah, yes. See Chico's nose? Vell, zat scar is also from a vild pig vich ve trapped in a cavern. Chico vent in to drag ze pig out. Other times he has almost been killed by peccaries. Zey are pigs zat go around in herds, trampling through ze vegetation. I am telling you: if you hear a rumbling, crashing, drumming noise you had better be vatching out. It means ze peccaries are on ze move, and maybe you had better start running out of zere path. Zat vas von vay in vich I nearly lost Chico, but I nearly lost Chico anozer vay too.' He stopped on the path and told me the tale.

'You have noticed zat I know vat every bark of zis dog means. I know vat is his varning yapping, his pained yelping, and ze vimpering he makes ven he is scared stiff. Vell, von day in ze forest I am hunting ven I hear his special bark – half danger, half excitement. I am raising my eyebrow. Vat can zis mean? I come nearer through ze trees, and I see Chico staring face to face with a hairy animal vich is two times bigger. Ven I am looking closer I see zat ze animal has a long snout, like an elephant's trunk but only a foot long. Unt I see zat ze animal Chico has found is an ant-bear.

'I knew vat vas about to occur, but I vaited, and vatched. Chico is dashing forvard for a vile, prancing and teasing ze ant-bear, and showing himself off to me, telling me how brave he is. Zen Chico goes up to ze animal unt starts to grapple vith it, unt immediately has it pinned to ze ground. Chico is vagging his tail, unt ze ant-bear is lying on its back vith its arms outstretched, looking hopeless. It is doomed, you might sink. But zis animal is not as stupid as zat. All of a sudden Chico has stopped barking. Unt in a few moments he is giving his vimpering, frightened call for help.' Fritz stopped speaking. His eyes were staring ahead, his brow was creased up, and he had stiffened his spine. Something was worrying him, but I couldn't see what. I stood on the path, not daring to break his concentration.

He spoke slowly. 'Flick zat black ant off my arm, vill you?' I saw an ant, the length of my thumb, twitching upside down on Fritz's elbow. I spun it off with the back of my hand.

'*Mein Gott.*' He wiped the sweat off his eyes with a sweep of his hand. 'Zat vas a *ventiquatro.*'

'A what?'

'A *ventiquatro.*' He stamped on the ant and crushed it into the ground with the ball of his foot, extinguishing its life as if it were a cigarette end. 'If von off zose is nipping you, you are getting a fever for a day, and are flat on your back in dreadful pains.

'Anyvay, zere vas Chico and zis ant-bear, wrestling on ze forest floor, scaring all ze vildlife for miles around. Unt ze reason vhy Chico vas vimpering now vas because ze ant-bear had vorked its arms around ze back of Chico's neck, unt had its claws crossed over, and pulling at eiser side of Chico's throat like razors. Slowly, slowly, slowly, slowly, ze ant-bear vas tightening ze claws unt ripping open Chico's neck. At zat moment I stepped in and I am bashing ze animal vith ze stick until it is letting go.'

Fritz reached down for Chico's ear and scratched it. 'Now Chico is as right as rains, but he is never forgetting zat day.'

I said, 'Unt vat is happening – I mean, what happened to the ant-bear?'

'Ze ant-bear?' Fritz smacked his lips, and started off down the track. 'He vas dinner zat night.'

– 6 –

On the mountain

Fritz enjoyed his lectures, and never excused either the dog or me from them. But I was learning.

His was a no-nonsense world, stripped of folklore and romance. The jungle around the hut clearing was his garden. He waged a brutal war against any pests or weeds that disturbed it. Everything in sight of his doorway, he said once, had some use: medical, nutritional or household. Everything else that encroached was exterminated. 'Just sink,' he said one day, sprinkling yellow poison over a nest of scurrying leaf-cutter ants. 'If I had had ze misfortune to be born von of zos dumb savages, my house vould have been viped out by ze jungle by now.'

When we were hunting, it was 'Now, ask yourself vat chance I vould have had picking off zat monkey vith ze bow and arrow'; and while gathering fruit, 'Do you sink ze savages know vat a goot fresh orange is tasting like? Do you sink zey know vat a vitamin is?'

There had been changes since my visit. Fritz's lifestyle was deteriorating; almost collapsing. Leaves lay scattered on the paths. Spiders hitched webs across the clearing. Chico sulked and went off his food. The stream got blocked with leaves, and the tortoise nearly drowned. All this hadn't escaped Fritz's notice, either.

'You see zis spider?' he would say. 'Zis is your fault! I told you to sweep ze path.' He had ordered me never to touch it.

The truth was that Fritz's existence here was on a knife edge. 'Nonsense,' he screamed when I suggested it, and that night we ate in silence.

Was he any better than the Indians? Alone, he could maintain his civilization, but with a companion to distract him, he lost all the time he needed to maintain his jungle niche. He was scarcely able to keep his head above water.

One night something happened to change all this. Fritz as usual curtly muttered, 'Sweet dreams', as I spread out my hammock and pitched it under the sky. Then, as I bent to unlace my boots, I sensed a movement nearby, a rustle in my hammock. I fingered in the darkness for my machete, then crept back across the clearing on all fours. Ten yards back I sprang up and ran to the house for a torch. When I got close to the hammock I saw it was still here, the creature. I caught it in the torch beam – a black scorpion, twitching in the hammock cotton, tangled in the threads and stabbing the air with its sting.

I clubbed it with the machete, and only then saw that it had been tied down at the torso by a strand of white cotton. It was secured with a neat double reef-knot – the loose ends snipped tidily away – and placed in the central sag of the hammock, like a gift, where I would have lain.

'Sleep vell?' asked Fritz next morning. He looked unusually radiant, I thought.

'Yes, very well indeed, thanks.'

'Zen I am sinking it is time for you to leave for ze Amazon.'

'Sudden, isn't it?'

'No furzer point in you staying. Nosink much more zat I can be teaching here.' He hadn't mentioned the scorpion, but we both knew that I had passed his little test; for the first time he looked pleased with me.

'You have been listening very vell to all my talkings. I have been putting all ze pressure I can manage on you, but you are vinning through. Ze jungle is tough, so I vas being tough.' He released a glimmer of a smile. 'Pack up your bags. I vill show you a path back to ze river Icabarú avoiding zat crazy imbecile with his bats.'

He led me down to a track, then said, 'Gootbye, unt goot luck vith ze Amazon.' Before I could get in a reply, he turned to his dog and said, 'Come on, Chico, let's go home', and they raced back up the path to the hut without looking back.

Roraima, the tower-block plateau I had seen coming over the Gran Sabana, commended itself as a place to be alone. I very much wanted to be alone before entering the Amazonian forest. Once again I took out the pair of paratrooper boots I had brought along for the jungle and squeezed them on.

I walked from Colonel Llabanera's red dust road, taking a sandy track for a day through the grasses and *moriche* palms to Paraytepuy, a Taulipáng village of pastel-pink huts capping a hill. I'd heard that the bark of the palms is cut to make a sandal, the *paray*, which gave the village its name. The day I came, I saw only one *paray*, which had been kicked off on a hillside path; the Indians wore baseball shoes.

The village did not stir on my arrival. A boy with a white T-shirt emblazoned with 'I Love New York' continued practising with his bow and arrow on some cream-coloured cattle, which were plodding through the village, kicking up the dust with their black hooves. A man whittling a green stick with a penknife shouted out in Spanish that I would need a guide to find the one route up the cliff face of Roraima. I said I didn't need a guide, and under pressure he drew a map in my notebook for me. Then he asked if I had an aspirin, and took the whole bottle, 'for his family', the ones who had not left for the golden-bedded river.

'Which golden-bedded river is that?' I asked, but the man shrugged his shoulders. He thought it was a river called Iggabarú, or Icaparú, something like that. Everyone, they were told, had been finding their fortune down there, so his children had gone to find their fortune too. They would return rich, he said, maybe even with cassette recorders.

The savannah was as lifeless as it had seemed through the dust of Peña's truck. The grass rustled with occasional lizards or springing grasshoppers, but otherwise moved only in the breeze. On the track there were ants building defensive turrets the size of pipe bowls at their tunnel entrances, and I followed the three-toed prints of ant-eaters. An Indian boy in blue jeans had told me what they were, back in the village, drawing pictures of them in the sand with a twig and giving me a stick of sugarcane to chew.

The grassland buckled into hills at the foot of the mountain. Snow-white mists curtained the sheer face and whirled off the plateau summit. I made a camp fire at the mountain's base and slept the night rolled up in a blanket.

Further up, there was forest. It was a mossy, cramped mess of frogs, ferns and tortured trees with cutinous leaves, fed by the cloud. It smelt of ditchwater. A diagonal fault was the ledgeway path up the cliff face to the summit.

I did not reach the top until hours later. The track ended in a spartan platform.

The rocks were pink, blackened by the driving mists, and shaped by them into caves and statues. Soil clung to the mountain in the shelter of nooks and ponds. The only sounds were of dripping and of lost, twittering birds swept up from the forest below. If a tree grew, its wood was deformed and twisted. The sedges looked pained when I trod on them, and the succulents cracked open under my boot. Two plant species in particular thrived here – pitcher plants and sundews; both carnivorous and the colour of fresh blood.

I walked for a week in the cloud, sleeping in the caves with necklace-length centipedes, and blue and black frogs with yellow underbellies. I found my way with a skein of cotton like Theseus, unwinding thirty reels of it in a trail behind me as I went. It was a labyrinth. Without the cotton I would never have found my way down.

When I did, I felt clear-headed and sobered. But ready? I wasn't sure. Peña had said that I wasn't to look back, so I didn't.

Part Two

The Acceptance

– 7 –

Boa Vista

The Brazil that rolled off the Pacaraima hills was cattle land. The dust road from the frontier was fenced with barbed wire, and behind it cows scratched their backs on the ant-hill pillars. Only beyond Boa Vista had the jungle been permitted to stay, for the time being.

Boa Vista was a spreadeagled town whose government clerks smelt of cheap soap. They knew little of my jungle. I drank a thousand coffees, it seemed, before I knew all I had to know of it. Now I could picture the forest for the first time: Amazonia was no longer a dark mysterious cloud in my mind. I'd seen it from a plane and it was a sea of ordinary trees; nothing frightening, just an overgrown forest.

I had done my research on the jungle, but I still had no contact with the Wai-wai Indians of the interior. My funds were running low, and I had tired of slinging up my hammock in hotels that doubled as malodorous brothels.

I sat in a bar in a small jungle-frontier town much like all the others: men in sombreros at tables clacking dominoes, or strumming *brasileira* music; bar girls draped around them; flies and smoke; a dirt floor; bottles in clumps on the tables. Many days before, I had dyed my hair a deep mahogany to look less like a gringo. Now the dye was fading, but no matter, because I'd learnt to drink *cachaça*, a sugarcane rum, without wincing. It was taken with a slug of lemon juice, squeezed straight down the throat, or sucked from the back of the hand.

The streets were washed with rain; the roof crackled under the pelting. I thought back to the Gran Sabana, thought of it breathing again, and of animals hopping about in the freshened air. One day it had been the dry season, the next the wet. The change had been as quick as that.

'Mind if I join you?' A voice spoke in Portuguese.

A man was bending over me, blocking my light. He stooped, and had a thin, bony face. He was wearing a black felt hat, a grey suit with dark rain splashes down the shoulders and a white shirt with no tie. His clothes were too well cut to be a farmer's, but his skin was too brown and fly-bitten for an office. His upper lip was thin, the lower one fat and bulged out, showing a neat row of sharp incisors. He was armed.

'If you keep that knife tucked away in your belt, certainly you can,' I said. I pushed a chair out with one foot. He sat down and asked if I was alone.

'Perhaps.' I shrugged. 'If you think I'm worth robbing, forget it, but I'll buy you a drink.'

He took off his hat and hooked it on to a rum bottle. The hat showered the table with water droplets, which were red from the dust. 'Thanks. Could do with one.' He flung the dregs from a glass smeared with two different shades of lipstick over his shoulder, and I tipped out a shot of *cachaça*.

'Heard you're looking for someone to guide you through the forest to the Indians out there.' He was looking out through the open door, into the rain and dark. He swigged the drink down in one go.

'Here, have another.'

He slid his glass forward. 'I think I can help in a small way.'

'Know anything about the jungle?' I asked.

'No.'

'Anything about the Indians?'

'Not any around these parts.'

'What about cooking?'

'I can't cook anything other than beans and rice and coffee.'

'Can you ride a horse, read maps, carry loads, anything useful whatsoever?'

'No, *senhor*. Just thought you might like to forget about your expedition for a while, and spend a night on the town before you leave. I know all the spots.'

'Well, well.' I held out my hand. 'Let's finish off this bottle and get another.'

Before long he could hardly say his name.

'Orrgge.'

'Jorge? Good health, Jorge.' We clinked glasses once more, and gulped down the last of another bottle. 'Jorge, what do you do exactly for a living?' But he couldn't get the words out. His cheeks looked pale, and I led him outside for a dose of fresh air. The sky had cleared, the mud of the street was wet and slippery, and water flowed along the gutters in rivulets. I had to prop Jorge up.

'Come on, Benedito, let's go dancing.'

'I think you've had a fraction too much to drink to dance with anyone.'

'No,' he said. 'On second thoughts, I think I've had a fraction too much to drink to dance with anyone.'

He was pulling me down a dark potholed back street.

I asked where we were going.

'Don't know. Let's just keep walking.'

We walked on, arm in arm. Occasional open doorways splashed light across the street. Women in tight skirts slouched in the doorways, jangling their bracelets, tapping their feet to music drifting across the roofs.

'Nice, eh?' said Jorge, wolfwhistling at a girl. She smiled, unfolded her arms, and inclined her head to Jorge.

'Just keep moving,' I said.

By day this town was just tin shacks and wall plaster, with the streets empty but for the dogs knee-deep in stewing gutter slurry. Its life was at night, when the men were in from the forest and fields, and the women came out to entertain and serve them.

'Where are we going?' Jorge asked.

'You said we should just keep walking.'

'Did I? Well, I've got an idea. Let's go dancing.'

The rain began rattling on the roofs, and we ducked inside another bar which looked out on to a river. Just as we got inside, a girl was pitched out into the street by two men. They blew her a mocking kiss, and laughed.

'This is my favourite joint in town,' said Jorge. We pushed through a crowd of men with bottles in their hands.

'Don't they have glasses to drink from here?' I asked.

'Want to catch a germ or something?' said Jorge. 'Just stick to your own bottle.'

We were steering towards a table decked with *cachaça* bottles. On the other side of the room, around the corner and beyond the bar, men were stomping in the dust to a samba rhythm. Someone was twanging a guitar. Other men were marking the beat by knocking bottles with nails the size of knitting needles. We cleared a space at the table and sat down. We had been alone, but two women descended on our table from the crowd and snuggled up to us. My girl had heavy earrings studded with paste diamonds bigger than any real ones unearthed in Peña's Gran Sabana.

'Are one of you two going to get us girls a drink?'

'I'll go,' I said, and went to the bar. I was back a few minutes later, and by then two more girls were around the table. Jorge said they'd have to share out the two beer bottles between them.

The oldest girl must have been sixteen, the youngest thirteen, but they were all professionals, and had heavily creased eyelids. Smiling looked a real effort.

'Beautiful, eh?' said Jorge, 'Now choose one.' He gestured to each, as if they were prize peaches in a shop window.

The oldest was a Negro, with light bones and plucked-away eyebrows. Another had green eyes, and crinkly hair that was a brown seaweed colour; she was gap-toothed. The third I remember only as having hard eyes, fat lips and bad breath. The fourth was the youngest, and her blood was pure Indian.

'*Vamos dançar*. Let's dance,' said the gap-toothed girl, breathing into my ear.

'*Não*. Let's not,' I said.

'Yes, let's,' said Jorge, and the gap-toothed girl strapped her arms around his neck. They slumped off to the dance floor.

'Come on, then,' I said to the flock of girls, and went after Jorge without looking back. The only girl still behind me at the dancing space was the Indian girl. I took hold of her hand. It was thin, and her fingernails were hard and spiked. We moved into a sweaty forest of entwined men and women. The girl softened her eyes.

'I will give you a good time tonight,' she said, thrusting her pelvis up against mine and locking her hands behind my back.

'Are you good at teaching things?'

'Tonight, I will teach you many things if you want.' She squeezed her knee up between my legs.

'Can you teach me to salsa?'

The girl thought this was very funny. She unbuckled her hands and, still tittering, taught me the dance steps.

Men swilling back bottles knocked and bumped us. Some danced without partners, but most were tightly wrapped up with girls. Once we bumped into Jorge. The gap-toothed girl had one hand pinching the scruff of his neck, and one hand splayed out, over his chest, feeling for his shirt buttons.

My girl said her name was Maria, took my wrists and cupped my hands on to her hip bones. When I asked her if she'd always lived in this town, she said no. Up until two years before, she had been at a good Catholic mission school. And before that she had lived with her family in the forest. Those were the days when she was called Mawa, which was a good name to be rid of anyway. A *mawa* was a sort of frog. Then one day some Franciscan missionaries came to the village and offered to bring her up and educate her. Her family thought about it, said it sounded like a bargain, and packed her off. The *padre* was a good man, warm and truly possessed by the holy spirit. It was he who had christened her Maria, and to be quite honest she'd forgotten her other name completely before I brought the subject up, she said. But two years before, when she was ten or eleven, she'd run away to the bright lights.

'Why?'

'More money. More money for perfume, clothes and all the things a girl wants.' She said that soon she would be rich, richer than she'd ever dreamt, and if her family knew they would be proud of her.

'You are a Wai-wai, then?'

'Was.' She stopped dancing and dropped her arms from around my waist.

'Would you be able to take me to your family in the forest?'

'No.' She stared at her feet.

'Please. If I paid you as a guide?'

'No. I'm not seeing my family again. I don't want to go back to the forest. I have a new life. I'm not going back.'

'Please. Just give me directions. Where do they live? It's not asking much.'

'I said *no*.' She stamped her feet.

'Then, do you know anyone who can help me?'

'No, no, no!' She pushed me back, kicked out at my legs, and dived into the crowd.

'Please,' I said, catching her hand. The palm was wet and hot.

'That's the man you want,' she said, 'over there. Now let me go.' I released her, and blinked through the smoke to where she'd pointed.

'Complete nutcase, that girl,' said Jorge over his shoulder. 'Should have warned you.'

'Know anything about that man over there, Jorge?'

'He's a brazil-nut gatherer. Stay well clear of him. Bad sort.'

The man in question had a thick, shaven head and wore thigh-length black boots. Silver spurs jutted from his heels like penknives. He looked the epitome of a thug, and was too big for his stool. On the table before him was his hat. It was lilac green, and a black and white spotted jaguar's tail hung from the rear. Two other men were at his table. One looked unconscious and his head was resting on the tabletop. The other had a heavy girl clinging to him. He was bouncing her up and down on his knees, and she was bellowing with laughter. The bald man was spinning coins at her, cheering when he got them to slot down her dress front.

'Come on,' said Jorge. 'Fatima and I are going back to the table.' I said I'd join them in a minute, bought a bottle of *cachaça* at the bar, and went over to the bald man.

'Can I sit down? I'm told you may be able to help.' The man spat at the floor.

'And who might you be?'

'Call me Benedito.'

'Who?'

'I'm told you know the forests. Is that true?'

'What if I do?'

'I'm looking for a guide to take me to the Wai-wai Indians.'

'What are you, some kind of lunatic? That's a month's walk, unless you know the paths.'

'How long if you know the paths?'

'Look, I'm not interested in taking anyone anywhere. I'm a nut gatherer. I just follow the trails and scrounge around the jungle floor picking up nuts. So I can't help. That's that. Hey, *amigo*.' He flicked his fingers across the table, to his friend. 'Bring that girl over here for me to play with!'

'Have a swig of this,' I said, placing the bottle in his ham fist.

'You still here?' He wiped the bottleneck with his fingers, then sucked it into his mouth, gulping some down. He knocked the head of the lifeless man with the bottle, who sat up and took a swig, dribbling it down his chin.

'You'll take me, then?' I repeated.

'That's not what I said.'

'Good. Here, have another drink.'

'OK, but I don't know the first thing about Indians, so there's no point in you asking.'

'I'm not asking. Pass the bottle to your other friend. Perhaps the lady wants a drink? That's right. Drink it all up.' She did, as if the *cachaça* was lemonade. 'Right,' I said. 'Where can we meet to discuss it?'

'Are you deaf or something?'

'That bottle didn't last long, did it, *senhor* . . . ? I didn't catch your name.'

'That's because I didn't give it to you. It's Pablo.'

I went away, gave the drink half an hour to work on him, then strolled back.

'What time did you say we'd meet tomorrow, Pablo?' His eyes were confused, and he frowned under the effort of focusing on me.

'Damn you. Why don't you leave me alone?' He clapped his head in his hands.

'I will in a minute. What time?'

'Ten o'clock, outside here tomorrow.'

'Promise?'

'I never promise.'

'Ten o'clock, then.' I picked up his limp hand and shook it. When I let go, it flopped down lifelessly.

On the way back to Jorge's table, I was clipped on the ear by a flying bottle. The tables and walls were rocking with the beat of bottles and fists. Men and their women, tone deaf with the *cachaça*, sang like cats. Jorge had Fatima on his knees. His hair was ruffled, and there was lipstick smudged over his face and neck. She was tickling his chin. The black girl with the light bones was playing with his fingers.

'How are things going, Jorge?'

'I've been warming a girl up for you. What's your name, girlie?'

'Rosa.' The girl snaked her arm across the table towards me. I was just out of reach.

Jorge said: 'You took your time coming, Benedito. I think I've been robbed.'

'Are you going to fetch it back or am I, Fatima?' I said.

The girl dipped her hand down the front of her dress, and plucked out Jorge's wallet. 'You beautiful girl, Fatima, where did you find it?' he said. He gave her a peck on the cheek, and the other girl tugged at him for attention.

A fight was brewing on the dance floor. Pablo was swinging punches at a skinny youth with a knife. The youth was being held in restraint by a crowd, and the knife was wheeling pathetically in his hand. 'Plenty of action here,' said Jorge. A passing man had got in the way of one of Pablo's right hooks and lay on his side with his hands to his nose. Two or three men moved in on Pablo. Pablo's two friends got up from his table. The music stopped. A bottle smashed. A clutch of bar girls ran to the door screaming. Then the lights blew.

The barman had an oil lamp ready.

'Time to leave, Jorge?' I said.

'Yes, time to leave.' Fatima winked at Jorge. She tugged his cheek, giggled, and teased the wallet from his trouser pocket again, passing it in front of Jorge's eyes for the other girl to take. I got to it first.

Jorge stepped outside, supported by the two girls. It was first light. The rain had stopped. The river was steaming, and fishing boats with dewy rigging and rattling engines chugged through the grey water.

'Sleep well,' I said to Jorge. He grinned and squeezed the girls. I said that I'd see him first thing tomorrow. The three lurched off down the street.

Back inside the bar I had to brush off the fingers of girls who'd lost their customers to the fight. Several men were locked together on the floor, rolling in the beer bottles. The crowd that crouched over them was thick and I couldn't see much. But there was Pablo. He was sneering at another man, who was lying writhing between his legs in the dirt. Pablo was slowly clamping his heels into the man's loins. Then I remembered the silver spurs that he wore. Good God, I thought. Then I went off to bed.

I came back after the sun was up, and saw a crowd of people standing by the river. Looking through the gaps between them I thought that the subject of interest was a street seller. I thought he'd stretched out his wares and was bartering with passers-by. Then I saw they were watching a man who was flat on his back. He looked as if he was praying. He was lying with his hands held up high in the air, in meditation. White candles were burning gently in a circle around him. Near enough to smell the burning wax, I saw the wetness of his clothes. Then I saw the blood. He was dead. No one was crying; no one was hysterical.

Women were standing goggling at him. Children were daring each other to touch the skin of his face. It looked cold and slimy to the touch, like a fish's scales. Water weed was tangled up in his hair. An old man with a bent back pointed with a loaf of bread to the spot where they'd dragged him from the mud. He said that many had hoped it was a *pirarucú*, or some such large fish. But no, it was this corpse, and just this second they'd taken the nail out of him. That was what had been his undoing. I looked and saw it was of the type used to bang out the music the previous night in the bar. It had been pushed up through the roof of his mouth.

Spectators at the corpse

'An accident, surely?' said the old man, then doddered off down the street.

Jorge appeared before Pablo did. We drank coffee at a table in the bar. 'How do you know Pablo is going to turn up?' Jorge asked me.

'Because of this.'

I showed him what I'd collected the night before. 'He's sure to come back for his hat.' Jorge took the hat and stroked the jaguar's tail. He repeated that he thought Pablo was a bad sort and he didn't want to be here when he came.

I said it was a miserable business about the killing last night.

He said: 'Yes, may the Lord have mercy on his soul.'

I said I'd been to a little village called Beiradão, on the river Jari, and the police there said they had well over one hundred official killings each year. That meant you had a one-in-a-hundred chance of being murdered each year, more if you didn't count babies and children. And the official figures were bound to be an underestimate because crocodiles probably chewed up most of the evidence.

Jorge didn't bat an eyelid. He was nursing his head in his hands. He wondered how much he'd had to drink last night.

'What's your job, Jorge? I never asked.'

'What?' He looked up blankly. His eyes were dull and watery.

'I said, what sort of job do you do?'

'Me? I'm a missionary.'

I snorted. 'No, come on, tell me.'

'I'm telling the truth. A missionary.'

'Prove it. I don't believe it. A man who drinks in a seedy place like that, who frolics with women, tells me he's a preacher! What sort of religion is that? Do you worship Bacchus or something?'

In a deadpan voice Jorge said, ' "God works for good with those who love Him." ' This man walked around with a knife in his belt. Good grief, I thought. He said it was from Romans 8:28.

I gaped. 'You really *are* a missionary, aren't you?'

' "Repentance and remission of sins should be preached in His name among all nations." Luke 24:47.' He nodded, with knitted eyebrows, as he said this, then he smiled. 'You see, Benedito, to survive here, you must modify your principles, take account of local values. Bend with the wind, that's my motto, bend with the wind, or else – ' He clicked his fingers sharply '– you snap.'

'Is that what you were doing with those girls? Bending with the wind?'

Jorge shook his head. 'Benedito, Benedito,' he said slowly through his teeth. 'You don't understand how things are here. You see, you're judging me from an outsider's point of view.'

'It's not *my* judgement you ought to be worried about.'

'Look,' said Jorge, rising off his chair. 'This is my home. It's where I let my hair down. When I'm refreshed, I'll be back to work in the Amazon, preaching God's love to the Indians. You know there are people out there who haven't even heard of the Lord?' Jorge thought I was mocking him, but I really was interested. He had changed overnight. It was fascinating, like watching a butterfly in metamorphosis, except here was a creature who changed not just one way but backwards and forwards, 'with the wind'.

'I'm talking about saving people for Christ. *That* is how important my message is. You just don't understand.'

He was right; I had gone further than intended. I hadn't wanted to cast judgement or hurt him – we had had a good time together. Now, standing there, he looked hunted and desperate. I felt pity for him and said, 'Sorry, Jorge. Sit down again. As you say, I'm talking from an outsider's point of view.'

'Thanks, Benedito.' Then he smiled too victoriously, with self-righteous gloating.

So I said: 'I'll pray for your sins tonight, before I go to bed.'

He looked about to explode.

'Only teasing,' I said.

Pablo came dead on time, before Jorge could get away.

'You got something for me?'

'Ah, Pablo!' I said. 'Sit yourself down. I've already got you a drink.' Pablo grabbed the hat, and scrutinized it. Then he sat down heavily and took the beer bottle in his hand. He felt the coolness of the glass and smiled.

'I'll be going, then,' said Jorge, getting to his feet, 'if you two are about to discuss business.'

'I didn't come to discuss any business. Just to pick up my hat.'

'Well, I've got things to do anyway.' Jorge extended his hand to me. He wasn't inviting me to shake, he was giving me something. 'A present for you, Benedito.' It was the knife. 'It'll come in useful. Hide it in your boot.'

'Thanks, Jorge, that's very kind.' I said I was glad we were still friends and asked him to slip 5000 cruzeiros to the Indian bar girl I'd upset, and to tell her it would pay for the income she'd lost the night before through spending time with me. Without thinking, I used her Indian name.

'Mawa?' Jorge shouted.

Pablo let out a curse as his beer bottle chinked on his front teeth.

'*Mawa?* How did you know that was her name?' Jorge was leaning forward on his knuckles, like an ape, rocking the table and fuming into my face. '*Maria!* That's her name. A good Christian name. *Mar-i-a.* What right have you to come along and remind her of her primitive upbringing? Just tell me that. OK, I grant that she's a bad influence on the town, but now at least she has the comfort of the Lord. At least she knows His love, Benedito.'

The veins on Jorge's neck had risen into blue electric flexes. I could feel the strength of his feelings, but his message was confusing: just who was doing the sinning? Me, the girl or him?

His head seemed suddenly heavy. He propped it with both arms. 'Let's all just hope you haven't done too much damage. It's unlikely, but who knows? Now she may think of going back to the forest to live her life out there. What then, eh? What then?'

I couldn't think of anything to say.

Pablo said, 'You're spilling my drink.'

Jorge stomped off. Pablo was cackling with laughter. 'You know what, Benedito?' he said.

'What?' I was still watching the dust cloud behind Jorge. He hadn't said goodbye.

'You might have earned yourself a ride into the forest.'

I wasn't sure I wanted a ride into the forest with Pablo, after I'd seen the use he put his spurs to. 'Why is that?'

'You see,' he said, 'Jorge and I are not what you might call friends.'

'I'd gathered that.'

'He did something unspeakable to an Indian tribe I knew, on the far side of Amazonas.'

'Unspeakable?'

'Yes, unspeakable. Unless you get me another drink.' I went and got one.

'In what way unspeakable?'

'Christianized them, that's what he did. Flew into the jungle, spotted a village, built a church overnight, told the Indians they'd be damned if they didn't pay it a visit every day of the week. Handed out T-shirts. Told them they'd be on their way to Hell if they didn't cover themselves up. The women, he said, were tempting men to lust. Their bare breasts were tantalizing them. Jorge taught the village a shortened version of the Lord's Prayer and told them to recite it every day before going fishing or hunting.

Then he decided it was time to spread the Word elsewhere, so he handed out Bibles and told them to get reading. Everything else they needed was in there, he said. Do I have to tell you that these Indians could hardly read? Anyway, Jorge flew away in his little aeroplane, on to the next tribe. He had told the headman to ostracize anyone who didn't obey these rules.

'Five years go by, and that's when I turn up. I was just passing through, looking for better brazil nuts, but what do I find instead? I find a handful of puny, bony people, amid a junkyard of huts and burial mounds. Most of the tribe were dead. Why? I'll tell you why, because they'd killed themselves. Their clothes had worn through, and they'd been naked and because of that ashamed. Others had died of starvation, because the need to go to church meant the village couldn't be moved on to fresh fertile land, and they wasted all the valuable hunting time in front of the altar.' Pablo emptied another bottle. 'Yes, you can say that Jorge has a funny idea of pastoral care, all right. But do you know, I've seen worse sorts than him out there. They are working on the Indians at this very minute.' He sighed, then spat into the dirt. 'My glass is empty,' he said.

Refuelled, he went on. He cited an incident he had witnessed off the Orinoco, when a young man of the Panare tribe had failed to 'see the light'. The tribe was informed by this North American sect that the Indian boy was the devil incarnate. His body was found swinging from a tree first thing the next morning. He'd hung himself like Judas, the tribe was told at worship. Of course some missionaries were not like that. They were warm at heart and had open eyes. Their intention was to improve the Indians' lot; nothing more. Had I read any Mark Twain? Pablo asked. '"Soap and education are not so sudden as a massacre, but they are more deadly in the long run." And just think of poor Mawa.'

Pablo, the shaven-headed thug who minced people up with his spurs, had, it turned out, been to university in Brasilia. There he'd specialized in English literature. He had grown up poor, on the forest edge, where his father scratched a living from the land. He had kept the forest life in reserve if all else failed with his city career. It did, so now he was a brazil-nut gatherer.

'You'll find I have a soft heart underneath – if I'm handled right.'

'Does that mean you are going to help me?'

'You'll have to show me your plans better first. But I should be able to. Ten minutes ago I wouldn't have held if you'd offered me a fortune. Thought you were something to do with that priest. Know why he carries that knife?'

'Why?'

'Because once I whispered in his ear that I'd kill him.'

'Any reason in particular?'

'For what he had done to those Amazon Indians.'

'And *would* you kill him?' I said.

'Depends how the mood takes me. Might have last night, but he got out when he saw the fight start. Wise move.'

'Pity about the killing, last night,' I said. In response to this Jorge had said, 'May the Lord have mercy on his soul.' I wondered what Pablo would say.

He said, 'The killing? Yes, a pity. That's life, I suppose.'

I unpacked my maps and flattened them out on the table, weighting the corners down with beer bottles. 'Bit rash of Jorge to give us his knife, then?'

'It was a bit. Though he knows he's safe during the daytime.' Pablo tipped his most recent bottle upside down. It was empty. He was frowning at it. 'And yet, you know, I do believe I'd kind of miss him around the bars, pillaging all the girls, if things didn't work out between him and me.'

– 8 –

Contact

Pablo pushed away the maps. The cartographer's interpretation of the forest – a web of vague gullies and tracks, dreamed up in air-conditioned offices, he said – made him laugh. The plan was arranged. He would take me to a bunch of goldminers, *garimpeiros*, deep in the forest. They knew the Indians well. From there it would be up to me. We agreed a price for his pack-horses.

'And terms of payment?' he asked.

'I'll divide each note in two,' I said, 'and give you the left halves now. You'll have the right half once we get to the *garimpeiros*, and we're within reach of the Indians.'

'Suits me,' said Pablo.

I split the cash with Jorge's stab-knife, a double-bladed instrument which carved through the wad as though it were a pat of lard. He reached for the money, thumbed through the notes, and packed them into his breast pocket.

I needed only one day for final preparations, but Pablo said he needed a dry day before entering the jungle. The going was treacherous where the farmers were waging war with the vegetation and he couldn't afford one of the horses slipping in the mud and breaking a leg. He gave me three days from now. If by that time it hadn't stopped raining he could not ferry me through. 'So you'd better start praying for sunshine.'

We were to rendezvous on the first cloudless daybreak, in the village of Paraiso.

South from Boa Vista, down into the Amazon basin, the main road split; this was Paraiso, two dozen huts by the road.

Most of that road went on south to the city of Manaus, an Amazonian riverport which had been the vanguard of the rubber boom in the 1900s. Rubber barons had milked the forest for its latex and achieved such opulence from the trade that they erected baroque mansions in the jungle; they cobbled the streets with imported stones and mosaic pavements, and sent their linen to Ireland to be laundered. That was Manaus, where the main dirt road led. The other road spluttered east from Paraiso for a few miles, then stopped. That was the frontier of cultivation, and the beginning of my jungle, a dark wall of one-hundred-foot trees. Seven hundred miles to the east lay the mouth of the Amazon.

I was ready within a few hours, but the sky billowed and swelled with slate-grey cloud and sluiced the streets with rain, splattering the huts with red blobs of mud.

I had my supply stacks waiting. Everything had been thought of: flour, rice, coffee, sugar, beans; enough food, even without jungle meat, to last three people for four months. The sacks had been heaped, unheaped and heaped again on the dirt floor of my room in Paraiso, but still the skies were thick with cloud. On the medical side my strategy had been based on a defence against jungle fevers. I had brought most drugs from home, but topped them up with a few local tonics, such as Licor Amazonia, the '*fórmula do Dr Manoel de Morais Bittencourt*'. Bittencourt had been a strait-laced Victorian, judging by the photo on the bottle, who wore a brutally stiff butterfly collar. His was a jungle concoction of roots, nuts, leaves and fruits, 'all most rich in medical properties'. I'd reinforced my stock of presents for Indians with trinkets. I'd memorized the maps, and homogenized their discrepancies. I'd sealed up my survival belt – an emergency bag which would be strapped around my waist, stuffed with fishing lines, a compass, hooks, matches and so on.

There was nothing more to do but wait. Still it rained.

I sat on my pile, the size of a cot, and stared at the dark sky all that day. The next was as wet. The dozy hotelier said he'd never seen it so wet at this time of year and it was incredible. I ran my sweaty fingers up and down the equipment lists until the typed ink wore off. Still the rain fell. The drumming on the tin roofs was driving me mad. I could barely keep still. I paced the bar, or drummed my fingernails on the counter.

The following day was no better. The streets were awash, the sun blocked from the sky. The rain pummelled the roof without a break, all through the next night. I could not sleep and lay damp in my hammock. If at dawn the rain had not cleared, I would not be going at all. This was my last chance. I looked through the dark to my stores. Why was I making this journey anyway? I could not think of a good reason, and then I asked myself who would mind if I turned back and went home. The answer was no one. I wanted to express all this in my notebook: the rain squalls, the clattering of the roof, my stores waiting beside me. I opened a fresh page and wrote: '*2nd April. Lonely.*'

Later I did sleep, and later still I realized why: the roof was no longer rattling.

Waiting for Pablo (1 minute sketch)

At dawn I swung from my hammock, unbolted the wooden shutters, and looked out into the street. The road was lit gently. The sun was still below the treeline. Blue mist was steaming from the walls, street and roofs. The air was sharp and bitterly cold, but the tinbox houses looked magical, veiled in pale wisps of mist. I felt like skipping through it, down the street. There was not a cloud to be seen. The sky was a smoky blue, and quite clear.

Before long I was sitting in the street with my stores beneath me in the dawn sun. Soon Pablo would come with the horses and we would be away. I paced the gluey mud of the road. Where was he? Where was he?

*

Another brazil-nut gatherer called Raimundo came with Pablo to manage the horses, which were aloof beasts with tub bellies. Raimundo had small eyes and a small mouth that hardly ever opened. He had a monkey face with thick eyebrows that met in the middle and were like moss. He had a bristly neck; his ears were like gristle.

It was a full day's walk from Paraiso. Along the way, the forest had been bruised and scolded by small farmsteads, whose crops were all failing. The road ended at a small river called the Jatapu; shortly after, there was the jungle wall.

We slept at its foot, on the land near one of the last farms, Villa la Tapolandia. We were embraced by a farmer who showed us his children's rib cages, and ran his fingers over their bones as if they were xylophone keys.

The next day we had another look at the jungle wall. Pablo seemed to dip into it at random. He probed about, forcing the lead

Entering the jungle

horse ahead of him, batting it from behind with a stick, and shoving its head into the leaves. Each time, the horse refused to enter. Its eyeballs rolled, its nostrils widened, and it whinnied and stamped, with its nose in the air. 'The path has grown over a little bit, perhaps,' said Pablo. The truth was that the jungle had sealed it up completely.

'The jungle is fighting back,' said Raimundo, nodding at the charred remains of the field behind, the farmer's latest assault. 'But don't worry, it'll lose in the end.'

Eventually, we penetrated the wall. It was warm inside the jungle, as choking as a hot-house. The air was still; it pressed against the skin, and its moisture clung to the back of my throat. Light came in splashes for a while, but as we entered deeper none of it broke through. The sound of our knives hacking was sponged up by the leaves, and the insect buzz muffled the crunch of our boots. Deeper, the undergrowth had mostly given up hope of light, and the horses nosed their way without prompting.

Pablo said we were northward bound for a while, following the Jatapu river. Not far from an Indian village called Anauá, we were to swing east. I stayed close to Pablo, keeping my eyes on his green hat, and on the black and white jaguar tail, which flapped from it, through the leaves. We moved at a trot to keep up with the horses, slicing at the creepers with our machetes to trim them back. If we came across birds or monkeys, Pablo blasted at them with his shotgun, but we were moving too fast to take hunting seriously.

We stopped only once, during a cloudburst, when we pulled banana leaves over us as umbrellas and crouched under the horses in their steam.

That night we drank *cachaça* by the fireside. Pablo said he was off to find some brazil nuts for our supper, and later he came back hugging casks which looked like cannon balls. Inside there were the nuts, lying snugly like orange segments. We cracked them with our molars, and roasted them dipped in sugar. Pablo said we had made very good progress and should reach the goldminers before the next nightfall. They lived in a decrepit shack nick-named the Palace. They kept a turkey as a companion. Pablo said it was a waste of good meat, their letting it trot around, and this time he was determined to get it into the cooking pot.

We stoked up the fire, tied up the horses next to it, and fenced them in by hitching up the hammocks in a large triangle around them. Pablo said the jaguars knew him well in these parts and had been craving his blood for years. So far they had dared only get their teeth into his horses, and this was why he wanted them on the inside. How could the jaguars resist going for him tonight? I was not to worry myself, he said; he would be wide awake and waiting for them.

Later I heard a purring, and was scared out of my wits. It was not a jaguar, only Pablo snoring, and I got up and cuffed him.

We were on the move before dawn and before the blisters on my knife hand had recovered from the previous day. Raimundo potted a spider-monkey, and as it tumbled down he muttered, 'That's one less person after our brazil nuts.'

The *garimpeiros* were Negroes, but their skins were palish from lack of daylight. There were three of them and they were excavating a pit. Their Palace was a palm lean-to which stood in a clearing paved with dead leaves and stunted cottongrass. They blinked like moles when they came out from the trees in answer to Pablo's hallooing. One took the monkey away to prepare it; another – who looked identical to the first, with the same fleshless body and limp wrists and neck – asked if we had any alcohol. The third, Antônio, was hairier, but otherwise much the same, and ran up to Pablo to hug him. He whisked off Pablo's hat, patted his smooth fat head, and laughed. He asked what month it was – surely Pablo had made

Tatty Palace Turkey

a mistake coming at this time of the year? – but it was wonderful to see him so soon, and by the way, unfortunately their dear mutual friend Jamarillo had drowned last week; it was most strange because the water had been only as deep as the bottle he'd had in his hand at the time, but there you are.

A tatty bird skipped into the clearing and pecked at my boots.

'Ah, good,' said Pablo, 'the Palace turkey. And even more meat on him than before.' The Palace turkey had a tarantula – hand-sized and kicking – in its beak. It dropped the spider on to my boot. Pablo stepped forward, sniggered, and smeared it into the dirt with the ball of his foot.

But the tarantula pulled itself back together again, reassembling its crushed black fingers, and stroking down its bristles, like a cat its whiskers. Pablo gave it another grind with his heel.

Pablo and monkey's arm

The monkey, once skinned, was pink, and its bandy legs and arms made it look like a starved human baby. We ate it boiled in a clay oven. Dinner was a heap of limbs in fatty yellow water. They tasted rubbery, and chewing the fingers made me cringe. Nevertheless, I piled my bowl full so as to avoid eating the monkey's head. It stared up from the serving pot with the same look of blind astonishment as the sloth's head wore as it went spinning in the Icabarú river. Pablo took a spoon, cracked the skull open like an egg and ladled out the brain in equal shares. He sucked his portion on his tongue and said, 'Hmmm. Almost as good as that turkey's going to be.'

'No!' One of the men banged his fist on the plank table. 'He ain't for eatun. Dat turkey's a good friend, and nobody's gonna lay a finger on im.'

The Negroes came from Guyana, whose border was only a stone's throw away to the north. They bragged they knew the jungle by heart. When they heard where we were going, one of the two identical ones said, 'You ain't never wantin to go near dem Injuns, man. You know, dem folks have tails. Dey swings just like monkeys.'

Pablo laughed at this.

'It's true, man!'

'I know for sure, and de women have busoms like pumpkins, and dey make love wid de monkeys when de men are away ahuntin.'

'How do you know all dese dings, Joshua?' the other twin said.

'I hears all dis from my friends back home in Georgetown.'

'So you ain't seen nothun wid your own eyes.'

'For sure I ain't seen nothun wid my own eyes, Moses, but I knows it for true.'

'Well, Joshua, I seen de Injuns and I tell you dis. Dey ain't got no tails. But dey got skin as white as bone. And somethun else. Dey skins you alive if dey is catchun you on dere land.'

'Dat's true, Moses,' the other said shaking his head. 'I ain't approachun a million miles near dere.'

'Funny you should say that,' said Pablo. He winked at me.

We had to use up a lot of *cachaça* to persuade them to take me to the Indians. Once they had agreed and were flat on their backs snoring, Pablo and I sat down and talked.

Pablo said he would wait here with Raimundo while Moses and Joshua were taking me, and leave for home only once they were back and he had a sign from me saying I was safely with the Indians; the jaguar's tail from his hat would do fine. He plucked it off and pushed it into my hand. I said I thought Joshua and Moses might not turn out to be the best guides in the world, and he agreed. He'd been thinking the same thing. The trouble was that both he and Raimundo had had a slight misunderstanding over some gold they'd come across near the Wai-wai village, and they weren't keen on being seen. But he would persuade Raimundo to accompany us part of the way. If Raimundo dropped me off with Joshua and Moses just short of the Indians, everything should be fine.

Later I bought two fistfuls of gold dust from the *garimpeiros*, as extra currency for trading with the Indians. I paid with five bottles of São João, and 500,000 cruzeiros. That gave me 100 grams of gold at a rock-bottom price. If I threw in another bottle, they said, they'd take me to the Indians for free. I gave up my last bottle, and we drank to the deal from tin cans of Lubrax MD 300, an engine-oil lubricant. They apologized. All the good cups had been washed away by the river with the body of their friend.

In the coldest part of the night, there was a shriek in the darkness. It was the bitter cry of someone whose trust had been betrayed, and I knew who it was. The poor Palace turkey hung limp with a noose around its neck next morning. 'Trod on it when I got up in the night,' said Pablo. 'Complete accident. Had to put it out of its misery.' He dangled it in front of Joshua's face, then hung it up again from the roof beam. Joshua was stunned by the sight; he put his hand in front of his eyes and gulped air like a fish.

'We must give de Palace turkey de proper decent Christian burial,' he said slowly, his eyes on the ground.

'What? And waste all that meat?' Pablo cut the bird down with a whirl of his machete and began plucking it like a harp over his knee. If Joshua had nothing better to do than stand around gaping, he said, then he could go off and find some jungle leaves to garnish it.

'He was de best friend I had,' said Joshua later, snuffling at the sight of the roasted corpse, as Pablo carved it up at the table.

'Let's hope he's not too stringy,' said Pablo.

Antônio was supposed to be Pablo's best friend. He had an unnaturally high forehead, poky eyes and a hooked nose; even when he smiled he reminded me of a vulture. He also dabbled in medicine.

'Hey, man, I got somethun for you,' he said, while the others were packing the horses. 'Come wid me.'

'Where are we going?' I said.

'Just you wait un see.' We were walking towards a straw house made of freshly cut and dried grass. 'Step right inside.'

The little house was murky. It smelt of spring cow-parsley. The grass walls were still green and sprouting shoots. They were stacked with sheaths of dried herbs, barks, and nuts. This was a jungle medicine cabinet.

'I got potions for you. Dey will help you good. Dey is magic.'

'What sort of magic?'

'Good magic, man. I got so much magic I keeps all de spirits locked up here away from de Palace.'

On the wall was the head of a toothless alligator, grinning. It was dried solid, but Antônio wrenched open its jaws to see if there were any back teeth left. There weren't. It was a crying shame, he said, because if you sucked one like a lozenge it would cure almost any bladder problem.

I said I didn't have a bladder problem. 'What else have you got?'

'Dis is what I wan you to take along wid you. For true, man, dis will give you good luck.'

'What is it?' I said. It was a hard, scaly, bony thing; a trumpet, I thought.

He said it was an armadillo's tail. 'Dis give you de hearing of a jaguar. You grinds it up and you drinks it in hot water like cocoa. Mark my words, man, you gonna need dis ting good.'

'Got anything else?' I was eyeing some purple berries, which looked like overgrown bilberries. As a medicine they looked a sight more promising.

'Dat's my supper,' said Antônio. They were marajá berries from a palm tree. He had been shinning up and down palms since he had been a boy, he said, and he narrated an elaborate story about how the trunk of a palm had snapped below him once and he'd fallen from the sky, into the arms of his wife below. It had been lucky for her his hobby was medicine.

Antônio put out his hand to say goodbye. I took the hand; it was hard and bony and had long crusty fingernails. I wanted to drop it. It was lifeless and cold. When Antônio moved away and I still had his hand in mine I almost screamed. He'd left the thing behind.

'Dat's a monkey's paw,' he said. 'Now, dat give you plenty of breath when yous needin it. Makes your lungs strong. You gonna need both dese tings good. De armadillo tail let you be hearin danger, and dat monkey's paw helps you run good from it. Keep

Antônio collecting berries

dem by your side.' Antônio clasped my arms and shook me. 'Now you be lisnin careful.' His eyes were bulging at me. 'Bad luck walks wid you, man. Any folk ever told you dat before?'

I scoffed, but the memory of the sloth's head made my palms sticky. I promised to bear it in mind, and said I was sure the monkey's paw and the armadillo's tail would come in useful.

I backed out of the hut and hurried up to Pablo. 'Your friend Antônio,' I said. 'Is he, er . . . mentally sound?'

'Not really. None of my friends are.'

'That's all right, then. But it's strange – I've had an unlucky run on madmen so far on my journey.'

I stuffed the gold down my boots, trouser linings, and saddle bags, stashing it away in cigarette-lengths. I then gave Pablo the remainder of his money. He said he'd already spent the left halves, by gluing them together. The people he mixed with were too drunk to notice, and with that cash he'd wiped out all his debts to bar girls in one fell swoop.

He wished me luck and I promised to send back the jaguar tail to show I was safely with the Indians. 'Come out of the jungle again, won't you, Benedito? I admire your pluck.'

'Thanks, Pablo.'

'Know what they used to say to me in Venezuela? "*La selva es una cárcel eterna.* The jungle is an eternal prison." Prove them wrong, eh?'

The others came without a word. Raimundo flapped the reins. The two horses we were taking with us lifted their heads reluctantly, wrenching away last mouthfuls of grass and savouring them. Sunbathing lizards rattled the twigs strewn over the clearing as we moved off. The last of the scorched leaves crackled under our boots, and then we were back in the jungle, in the dark again. Our hair was once more wringing wet, and we wiped perspiration from our eyes.

Three days on, an hour after the morning mists had lifted, Raimundo said we were nearing the Indians. He was walking at the back horse's tail; Joshua and Moses were at the front; I was wedged between the two horses. After a long silence, plodding on like this, Joshua suddenly said, 'Hey, I gotta bad thought. You think dat maybe Pablo killed de Palace turkey on purpose?'

'Now, why would Pablo want to do a mean thing like that?' asked Raimundo. He was trying to hide a smirk.

'Because he been wantin my turkey dead ever since I first introduced dem, three years ago, dat's why.'

'Yeah,' said Moses, 'I seen him lickin his lips, and I seen him wid a murderous kinda look in his eye.'

'Tasted good, didn't it?' said Raimundo, and Joshua burst into tears.

Ten minutes later, Raimundo said, 'All right. We'd better tie up the horses now. From here, we go on by foot.'

'But we ain't nearly dere yet,' said Moses.

'Near enough for my liking,' said Raimundo.

Joshua said, 'Yeah. Dem Injuns is bad people. Dey got monkey tails. Dey got noses like jaguars. Dey got skin as white as bone.'

'So you said,' said Raimundo. 'Now, you stay put with the horses, Joshua, and don't make a sound. I don't want the Indians ever to know I was here. They might not be too pleased about you two, either, you being goldminers as well.'

'I sure am scared,' said Joshua. 'One you men stay wid me.'

'Sorry, Joshua,' said Raimundo, 'you'll have to wait alone. Just keep calm. We'll be back soon to pick up the stores.'

'Man, I sure am scared.' Joshua put his fingers in his mouth. 'Shhhh!'

We tiptoed forward, leaving Joshua trembling alone on the track. I could dismiss Joshua's fear as ignorance, but Raimundo's worried me. I knew only that he had had a 'misunderstanding' with the Indians over the gold. That was what Pablo had said; knowing Pablo, it meant something far worse. The 'misunderstanding' had probably included eloping with the headman's most precious daughter or something. His pride and joy had been swept away in Pablo's arms, and the Indians were dying for revenge. It would be something like that.

Raimundo jerked to a standstill and stiffened. Neither Moses nor I had heard the sound, but sensing something wrong we listened with him on the track, not daring to breathe.

I caught it the second time. It came from ahead, in the jungle off to the right. It was only a crack of a twig, but both Raimundo and Moses had frozen solid, with their shoulders hunched up.

There were the usual jungle sounds: whistlings, chirpings and clickings; and far away a crash of leaves – monkeys passing through the canopy, yanking branches. Bird sounds, too – the squawks of parrots and the twitterings of smaller hopping insect-eaters.

What did the other two think? Should we run? I wanted to see Raimundo's eyes, read his face. But both men were ahead of me on the track and I could see only the back of their heads: Raimundo's straight, thick black hair and Moses's tight oily curls, rolling on to his heavy knotted shoulders, which dribbled with sweat. They still seemed to be waiting for the sound to come again. Or perhaps they could hear it plainly and were thinking out our next move. Both men knew the jungle. They could hear the false notes; I couldn't. This thought made me feel small.

We all carried machetes and Raimundo had a shotgun strapped over his shoulder. The sight of the knives worried me more than the gun because they were at hand. They held them loosely, like twigs of kindling wood, as if they had been using them since babyhood. The silver cutting edges flashed in the leaf-clouded forest, and I visualized both blades slashing through the Indians with the same easy swing they had used to clear saplings from our path, converting them to clean stumps.

The air was steaming with the sweat of leaves and branches. As we waited, yellow wasps darted about in the stale air around us, trying to settle and lick the salt from our skin. The silence and the waiting were unnerving me.

Raimundo bent backwards to Moses. He was taking care not to move his feet and so snap a dry leaf. He cupped a hand around Moses's right ear so that he was speaking away from the direction of the noise. They were a stride away at the most, but I didn't hear the whisper. Raimundo patted the air, as if slapping a dog down, and we all sank to the earth.

The path was paved with brown chips of leaf. They were soft crumbly flakes, which were damp against my cheek and smelt of old pipe tobacco. We had disturbed a passing army of ants, but now they had reassembled and began to trundle over us in long, unbroken chains.

I was still convinced it was not Indians we had heard. Indians didn't walk about the jungle cracking twigs. They walked on their toes, and left no trace.

I wouldn't be able to lie here much longer. Root knots were working dents into my skin, and now Moses's machete had scraped through the file of ants. They were having tantrums. I watched them fretting, dragging out the crushed ones, stroking the air with their antennae, and gnawing at Moses's black knuckles. He rolled his fist and crunched a few. Others were swarming towards me. They clamped their jaws on to my shirt; they pattered down my spine. My skin started to swell and burn with their bites. Now they were all I cared about in the world. I just wanted to spring up and pluck the tweezer heads of those ants off. I squinted with pain.

Raimundo rose to his feet. Moses and I did the same. The rust-freckled barrel of the shotgun came down from his shoulder. He cradled it in his arms, gave it a smile as if he were cuddling a baby, and signalled us to follow. We slinked forward. The forest had gone dead. The only sounds were our clumping boots. Were we going to be ambushed? I tried to prepare for it, holding my breath and bracing myself for the whooping shriek of the Indians. I pictured the leaves sprayed with blood, and prayed I wouldn't show myself up by jumping with surprise when the attack came.

Nothing happened for a time. When it came, it was the others who jumped. We were crossing a stream bridged by a fallen tree, swaying in single file with our arms outstretched for balance. We couldn't have made ourselves more vulnerable. The bushes ahead crashed open. I stopped dead, with my mouth wide open, half-way across the log. Raimundo and Moses spun around on the spot, while I stood petrified in mid-stride. They shot past me in a blur and sprinted along the tree trunk, with their hands reaching out for the forest.

Still tottering over the stream, I saw the Indian – only one, and he was small, with a short red loincloth and a knife. He had no bow and arrows. Joshua had been right; his skin was pale. I knew it was too late to make a run for it, and he was intent on the others, looking right past me. I could hear their boots pounding back down the track behind.

The Indian lunged by me on that tightrope of a log, and shot down the track, leaving me wobbling. I was surprised: not because he had gone by without even brushing me, but because of how clean the Indian had smelt; not like a mangy dog as Fritz had led me to expect, but more like unperfumed soap.

I sat down on the other riverbank and sponged down my ant bites with swabs of moss. There was nothing else I could do. I toyed with the idea of hiding, but what was the point? There was nowhere to go, the track was too weak for me to trace for the three days back to Pablo, and so I just sat there, awaiting the Indian. In the far distance I heard the whinny of a horse. What about my expedition supplies?

The Indian came back, running. I heard his approach: not his footsteps, but his panting.

He looked at me for a second from the other side of the stream, catching his breath. He was breathing so hard his tongue hung out, and all his weight was on the toes of his right foot. He cantered along the log. His skin was a milky caramel, but his hair was jet black, cropped into a fringe at the front and plaited into a tail at the back, which ended in a heavy clump of silvery egret feathers.

I got up slowly and put the handle of my machete in his hand. He took the knife and eased it into his loincloth.

There was blood smeared on his face. I breathed out. No, it was paint; greasy smudges of it across both cheeks. I noticed that his hand, still on the knife, was shaking, his knuckles white with the pressure he was putting on the handle. We stood there, eye to eye. I could not read his intentions. His face wasn't hostile, or curious, or kind. He looked me over, breathing out steam through flared nostrils. I tried a few chatty phrases in Portuguese. His expression didn't alter. I tried Warao, but when he still looked blank, it didn't surprise me. The Wai-wai, like the Taulipáng of the Gran Sabana, are of Carib stock, and belong to a different linguistic group.

Raimundo had told me I would be able to communicate with ease. Now what?

The Indian pointed the knife at my stomach – not threateningly, but carelessly, as if the consequences of stabbing didn't matter. I kept talking, trying to establish a relationship, while that knife-point pricked me like a blunt needle.

'*Tushau*,' I said, gesturing for him to lead me on. Pablo had said the word meant 'headman', or 'chief', in Wai-wai. The Indian grunted, then prodded me up along the track.

On the way, I remembered another of Pablo's words. I turned my head, still walking. '*Kiriwanhi*,' I said, pointing at my chest, '*kiriwanhi, kiriwanhi*. Me good, me good.' He spiked my shirt with his knife, and we continued in silence. I thought to myself: You have got the words the right way round, haven't you? And I felt my cheeks flush. *Kiriwanhi* meant 'good', *chichibé* meant 'bad'. Or had I got them the wrong way round? I said nothing else. Those three were my only Wai-wai words.

The path split and thinned. Walking in front, I took too many wrong turns, so the Indian took the lead. He became agitated if I lagged more than a pace behind, and when I did he would wave the knife in my face.

The forest became darker, the path veered, then we broke into dazzling light. I had to cover my eyes. Still blinded, and wondering where the Indian was, I heard the lapping of running water a couple of steps ahead. A girl screamed; a dog barked.

I opened my eyes and saw river water thrashing with running women. They were naked, and ran with cloth bundles and kicking babies tucked under their arms. They were sprinting for a group of palm huts, high up on the far bank. The huts were round and simple, with loosely plaited walls of leaves and drooping roofs with even looser thatching – just beds of heaped fronds. I could have made them better myself. I got the impression the huts had been thrown up in a hurry. These people weren't nomads because they weren't practised in the art of making speedy tents, and tents were all that the huts were. So maybe they were refugees; either that, or being drenched by rain didn't worry them.

I took off my hat. Beyond the village some children were mucking about in the river. They hadn't seen me. Some were diving into the water from an overhang of soft fawn rock. Others were cartwheeling down off tree vines, holding their noses and screaming as they dropped. When they did see me they ran like the women, yelling across the water, kicking up suds, leaving spray. When we came to the village the women and children were a wall of waving arms, legs and bosoms. My Indian bawled at them and they backed away into their huts.

We walked into an empty central area of bare earth. The ground, as smooth and hard as concrete, reflected the sounds of gossiping in the surrounding huts. In the doorways were hot ash heaps and pots with blackened bottoms. A slender hand came out from one of the huts and whisked the contents of a bowl with a stick. The steam smelt of boiled ham, but from the look of the white scum and bubbles I thought they might be trying to poach an egg.

The Indian stopped me, and jabbed his knife through the doorway of a hut much smaller and more tightly woven than the rest. I went in.

I had to stoop because of the lowness of the roof. The light coming through the door was blocked off behind me. The entrance was being stacked with spiky palm fronds, the spines along the mid-ribs like black hatpins. The walls were woven like a wicker basket. I leant against them, but they didn't give. This was not a hut, it was a cage.

I waited an hour by my watch, wondering when I was going to be allowed a drink. I was not worried, not as much as I might have been. The palm door wasn't fastened, and so I didn't get the impression I was a prisoner. But where could I have escaped to? I tired of squinting through the wall chinks, and so I listened to the women jabbering in their huts, or walking by, scuffing their feet, tired in the heat.

Later I heard men talking, and felt the earth vibrate under a stampede of feet. A hunting party had returned, I guessed. Through the hut walls I could see only the backs of children hopping up and down to get a better view over a crowd. The men

must have had a good morning's hunt. As they distributed the
meat, I heard one word repeated time and time again: '*Atchi*',
'*Atchi*', '*Atchi*'.

Two people with heavy steps were approaching. The doorway
was cleared, and two men stepped in. Their black silhouettes had
short thick legs, compact torsos, and hair cut into a clump above
their ears. One had a pigtail – he was the one who had put me in
this cage. They were talking loudly to me. I smiled, nodded and
listened patiently but I couldn't understand a word. They became
more and more worked up. The cramped cage was bottling up
their energy. If it wasn't released soon, they were going to lash out
at me. All I could do was put up my hands and say I wanted the
chief. '*Tushau, tushau, tushau.*'

The newer Indian bent down and joggled my arms. '*Garummm-
pppppooo!*' he said. His eyes were bloodshot. The hand on my arm
was quivering. He placed the heel of his foot on my chest and
pushed me back against the wall. He reached for my throat, but I
ducked in time. This was getting nasty. Then I caught the word he
had said before. *Garimpeiro*, he meant – 'goldminer'.

I shook my head. 'No, no, no. *Não garimpeiro!*' I said. I beamed
at them. I thought this had done the trick. The Indian was no
longer bearing down on me. We would soon have this little
misunderstanding straightened out.

He took a small package out of his red loincloth. I frowned.
They had been rifling through my supplies. Then I saw what he
had got and almost fainted. He held out his palm and sprinkled out
one of my phials of gold. I watched it spiralling down, and began to
fidget. After he had emptied every grain out, he brought the gold
up in front of my nose. I tried to laugh but ended up wiping my
brow. He sniggered, brought the dust even closer and blew it into
my eyes. Before the sting had worn off, the thick wrist of the
Indian made another grab for my windpipe. The situation was so
frustrating, and so stupid, and the grit in my eyes was so painful,
that I lost my temper and exploded in English:

'Get your lousy hands off me!' They were the words Fritz would
have used, and a string more came into my head.

The Indians stopped the scuffle. The hand in my grip went
limp. Something had happened. The nearer Indian said, 'You talk
English?'

I was stunned with surprise and relief; I could hardly breathe. I wiped my eyes, releasing the hand, and blinked out the gold. They were waiting.

I said, 'As a matter of fact, I do.'

They slapped their hairless thighs. 'Golly God. Dat make three of us!' And they both fell about laughing.

– 9 –

The pig duel

It was not a hunting party that had returned to the village, but a luggage party. The two men, still wheezing from the laughing, let me peep out of the hut. I saw all my bags spread out and scattered. The Indians had flocked to them, and were picking through my things like hyenas after a killing. One man was wearing my hat. He had tipped it to one side and was mincing across the clearing, showing it off. I tried to run forward to stop the rummaging but I was held back.

'For now you wait. When headman come, you talk good why you have gold. If you no explain, then bad for you.'

'Yes,' said the Indian called Anarau, who had escorted me to the village. 'If you no explain, too bad for you!' He flourished his knife.

We watched the looting of my stores. Some of these people, like the Warao, wore a smattering of Western clothes. I saw a pair of shorts and a nylon miniskirt. But these were relics – so threadbare they were see-through. All the newer garments were red and from a rough cotton: aprons for women, short loincloths for men. Beads and earrings of soft breast-feathers swung around nearly everyone's necks, though those on the men were heavier and brighter. The difference between the people here and the Warao was that the Warao decorated themselves brightly by accident rather than design. The Warao fished for their clothes in the Orinoco waterways. They dressed from whatever swept down in the current from upstream – whether purple cotton sheets or orange polythene shopping bags. Their wardrobe was garish, because dull-coloured objects went undetected.

Now, sitting in the white mid-afternoon sun, my machetes were being used to slice open the food sacks. While dogs and children

Village on stilts

Dawn

Mount Roraima

A dug-out canoe

Landing strip

Cashoe

Abandoned highway

Constructing a shelter

Headman Maipuri

Ak-ak

Anarau

Tautau

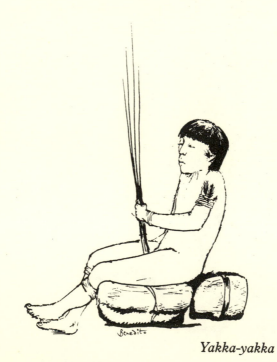

Yakka-yakka

Indian trying on clothes (With apologies to Picasso)

pattered in the spilt rice, two women were carving my short trousers up between them.

'*Atchi*', the word I'd heard earlier, seemed to mean 'what is it?' They picked up my thick woollen socks. '*Atchi, atchi?* What is it?' The women shared the socks out and tried them on until they could find somewhere they fitted. One was stretched over a husband's head. Another pair was squeezed over a woman's breasts, and my two men laughed so hard they had to clutch their stomachs to ease the cramp.

The headman was every inch a king. He walked majestically, and the villagers dispersed from what was left of my luggage to trail behind him as he strutted into the village. Two men walking humbly behind him were bearing between them a bristly pig which hung upside down with its trotters tied to a pole. It was the size of an overweight goat, and it was alive, because I saw it blink.

I was left alone, sitting crosslegged on the dust, while my two captors reported to the headman. He had a fringe and the rest of his hair was in a plait, which hung stiffly down his spine in a sheath of animal skin. Cotton wool covered his earlobes in white puffs, and his short neck was ringed with beads. He wore a white armband which pinched into the muscle; a machete with a muddy brown blade projected from his loincloth. He looked over towards me and stared. He came nearer, still staring. His face was old and withered, but below the neck his skin was firm and young. He had a hole in the septum of his nose, and peering through I could see the blue of the sky. The entire village trooped up two paces behind, squinting at me.

'You take Wai-wai gold?'

'No. I'm just journeying through.'

The headman smiled to the crowd. 'He say he just journeying through!' The crowd laughed. He said to me, 'Through where?'

'To the Trombetas,' I said, naming the first major river to the east.

'You want gold in Trombetas?'

'No, I'll move on east and east and east. I want to go to where the jungle stops.'

'If you go to end of jungle, you go wrong way.'

'Mmmmmmmmm,' said one of the hunting Indians, nodding. He had a shotgun balanced on his shoulder. 'Only way home is way you come.'

'No, I want to go east.'

'*You* not going anywhere,' he said, suddenly. '*You* staying here. Where your present to me?'

'I have brought many presents. Look over there.' He looked, I looked, and the crowd turned and looked, but all we saw was the dust clearing, and a few scattered grains of rice. Everything had gone.

'You bad man. You lie.'

'Your people have borrowed them. I'm hoping they are about to bring them back. If you ask your people, they will bring the gifts perhaps. Then I can present a special gift for you.'

'No.'

'No?'

'No. I will have *everything*,' he said. I groaned. He barked a few orders, and the villagers went away sulkily to bring back the spoils. A few men stayed on and stood around with their arms folded, their eyes on the survival pouch around my waist.

'What else you got?' asked the headman, who seemed to be called Maipuri. He made no mention of what he had in mind, but his eyes were fixed on my survival pouch as well. I pulled a couple of picture postcards from my breast pocket. I'd been entertaining Joshua with them that morning. I put one in his hand. It showed the Queen smiling in state, with Windsor Castle as a backdrop.

'What this say?'

'It says, "Greetings from London."'

'Your chief send *greetings*?'

'Er . . . sort of.'

'But she a *woman*.'

'Yes, she's a woman.' I showed him the other card. 'This shows her house, and a beefeater, who is a sort of warrior, and there's a picture of a big village called London, where she lives. That red thing is a bus. And that's Tower Bridge, and that's—'

'Buzzz?'

'Bus, it's a bus.'

'Mmmm. Your chief has big hut.'

'That's Buckingham Palace. She is very wealthy. She is the most rich person in all the world. She is waiting for me to come back safely.'

Maipuri scratched his navel, and looked down at the dark crescents of sweat spreading from my armpits. Two other men peered over his shoulder to look at the photos, but he flattened them against his chest as though they were a hand of cards.

'But she a *woman*?'

'Yes.'

The chief coughed uneasily, turned to his men, and muttered something in Wai-wai. The villagers began to laugh, but it was the women who were laughing most and also clapping their hands. When they didn't stop after a while, the men turned on them and waved their fists.

'When this woman coming here?'

'After I've got back home safely.' I repeated that she was waiting for my safe return.

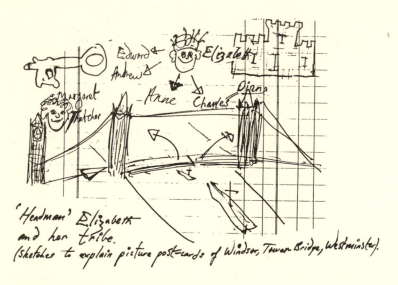

'Headman' Elizabeth and her tribe.
(Sketches to explain picture post-cards of Windsor, Tower Bridge, Westminster).

Maipuri frowned. 'What her name?'

'Elizabeth.'

'Lizbet,' said Maipuri to his men. 'She Lizbet.' To me he said, 'Lizbet like gold?'

'Very much.'

'Then you take gold from Maipuri to Lizbet? You agree?'

The Indians were standing looking at me on tiptoe, holding their breath, and very still. I basked for a while in their gaze.

'All right, I agree.'

The men gave heavy, whistling sighs of relief. The headman glowed at his coup, and the men looked at him with admiration.

'On one condition,' I said. There was a heart-broken silence and I felt cruel.

'What you say?'

'I will give her the gold on one condition.'

'What you mean?' said Maipuri, slowly.

'You must help me on my way. With my baggage of course.'

'That is two condition.'

I said I was very sorry, but that was the way it was.

Maipuri mumbled to himself, flexing his fingers at his sides. Then his arms stiffened. He marched right up to me and said, 'Baggages *mine*. I want baggages.' He stepped back again, folded his arms, and nodded triumphantly. 'I keep baggages. You my prisoner. So you make you quiet for now.'

'Mmmmm,' said the men. 'You quiet for now.'

They put their heads together for a good think.

My luggage was now back in a heap by my side; the Indians looked it up and down longingly. I felt stronger with it near again.

'I make decision,' said Maipuri, raising his right hand with his fingers to the sky for silence. 'My decision this. No one know where we are but *garumpo*. So you *garumpo*. You *garumpo*, so you thief. You thief, so you prisoner. You prisoner, so you in trouble deep. You in trouble deep, so you need Lizbet. We also in trouble deep and need Lizbet. She like gold, and you have gold. You take gold and talk with Lizbet. You talk that Maipuri is a friend.'

I said that the arrangement seemed satisfactory. Maipuri grinned at the men either side of him. One of them said that I looked pretty weak to his mind, and might not make it out of the forest anyway. Maipuri said he had already thought of that.

'You strong?'

'I can do a hundred press-ups. Shall I show you?' I began to bend down.

The men stepped back. 'What he doing?'

Maipuri said he had a better idea. 'We watch you kill pig.'

'You do what?'

'You kill pig with bare hand.'

This was just the sort of predicament I had dreaded ever since first setting foot in South America. I had broken into a cold sweat some nights having faced, in dreams, imprisonment by hostile natives, or interrogation in a foreign tongue, or a decimation of all my expedition stores. Today, one by one, all my nightmares had cropped up in real life; all except the test of skill and daring. That was coming now.

'Fetch pig!' the headman yapped. The two bulky youths who had been hunting with Maipuri loped off through the crowd.

How do you go about killing a pig? I wondered. I had killed some pelicans once. That was with Camahu and Narru in the Orinoco delta, standing stark naked on the grey flats with a mudpack on my shoulders to fend off the sun. We had snapped the bird's necks as if testing the breaking strain of a rope. Then as a boy I'd earned holiday pocket money on a turkey farm, executing turkeys for the Christmas market. But a wild pig? That was different. I thought of Fritz's wild boar, the one that made a mess of a tree even after it had been shot through its head. I said, 'You mean with a machete, don't you?'

'I mean with bare hand.'

One of the men with folded arms unfolded them and said, 'He scare easy.'

I said I wasn't scared. I tried to look him in the eye, but couldn't.

The crowd was stirring. A pathway was being made to let the pig through. It was causing quite an upset and must have been kicking out wildly. I imagined something the size of a horse, breathing in grunts, with yellow teeth jutting out like chisels. But what I saw was more moderate: a peccary, the fat, goat-sized animal I'd seen earlier, fresh from the forest. It was screaming, and the scream was a lonely cry for help. Never say die, piggy, I thought. Look who you're up against.

The men wanted me to take my clothes off and fight naked. They ripped away my cotton shirt, pinging off the buttons, and chucked it to the crowd, which divided it. Maipuri interceded on my behalf and said of course I had the right to wear what I pleased. I unpeeled the other Indians' fingers. I said in that case I'd like to slip on a new shirt to keep off the sun.

'No. That unfair on pig. How can he bite you good?'

I asked if he could hold on a minute because I still had gold dust in my eyes. The headman said I'd have more than that in my eyes before the fight was over.

I took a couple of steps closer to the pig, into the centre of the village. The crowd encircled me; only twenty-five or so Indians. We could see each other in the open for the first time. My view was of soft tawny skins, feathers, glossy black hair and rainbow hoops of beads. Their view was of a man a foot taller than anyone they'd ever seen alive, with blue eyes and green sweat-blotted khaki. They were lusting after my clothes, and confused by the colour of my eyes.

Some women had babies resting in the nooks of their arms like handbags. They were clambering for their mothers' nipples, jerking them down to their gums.

'What you waiting for?' said Maipuri.

The pig was forced to the ground, as an act of generosity. The Indians were blue in the face, and struggling to maintain their grip. One had the pig's ears, another its tail. Seeing me over it, the pig squealed again, and humped and flopped on the ground like a seal. The crowd was swaying for the best view. The noise was of the cockfighting crowd of Icabarú: jeering, taunting, daring. I felt as apprehensive as the pig, crouching in the middle of that crowd. Neither of us wanted to fight, but like the cocks we were going to have to.

I decided I'd go for a throttle hold. That was my best chance. First I'd hold the beast down with my weight, then I'd go for its throat, which was as thick as a mule's. I hadn't heard of anyone wringing a wild pig's neck, but I thought that in the Bible Samson had strangled a lion once.

Benedita   The Pig Duel

I took hold of the pig's ears. They were rubbery and damp, like bacon rind.

'Why you keep me waiting?'

The Indians leapt back. The pig and I were alone in the ring. Neither of us moved. I was on my knees; the pig was on its side, blinking its white eyelashes and blowing up dust with its snorts. The pig wasn't trapped, it was waiting.

'He clever,' said a man in the crowd. 'He know how to fight.' Who was he talking about – the pig or me?

The pig kicked out. I rolled on to its stomach and flattened it to the ground. I began to walk my fingers up through its bristly hair, against the growth, in the direction of its throat. The skin was dry and hairy, as well as prickly, covered with what seemed like chronic eczema. The pig rolled its eyes when it realized my fingers were slipping down towards its neck; it bucked and jolted to dislodge me. Soon I was winded and had to bring back my hand to keep the animal under me.

The crowd crept in, and roared, thinking the pig was gaining the upper hand. I could feel the strength of its lungs under me. A man's foot stamped near my nose and sprayed sand into my face. I thought it was deliberate. The crowd roared as I winced. Were they for me or against me? I had no way of telling. One girl at least was egging me on. Our eyes met, as I was winded again by a loose trotter. She grinned – her teeth were a brilliant white and unusually sharp – and nudged a girlfriend. But now the pig was working itself free.

It was slippery with perspiration, and my fingers were numb. I lurched back on to the animal to give my fingers a rest. The crowd swelled forward in a tide. Now they thought I was moving in for the kill. I had heard the same gasping roar a second or two before the end of each cockfight; but this crowd was wrong. I was weakening and the pig was strong. The men at the front of the crowd were again flicking up dirt in my face. One foot trapped my hair. It *was* deliberate this time. I was so annoyed that I thought, right, if *they* are going to cheat, then so am I. I loosened my grasp on the pig. It twisted itself up on to its hindquarters and took a deep breath. Before it was away I butted it into the crowd. We were right into the forest of legs, in the shade of the Indians and their musky smell. The crowd tried to back off but several men and women toppled. In the confusion I hunched up, tugged

Jorge's knife from my boot and thumped the butt down on the pig's nape. As the animal flopped into my arms, I smacked the knife-blade up into its throat.

The pig's screaming stopped. The blood-lust roar of the crowd stopped. I hid my knife away. Had anyone seen? The blood was spouting everywhere; it speckled my face, hair, the dust, the silent crowd. It was warm, and made my fingers stick together.

The crowd was stunned. It had missed the kill. It had been cheated. The girl who had been egging me on smeared the blood on her cheeks in bold stripes, and laughed. That was the only sound. Perhaps they had all been betting on the pig to win.

I got to my feet, wiping my face on my shirt sleeve.

'You got strong teeth,' said the headman.

'Strong teeth?'

'Yes. You got strong teeth. You bite deep into pig.'

I smiled and touched my canine teeth. 'Mmmm-mm. Sharp,' the crowd agreed.

'He kill like jaguar kill,' said one man.

'Mmmm,' said a third. 'He dangerman.'

'You stay for ever and ever if you like, Dangerman,' said Maipuri.

I might have been Dangerman for ever here, but I asked Maipuri not to call me that. It might lead to trouble. 'Call me Benedito.'

'I call you Mad Benedito, because you mad to leave forest the long way.' I said '*louco*' meant 'mad' in Portuguese, and so I became Louco Benedito.

I went for a dip in the stream, leaving the men behind to poke at the pig carcass. A few women had stripped off their dresses and were scrubbing off the blood. They saw me, but they didn't bolt; they tittered, and made play of removing the blood from their bottoms.

A very long way downriver I threw off my clothes and dived in. The cool bite of the water was invigorating. It was smooth as a mill pond here, and as green as the overhanging leaves.

I had wanted only a short bathe, but I was kept in the water by the appearance of the girl with red smears of blood across her cheeks. She came skipping along the bank while I was up to my neck amongst some ropy tree roots on the other side. She came to my pile of clothes and stood looking around for me, smoothing back her hair. I kept still, and her eyes missed me, so she bent over and began sorting through my garments. She discarded the shirt and trousers over her shoulder. It was the boots she was interested in. She tipped them out, one at a time, rolling back their tongues. I knew that she was after the knife. She must have seen me use it. Was she going to tell the others, or just keep it for herself? Whatever she wanted it for, she wanted it badly, and she shook the boots aggressively. Nothing dropped out. She hurled them down, kicked through the other clothes again, looked about her and sprinted off, leaving everything strewn on the river's edge, soaking up water.

The knife was tucked into my survival belt around my waist.

I passed the girl on the way back along the riverbank, and walked loudly so she had time to escape. She had stepped out of her red skirt, and was splashing water over her face. Her nose was touching the water and her bottom was pitched in the air, away from me. Her hair streamed down between her cinnamon-brown legs and flowed like weed in the current. She must have heard my footsteps, but she didn't open her eyes.

It was time for presents. The pig was on the chopping stone, and the fires were being stocked up, and everyone was seated in family clusters at the headman's feet. My stores were beside one of the huts, in two neat mounds. The two halves of my split trousers lay on the crest of each; the beans had been mixed in with the rice and sugar; ants were sawing through the coffee bags, but not a thing was missing.

To the headman, Maipuri, I presented one of my Brazilian machetes. He showed me his own. It was better, tempered from Sheffield steel, like mine. I doled out ten cartons of Benson & Hedges cigarettes. They bit off the filters and chewed them, pulling faces. Then they sat dumbly, with downcast watery eyes still on my luggage pile. Needles, fishing hooks, cotton and beads – whatever I produced was a let-down.

Maipuri eventually said, 'Lizbet. We want see Lizbet more.'

I brandished a stack of pictures: Buckingham Palace, Piccadilly Circus, Tower Bridge, the Houses of Parliament and 'Lizbet'.

Hands snatched them away. I heard them ripping, but the men and women sighed with heads together. 'Mmmmmmmmmm. She beautiful.'

That night the sun melted like butter over the sky and left yellow oily smears over the clouds for a while, before they were mopped up by the trees. I squatted with Maipuri by the fireside and drank soapy cassava beer from a gourd, while we ate some of the richest cuts of the pig. I reminded him that he had said the group was in trouble and needed the help of my headman. What had he meant?

Not many rainy seasons back, Maipuri said, they had lived in the land called Guyana, on the other side of the Pacaraima mountains. They had picked up scraps of English there, on the upper reaches of the Essequibo river, from a 'Godman', a Christian missionary. The man had been good to them in many ways, but he had evicted the witchdoctor, sending him off into the forest. 'But *more* terrible,' said Maipuri, 'he say is wrong to take two wives.' That was the final straw. They decided to lose the Godman in the jungle. The plan was less than half successful, though, because most of the tribe had drifted back in dribs and drabs. The Wai-wai have only one weakness, Maipuri said, which is that they like decorating themselves – especially the men. Some had got hooked on wearing clothes. Anyway, his group of five families had walked on into the forest. Unfortunately, the government had also decided it was development time for the Indians, and sent a junior office clerk off on their trail to do the job.

'Well, dis poor boy arrive. He never seen Wai-wai before, and he very afraid. His knees quaking. He think we going to eat him. But we calm him. We sets him drinking cassava beer, and more cassava beer till he bursting. After one moon go by we gets him sleeping in a special hut with woman. We ask him if he want to join us and live wid trees. He says he can't do dis. "Orders is orders." Den we break de news. We not hanging around no more. We going many moon into forest. He say, "Please don't do dis to me. Please don't leave me here alone. My career die." He been sent out special to tame us. "Well," we says. "Sorry, mister, can't do dat, we gotta go, we Wai-wais." So dat night we disappears, as quiet as jaguars into de forest, and next morning he wakes with de sun high, and we all vanished, Benedito. Mmmmm, he all alone. Maybe he die out dere wid his career. We dunno. We walks to here. We here now, but we always keep moving. Soon we go to river Mapuera. Mmmmm, Louco Benedito, *dat*'s why we here.'

This group of Wai-wais were on the run, as I'd originally thought. That was why they built their huts like flimsy tents, though I now guessed them to be several years old.

Maipuri said that one of his two wives had died. She had been struck down by a jaguar while strolling back from bathing a few sunrises ago. It was a shame, but she was an old woman anyway, and no Wai-wai was afraid of death, or sorrowful after it like the Godmen. That particular woman had married him when he was only a small boy, and had brought him up. He had taken another woman much later when the old lady had lost her vigour and was not able to satisfy him.

'Didn't she mind you having an extra wife?'

'Mind? Why she mind? She *like* it. Now she more important wife. She get second wife to do all work. Mmmmm . . . she happier dan ever, Louco Benedito!'

My hut was downwind of the fire. That night I slept in its warm wood-smoke draught, in the sweet smell of sap and the sound of crackling sparks. I slept late. When I came out into the morning sunshine, my hair smelt of smoke. The women were already milling around the pots, and the fires were hissing with dripping pig-fat. The ground was sticky from a night shower, and my boots were clumsy. But I kept them on. I had grown sick of having to dig parasites out from under my toenails with a needle. Most were planted there by jigger fleas, which left the eggs tidily under the skin to incubate.

I took a stroll behind the village to a scrubby patch of jungle. I had to beat through what I thought was a thicket of bamboo to get there, but suddenly I realized it was a garden, and I had wiped out a tract of sugarcane. I found I was trampling on another grass, which later turned out to be arrow grass for making arrow shafts. The plants which told me this was a garden were the cassava and yams swelling in the soil like oversized potatoes. I walked along their furrows, whistling, and just when I thought the garden had got to an end I trod on a ripening gourd. I squelched another underfoot before I could find a way clear of them, then came to some cotton plants, with the white woolly puffs fixed on to their twigs. Three women came by, buckled up under the weight of banana leaf stacks. They propped them on their backs, with their arms out like wings. They smiled at each other when they saw me, but kept on walking.

I went to see where they'd come from and, through a bed of trumpet-flowered, sticky-leaved plants, which I knew were tobacco, saw the girl who'd tried to steal my knife. She was beyond what looked like a gooseberry bush, facing me but with her head up in a banana tree, cutting down more fresh leaves and laying them in a heap by her feet. Her skin was camel coloured, and paler than I remembered, but perhaps that was because I was comparing her in my mind to Zorola of the Orinoco delta. I couldn't see why. This girl was older, fifteen or sixteen, with a fringe right into her eyes. Their pupils were bright but black. She was stronger than Zorola, with thick shoulders and heavy, swollen breasts. Yet her ankles and wrists were slender.

She shifted the tarpaulin-sized leaves as though they were feathers. Her body was so powerful and she moved with such finesse, I couldn't help but gawp.

I ducked my head and crept away, back to the village. I wandered around the huts stalked by children, and afterwards lay in my hammock daydreaming. All I wanted to do was go back to the garden and take another peep at the girl.

– 10 –

The Godman's spell

In the village I was plagued by flies and children. The flies came from the forest, the children from the mouths of the huts. Peering into these I saw floors of shredded bark and straw, and babies being rocked in hammocks. I usually caught a muggy whiff even at midday when the sun had burnt up most of the smells outside.

The children often had dogs under their arms: underweight but happy mongrels with brown-and-white splodges. When the children were around, the dogs were everywhere, and even when they weren't it was hard not to tread on them. They were perched in hammocks, snug against the babies, or snoring on shelves up in the palm roofs, or diving into rock pools down by the river with the children. They were part of the family. In the entrance to a larger hut was a woman suckling a dog. In one hand she had a skinny, bald baby with wasted cheeks, and in the other a fat puppy. They were kicking at each other for space, stretching the nipples.

'My wife,' said Maipuri, coming up behind me. 'And those my children.' Where he was pointing I saw only the dog and the baby. I smiled and said they were beautiful. The woman was thrilled to bits, but Maipuri couldn't get her to hand either of them over to me.

Maipuri sat down with me and said he knew some Wai-wai Indians on the Cafuini, a tributary of the Trombetas. He would let me take two of his best men. Whether the Indians there knew anyone further away, over to where the sun rose, he couldn't say. I would have to take a gamble. He wouldn't chance it himself, but it was up to me.

'Come, Louco Benedito, I got thing to show you.' We ducked into his hut. The ground was strewn with fishbones. Maipuri kicked a track through and tutted in the direction of his wife. The air was dark and stale, though there was a cool draught through the pole walls. Three hammocks of bark fibre were looped across the centre. Maipuri pointed at the middle one.

'She beautiful?'

'She beautiful.' I nodded. She was a black hen with clean, glossy black feathers. She clucked when you tickled her neck.

Maipuri said she'd belonged to the young office clerk they'd left behind in the jungle. 'He surely miss her,' he said. 'She so beautiful.'

'Yes, I'd have missed her. Especially if I was left alone in the jungle.'

'Mmmmmmm. She his only food.'

We stepped outside. Maipuri said he wanted me to go off hunting with some of his men for the day. I must pick two of them as my guides for my expedition. He hoped one would be his son. It would be an honour for the boy, and for himself. He squeezed my shoulder, and looked up into my eyes.

'Maipuri be mighty sad, Louco Benedito, if my son not chosen.'

'Maipuri must not fear,' I said. 'Any son of yours will be strong and brave, I'm sure.'

I hoped his son wasn't too much of a fool, and thought it shouldn't be too difficult to fix up. I'd find out who the son was, and make sure he was honoured; a piece of cake. Everyone would be as pleased as Punch.

'To make justice good, I telling my son not to be telling who he is.'

Damn.

'He sleep with another family. But now Louco Benedito wait here.' Maipuri pottered back into his hut. There was a frightened squawk, a clacking of wings, a satisfied grunt from Maipuri, then silence. I expected Maipuri to come out with the poor chicken, limp at the neck and purple faced, like Joshua's turkey after its execution. But he held only a tail feather, and through the wall I heard the chicken settling its feathers back into place. The headman reached to my left ear and tugged the lobe. He coughed in disgust.

'Why no hole?'

He went away again and came back with a strand of my green 'rot-proof' cotton, and tied the feather to a lock of hair at the back of my head. 'That give you luck, help you choose well.'

I waited by my hut, in the black shadow of the roof's eve. Maipuri sent a boy to fetch the men from fishing, clouting him on the back of the ear to make him run at the double.

The women were spinning cotton, twiddling fluffy balls of it with spidery fingers, and stretching it out into thread with their toes. Little naked girls fed it to the women's hands and bundled it up at the foot end. The children looked bored. They watched me swatting flies, and tweaked the dogs sitting on their laps. The women's faces were creased up with concentration; they drew out the cotton without ever glancing up. A pair of small dark and dirty birds, with stumpy rounded wings and turkey wattles, flew over, croaking.

The art of cotton spinning

'*Hannaqua!*' screamed a child, pointing at the birds, which looked ungainly and prehistoric.

'*Hannaqua! Hannaqua!*' the stupid birds called back; a baby awoke and started to bawl.

The earth was baking to a dust pan, and the cotton spinners got up to move out of the heat and the sun's glare. I suddenly wondered why I had seen no old people here; not a single fleck of grey hair.

A train of boys ran into the village, whooping. They dived into the huts and bounced out again with parrot feathers speared through their ears and white bands around their arms and legs.

'This your hunting party,' said Maipuri. 'You choose guide from these.'

'But . . . but they're only *boys*.' I simply had to put my foot down here. I required skilled guides, not children.

'They *good* boys.'

I closed my eyes and said, 'Good grief.'

'And you take Tautau, if you like,' said Maipuri, jabbing a finger through the air at a man who was striding up from the river with a fistful of arrows. Maipuri explained that this man Tautau would be the lead guide, and I was to choose one boy and have two other porters.

Tautau was a brawny man in his mid-twenties. His hair was plaited into a tail interwoven with white duck feathers. He wore shorts, leftovers from the Godman, he said. They looked it; he must have been given them as a child. The hem had worn away between his legs, and there was a cotton loincloth beneath.

I went to get my machete. When I was back, Maipuri put a shotgun in my hand. It was also a 'leftover' from the Godman, along with all the cartridges, a canvas bag for them labelled 'Your souvenir from Chicago', and a tin crucifix, which was kept in the bag as a lucky charm. The Indians said it was the very one the Godman used to wear around his neck. They took it from him while he was asleep the night they fled.

The shotgun barrel was sprinkled with dirt. Maipuri tutted when I said it wouldn't do, and snatched an arrow from Tautau, which he rammed up and down the barrel from both ends. The barrel looked spotless but now needed a good wipe over with oil. Maipuri was looking at me with disdain, and I didn't dare mention it. I had ruined a perfectly good arrow, he said, and he broke it over his knee.

The arrows were made from the 'grass' I had seen in the garden. They were like the canes you use for running garden beans along, taller than Tautau, but a lot shorter than me, and they were smooth and balanced. They had flights of beige harpy-eagle feathers, which were curved to set the arrow spinning to its target.

The tips were poisoned with a blend of curare, and kept safely in a separate quiver. The poison must be brewed for many days, Maipuri explained, looking grave.

It is a secret process, and the brewing is done in a special little hut, well away from women. Some of the poisons are from the worst snakes, like the fer de lance, and a bark, a vine and a leaf. All are pounded and mashed up in a pot, brewed and brewed for days, and kept on the boil until the mixture hardens into a treacle. Then the tips are dipped in. That was all Maipuri would tell me. Later he confided that other Indians, the Wapishanas, had made this batch. They had swopped the poison for a Wai-wai cassava grater.

The four boys were ill-disciplined, over-eager and noisy. Tautau ordered them to tag behind, out of politeness, which meant they kicked my heels and shunted me along the riverbank path at jogging pace without letting me pause for breath. I was in a huff. We were not going to catch anything. I had never known such a riotous hunting party. I did not want a boy guide for my expedition, and I didn't know how I was going to select the headman's son. At least they were all physically fit, so far anyway.

The boys knew they were being watched, and were all desperate to be chosen as my guide. But they were also under observation by Tautau. They were being initiated into adulthood. Today's hunting was one of a series of tests. So why on earth were we setting out when the sun was high, just as the forest animals were tucking themselves into their nests and burrows? It seemed stupid, and that was another reason for being fed up.

Tautau carried the bow unstrung. It was made from wood with a milky grain, the colour of ivory. He said he had shaped it only a few suns ago. He had a wife and six children to look after. That wasn't many for an Indian, and only one child was his own, all the rest being orphans. Tautau said the parents died because they had no witchdoctor to heal them with herbs or spells. The Godman had chucked him out.

We walked upstream. The boys kicked through the water, upsetting the birds from their nests miles ahead. I asked why Tautau didn't tell them off.

He laughed. 'We go on and on.' He pointed through the branches to the sun. 'When he strong, we at home of *maipuri*.'

Maipuri? But we had just left him in the village.

'We go and kill him, Louco Benedito.'

I almost dropped the shotgun. This was certainly going to be some initiative test. Kill the headman?

'*Maipuri* taste good.'

After a while I decided the headman shared his name with an animal. 'What is it, this *maipuri*?'

Tautau instructed the boys to imitate it, one by one, for me. They giggled helplessly.

'*Atchi?*' they squeaked, scuffling through the riverbank grasses, pawing the roots with hoof-shaped fingers. They showed how it cocked its head to listen, and scratched off ants from its back. The last boy, who had a gory red feather in his ear, was a clown. He reduced the others to tears by showing how the animal crouched to urinate, again and again, to encores.

It was a tapir. I guessed that from the way it smelt the air with its rubbery trunk-nose.

We were still on the river when the sun was high, but the river was only a weak and silent trickle. We were at the tapir's home. The boys had gone silent; they stepped delicately through the water as if they were herons.

The forest was fast asleep, snoring in an even hiss. Tautau spoke softly to us. Then he knelt and strung the bow. The force of bending it made his shoulderblade muscles swell and buckle. The boys stood to attention and pleaded silently with him for the bow and arrows; they were given to the one with the garish red feathers lancing his ears. His name was Ak-ak, the sound of a frog. He gave a snide smile at the three other boys, who pulled sour faces.

Tautau waved them away, and they merged with the forest on the left bank. We crossed over to the other side, scrambled up the crannies of a steep rock and looked back down, almost from canopy level. The river swung lazily around this rock, and here it was deep and had the duckweed smell of a weir pool. The four boys were worming up through the undergrowth. There above them was the tapir, mottled black and white and lying back dreamily like a cow before rain. It lay in an open patch; to get to it undetected was not going to be easy.

'No, not easy,' whispered Tautau. We lay down and loaded our shotguns. As their test of skill, the boys would each have to touch the tapir before Ak-ak fired his poisoned arrow.

'Ak-ak must touch it as well?'

'No. Ak-ak job easy. He just shoot *maipuri* here –' he tapped his neck ' – and best not shoot a boy either. Poison kill easy.'

They were closing in from the rear. Ak-ak was crouching in front where the animal would run to. Tautau had said that Ak-ak was a bit of a tyrant amongst his friends, but now he looked small, waiting by himself behind a bush. He was fumbling with an arrow, slotting on the poisonous tip, and hitching the arrow on to the string.

Tautau's instructions to me were simple: if something went badly wrong – if the tapir charged and crunched up a boy – there was nothing much we could do but watch. We should fire our shotguns only when the tapir was in the water and in full view. We had to score direct hits in the tapir's head. The animal was the size of a heifer, and only with the arrow poison would that be enough to stop it.

Tautau began to strum his fingers on the rock. The boys were taking too long. They'd lost their nerve. If they didn't act now there was going to be a terrible accident. We watched the four white, scared faces. From here we could almost see their trembling.

Then the tapir lurched in its sleep.

One boy jumped sky high. The two others thought he was making a dash forward, and sprang out. The tapir rolled to its feet, snorting. The two boys got to its rump, tapped it, and took to their heels. The third boy arrived just in time to catch the eye of the tapir. They were face to face, the tapir with its nose trumpeting and its jaws wide open, the boy with his mouth in a tight knot. The tapir bent its head, held its breath and charged. The other two boys weren't watching; they were on their stomachs clutching their heads, ducking the arrow. But the arrow was still in Ak-ak's bow, and he was waiting for a clear shot. We watched the tapir crash into the first boy's legs, and closed our eyes as the frail shriek echoed up from the water.

In my right ear Tautau was screaming, 'Ak-ak! Ak-ak!'

But Ak-ak's target was blocked by the mangled boy, who was draped across the tapir's neck, out cold. The tapir dived for the water, still jockeying him along.

'*Ak-ak!*'

The arrow flew. It struck between the tapir's front legs. The animal bellowed and pranced, snapping the arrow in two.

The boy slithered off and crumpled to the ground. The tapir plunged into the pool and, hampered by the water, made an easy target. My shot missed. The tapir cantered on upstream, streaming blood from Tautau's shot, with Ak-ak at its tail. There was also a sheen of blood on the wounded boy. He was lying like a dead sheep, head down in an inch of water. Tautau was already running.

He got there first. He hoisted him into the air and beat on his chest to get some life out of him. The boy groaned. Tautau laid him on the riverbank reeds, propping his head on a green boulder.

Once we had crowded round, the boy began to writhe and contort his face, bashing his skull on the rocks. Tautau held his head tight on his lap with the grip of one hand. Upriver there were high-pitched yells.

'Ak-ak catch *maipuri*,' said Tautau, but didn't look up.

'This boy called Yakka-yakka,' he said, in a broken voice. 'This boy, he my only son,' and he crooned softly.

I said I thought Yakka-yakka wasn't too badly hurt. He was not to worry. One of his shinbones might be cracked; maybe a rib or two. I glossed over what really worried me: Yakka-yakka was clutching his sides and trying to curl up like a loop caterpillar. We had to pin him down by the wrists and ankles. He bit into his tongue. I thought his liver or kidneys might be punctured.

Ak-ak came back running. He jabbered away to us about his fine shot, articulating across Yakka-yakka's body with hardly a glance down. Tautau said that the women of the village would be coming shortly to heave the *maipuri* meat back to the village. Ak-ak was to stay and fend off the vultures until then. Ak-ak scuttled off upstream without looking back. I flushed Yakka-yakka's cuts with water. Tautau sent another boy off to find a special herb. He returned with a sprig of silky-leafed plant, which we strapped over the bruises with a stringy sapling. Knotting it up tight, we made the boy convulse.

Tautau smoothed his son's stomach with the back of his hand and blew over the purple bumps. I wanted to stretcher Yakka-yakka away, or at the very least put his legs in splints, but Tautau scorned these ideas, and simply folded him over his shoulder. That was too much for the boy, so he was borne piggy-back. Tautau insisted on taking him all the way. To keep Yakka-yakka hanging on, I had to bind his wrists together with a vine, so they were locked around Tautau's throat. He hung like a hunk of meat at a butcher's window.

We met the women wading upriver after about an hour. Tautau wouldn't let anyone touch his son. He pushed away his wife, and stared blindly ahead.

'He my only child. He my only son.' He said it again and again as we went lumbering on. 'He my only son, he not die.' When we got to the village he was still mouthing the words, 'He not die. He my only son.'

Maipuri was thunderstruck by the news. The village had no witchdoctor to heal the boy. Ever since their flight from Guyana, they had had no one to administer medicine. 'My people dying,' moped Maipuri. 'Each new moon, one more die.' This turned out to be only slight exaggeration. With Yakka-yakka moaning softly in the background, Maipuri led me around the village to show me three ash-heaps of huts they had burnt down, each one after a death.

The village was wrapped in stillness. Children stopped romping with the dogs. The dust settled. Leaves fluttered into the yard and rattled in the evening breeze through the empty village. There was a feeling of desertion here, of missing friends. I saw the lonely faces of the men, lolling in their half-empty huts. The lifeblood of the village was draining away, and Yakka-yakka's pathetic cries were reminding them.

Yakka-yakka lay on a shelf in Tautau's hut. His bad leg was blue and spongy. I tied it in a splint of arrow grass, and I gave him a dose of morphine. The bone looked straight but the boy was sweating buckets, so we dabbed him with cold water. Tautau sat perched in a hammock holding Yakka-yakka's hand. Maipuri ordered a boy to fetch the Godman's crucifix. It was a last resort, and stooping this low grieved him. He hung it around the boy's forehead, as he'd seen the priest do to an old woman who had been gripped by coughing fits. She'd died, but Maipuri thought it worth a try.

He also remembered a little spell of the Godman. 'Our father's heart in heaven. Hallo be my name.' He mumbled this on his knee. 'Give us our tressle passes and those with tressle passes against us. And give us today our daily bread.' He sprinkled water into the confused boy's eyes. 'My king come. My will done. Honoured as it is in heaven. For mine is the kingdom, the power and the glory, heavier and heavier, our men.'

'Our men,' said Tautau, who was also on bended knees.

'Our men,' said Maipuri again, and looked at me.

I nodded. 'Our men.'

I left the hut for some more cold water, and for a quick bathe. The village was a liverish yellow in the setting sun and it was so quiet in the yard I could still hear Yakka-yakka's throaty breaths.

On my return up the river-path I met a cloud of tobacco smoke. I traced the smell back to Tautau's hut.

Yakka-yakka looked very hot. He was on the verge of a fever, and his groaning was desperate. Maipuri had been chain-smoking cigarettes, and puffing the smoke into the boy's face. It was a trick they had learnt from the witchdoctor, to clear off bad spirits. I pretended I thought Yakka-yakka was suddenly on the road to recovery, and they stopped. But his eyes stayed red and swollen long after the smoke had cleared.

'He cry,' said Maipuri, peering at the boy's eyes and running nose.

'No. He no cry,' said Tautau. 'He man. He my son. My son no cry.' The boy's face was quivering, and thick tears were dribbling steadily down his face. Tautau started to sniff also. 'He know he dying.'

I said I'd watch over Yakka-yakka for a while if they liked. Both men left me alone in the dark hut. The boy murmured something. When I didn't reply, he gritted his teeth and craned his neck to see who I was. He saw me and exploded into sobs. He was devastated that he had been left alone with only me, and sank back heavily on to the shelf, without drying his face.

I tilted a cup of cool water towards his mouth but he shrank back from it. I tried to insist; he clamped his lips together, his face tightened and he held his whole body stiff. I put the cup down, and heard him say 'Mooder.'

'Mother?' I said into his face, and he smiled. The effort made him wince.

'Mooder.' He wanted his mother. He had been too afraid to ask in front of the men.

I knew Tautau and Maipuri would be furious if I let his mother anywhere near him, so I just said, 'When you're better. Then you see your mother. Tautau wants you to be strong.'

'Mooder!' came back the cry. He felt for my arm, unable to see through his tears. He found my shirt sleeve and jerked it to his face, so I had to bend forward.

'*Mooder!*' he choked. He pulled my fingers to his face and made me feel his tears. I felt the wetness of his cheeks and the weak quavering in his lungs as he sobbed, 'Mooder! Mooder!' There was nothing I could do but squeeze his hand; I told him he would be better soon, and that Tautau would be proud of him if he was brave.

'Mooooder!'

Maipuri and Tautau came back in. 'You working good magic?' I released the boy's hand, but Yakka-yakka snatched mine back and wouldn't let go. I smiled awkwardly.

Tautau grinned. 'Mmmmmmmmmm. You working good magic, Louco Benedito.'

An hour later, when the night was lit with silver moonshine outside, the boy suddenly closed his eyes, and his face slackened. Tautau sank back into his hammock, lowered his eyes and moaned loudly. Maipuri ran from the hut without a word. I knew he would keep running till he was alone in the forest. But I had Yakka-yakka's hand in mine, and I knew the boy had only gone to sleep.

– 11 –

Gift of the night

The tapir was brought into the village in chunks, late that night. We heard the procession miles away, and the warbling songs of the women were louder than the night bats and river frogs. Maipuri was celebrating Yakka-yakka's recovery with cassava beer; he wandered out with an empty gourd in his hand to greet them. The dogs ran out with the children and came back ahead of the women. Everyone wanted to carry a piece of tapir. They came running, clutching wicker baskets of offal, snake-coils of intestine, and casks containing the liver and heart. Ak-ak danced in circles at the front, holding up the tapir's head.

The meat was smoked in the night fires, wrapped in the banana leaves I'd seen cut that morning.

When I awoke at daybreak – the fat had been spitting in the flames all night – the meat had been stuffed out of reach of the dogs in the roof eves, and Yakka-yakka was able to raise a smile. Tautau said he had a bad headache, and I put some aspirins on his tongue for him to swallow. Tautau himself looked worse. He had red blood vessels in his eyes and hadn't slept a wink. He kept tweaking Yakka-yakka's leg, even though the boy screamed, to see if he would be able to dance at my farewell feast that night.

I was called to Maipuri's hut. Through the gloom I saw the hen first, cornering a banana-coloured beetle. I wondered where Fritz's black cockroaches were, the ones he had warned me all Indians lived with. Maipuri lay in his hammock, and his wife in a lower one, within arm's reach of the fire.

She didn't look up. She was weaving a basket and breastfeeding a boy of three or four years old, with little white stumps of teeth, round eyes and thick knots of beads through his ears. The mother sat astride the hammock, the child across her stomach, swinging from the breasts and with eyes glued on me.

He was frightened when he saw my fair hair, and threw himself into the bowl of the hammock to hide, letting the bosoms bounce free and swell. When I turned to Maipuri, I saw from the corner of my eye the child crawling back up the woman and pulling down the nearest teat.

'You chosen guide for journey?' said Maipuri.

I coughed. 'Er. . . .'

'Well, you tell people tonight. You chose my son. He proud to be chosen by you. Tonight big feast. Tonight you happy. To-morrow you leave. Then you come back after many moons with Lizbet. Mmmmmmmmm, that good. Lizbet your wife?'

'No. Lizbet my headman.'

'But she *woman*?'

'Yes, woman.'

Maipuri began a rumbling laugh which developed into a nasty coughing spasm. He said: 'Mmmmmmmmm. Louco Benedito!'

'Yes?'

'Maipuri like you very much.' He gave a child's smile.

'I like you too.'

'Mmmmmmm. You like stay many, many moons?'

I said I couldn't. I just had to get home again.

'Maybe you want better hut. I make for you. It take only two suns.'

I had to decline the offer, but I walked into the sunshine smiling, with black children stalking out behind. In a couple of days I had become completely at home here.

'Or maybe you seen girl you like.' Maipuri's head was poking from the dark of the hut. 'Anarau, he got daughter who say she like you. She watch you. She say you strong. You make good husband she say.'

I was not in the least surprised to find out who Anarau's daughter, Yimshi, was. And now I knew why she'd reminded me of Zorola when I spied on her in the garden. It was because circumstances were conspiring to bring us together in the same way. In the Orinoco delta it had been the shoelaces, the welcoming ceremony, and a chance reunion in the forest with her brothers. Here it was the knife, the pig-fight, and the chance sighting in the garden. What was more, Maipuri had a lot to gain, he thought, by adopting me. By staying I might even secure his people's future. I was a man strong enough to bite through a pig's neck, a man with a woman chief, the richest chief in the world.

In the milky dawn sunshine the women were wrapping up the last of the tapir in parcels of rubbery green leaves. A girl was being taught how to drive a stake through a tortoise. The idea was not to give a mortal wound, otherwise the meat would spoil in the sun. It was just going into storage, being staked alive to the ground through its shell. The tortoise had tucked in its bald bird-head and stumpy legs and was bracing itself against the girl's protracted and inept blows. The men were smoking cigarettes and shaping arrows. They twirled the arrow grass in the smoke of the fire, to iron out the curves. Then, sitting on logs, they rolled the arrows along the length of their arms, squinting along the shafts; five feet long from the flight feathers, through their fingertips, through their toes to the wood shavings in the dust. Other men sat on their haunches, shaping feathers. Maipuri said that the only time

Mid-Morning

women squatted like this was when they were giving birth. It was more becoming for them to kneel.

The children were dressing up the dogs, weaving yellow parrot feathers into cotton and fixing them on as collars.

Tautau and Anarau were out in the forest, putting the initiate boys through another test of manhood. This time they were stealing honey from a beehive which was lodged in the crown of a cocoa tree. Yakka-yakka had been dragged along to stand at the foot of a tree and watch the other three boys knock out the nest. Maipuri said he couldn't risk me going to watch, even from a distance. 'Bee get angry. Bee hate thieves. Bee go killing.'

'What about Yakka-yakka? He should be lying down, taking some rest. Besides, he won't be able to run.'

Maipuri said, 'Even dead men run when bee coming after them.'

And the bees did come. They flushed the Indians through the trees – they ran like stampeding forest pigs.

The village turned out to watch them crash out of the trees. The boys didn't scream because they couldn't open their mouths in the swarm, so we heard only the furious bees and the tearing leaves and branches. They had not been allowed any clothes, and sprinted with one eye open and one eye protected with a hand, then dived into the water and stayed under. Maipuri was right; Yakka-yakka could sprint quite easily, even with a broken leg.

The four boys cried right through the stillness of the afternoon. Ak-ak's face was puffed up like a rotten tangerine, and Yakka-yakka was swollen into a hunchback; the nest had landed right on top of him. The bees wouldn't surrender; they smelt the honey in the village and pestered all of us. They became more and more irritable as the sun began to burn. They made the dogs whine and fret. The children made the noise of howler monkeys, and two babies had to be dipped in the river and then swaddled in a poultice of leaves, to deflate them.

Later a burst of rain drove the bees away into the trees.

From the hammock where I was dozing I saw the men begin to paint themselves. The camp now smelt of incense instead of hair and dogs. I traced the smell to the red greased paint they were wiping over their faces, chests and legs in stripes and spots. They highlighted their doodles with charcoal-black paint. Maipuri came from his hut with his hands on his hips and with red macaw feathers arching from his nose. His pigtail was cobalt blue with toucan plumes, clumped at the end with a parrot's yellow-and-spinach-green flight feather and the electric-blue breast feathers of humming birds. He had combed palm oil into his hair to give it a blue sheen.

'Louco Benedito, what you think?' He smoothed his thumbs along the length of his nostril feathers. 'Beautiful?'

'You look magnificent.'

'Mmmmmmmmmm.' He puffed himself up and strutted around the camp, purring like a cat, while the men studded their ears with mother-of-pearl and hung last-minute tassels over their buttocks.

The women took less trouble. Even the dogs were better dressed than they were. The few who bothered were the nubile ones, and they merely smudged red paint in lines over their cheeks and slung a few beads over their breasts.

There was one exception. At the other end of the village, Yimshi was catwalking in front of her girlfriends, twirling like a model, and lapping up compliments. She was too preoccupied with herself to notice me, and I was glad, because of what I had gathered from Maipuri about her ambitions in my direction.

She was looking down her body, smoothing her thin fingers over her skin, and assessing herself: the weight and balance of her breasts, her slender stomach, the pretty cut of her skirt, the grace and power of her thighs, and the delicacy of her little feet. She saw all that, and what she saw made her smile.

She sat down on a log with two other girls and said something which made them giggle so much they almost keeled backwards off the log. She pointed her arm across the village, at my hut, and shrieked something else. The girls clapped their hands over their mouths and rocked about in fits of laughter. While they were wiping the tears from their eyes one of them saw me watching. She jolted, her face reddened, and she nudged the others, who fidgeted with their hands, and tried to busy themselves with each other's necklaces. Yimshi was nonchalant. She sat with her hands in her lap, her eyes locking onto mine. Then she dazzled me with a wolfish grin. I dropped my eyes and the girl's laugh flitted across the village. I felt sticky under the collar.

I sat with Maipuri as the food roasted on stakes in the fires. He said he hadn't seen so much meat for ages; normally they gorged themselves the first day it was caught because it was so rare.

The jungle was a hard place in which to live – that was why the initiation ceremonies were taken so seriously. Every man had to prove he could support a wife by shooting straight, and so on. And for the women it was just the same; they also had to prove they could endure discomfort and pain, and at puberty were sometimes sent off alone to bring a queen bee back alive, which meant cracking open the nest and rummaging in its core for her.

He said he would never forget the time when Yimshi was ordered to do this as a little girl. They ripped off her apron and ordered her not to show her face again unless she had the queen between her fingers. Yimshi came back with the whole nest in her hands. The bees were so angry they almost wiped out the Indian village. And while they were swarming over her face, all she did was giggle.

I asked why she hadn't been married yet. Maipuri said it was the woman who chose whom she wanted to marry, and when she fancied a man all she did was sling her hammock in his hut and start cooking for him. Simple as that. Usually the girl's father persuaded him to move into her family hut. And, the very next day if possible, he would start cutting a field for crops.

But not Yimshi. She was biding her time. She valued her freedom. No one had seduced her, though many had tried and fallen by the wayside. I asked how much freedom this girl was allowed. He said all the freedom in the world. Maipuri told me he'd learnt from the Godman that non-Indians had children with twisted-up minds (he meant adolescents). That was because they were afraid of nature: afraid of their bodies mostly. Here everything was open. That was why the Creator had provided jungle medicines to stop girls having babies before they were married. He had got Yimshi to show both Yakka-yakka and Ak-ak how to use their bodies. Maipuri smirked. He said it had been the most gruelling initiation test of all. He hoped that Yimshi and the Godman would meet one day. That would soon stop the Godman being ashamed of his body.

'She's very persuasive girl, Louco Benedito.'

I said I didn't find it hard to imagine.

In the twilight, as the mosquitoes droned up from the river to the village for their night feed, fresh banana leaves were laid at the entrance to the huts. Maipuri's wife joined us, and one of Yimshi's girlfriends set down a gourd of stew in our midst and some mashed banana pâté. Before we had started on those, a girl came up and dangled ropes of tapir meat for us to cut off with our hunting knives. We were brought slabs of pig-fat, and more stews, pale this time and the consistency of wallpaper paste. Maipuri said it was sugarcane, chewed by the women to soften it up. We worked from dish to dish. It wasn't enjoyable; it was a tortuous marathon of sweet and bitter concoctions, which, apart from the meat, all tasted like boiled rhubarb. The four initiate boys were alone in a quiet circle, nursing their bee stings, and gobbling down the food. I had no way of knowing which was Maipuri's son. It wasn't Yakka-yakka, because he was Tautau's, so I plumped for Ak-ak. Maipuri was bound to have done a sneaky thing like arrange for him to take the shot at the tapir. No one gets to the top of a community without knowing how to fix the odds.

After nightfall I wandered amongst the family groups, being offered the food until I was bloated. The men put cassava beer to my lips and laughed when I said I felt queasy, and said then I must vomit to fit in some more. Anarau insisted on retelling the story of how he had come across me sitting by the riverside after chasing off Raimundo and Moses the day I was 'captured' (as he put it). He told how he'd thought I was a goldminer, and that I was so tall he was scared of me; how he'd almost fainted when I handed him my machete. The whole village came up to listen and had to return to their seats, ill from laughing, when they heard I'd used moss to dull the pain of my ant bites that day. And Cheroobé, the one who had joined Anarau to interrogate me in the cage, explained at length how he'd blinded me with gold dust. The villagers rolled on the ground helplessly.

I was sitting between those two men by the side of one of the fires, when Yimshi jumped down beside me. When I saw who it was I groaned. I heard Maipuri suppressing a snort behind me. Yimshi looked into the heart of the fire. She looked hot. Her brow was damp.

'She want kiss you, Louco Benedito,' said Maipuri loudly.

The girl turned her head to Anarau, and whispered close up to his ear, as if she was nibbling it.

'She say, how many moons to your village, Louco Benedito?' Anarau put his hand on his rib cage, and gave a short, pained laugh.

'Tell her it's too far to walk.'

This time his laugh exploded, sending spittle on to his lap. Yimshi leant towards Anarau, waiting to hear the reply. She stared into the flames, her arms down by her sides, while he told her.

'She wants to know if it's true your chief is a woman.'

I said it was.

'And does she really have more riches than anyone else in the world?'

As I said yes again, I saw vaulting ambition kindle in her eyes. Anarau had noticed it too. It crossed my mind that she might blackmail me about the knife I'd used to kill off the pig.

Anarau said that Yimshi's name was a shortening for 'baby', but that really she was more like a jaguar.

'Not!' she shouted, and glowered at Anarau.

'See? She even understand a little English. And you see her face? She got cat's eyes.'

I said, 'So you're a jaguar, are you?' Her eyes darkened and she shook her head vigorously. But she couldn't stop her lip curling in anger, and her sharp teeth showed.

I nodded. 'You *are* a jaguar.'

'And *you* . . .' she said, 'you are . . .'

'What am I?'

'Yes, what he?' said Anarau.

She pondered, looking me over. 'You are . . . Mad White Giant.'

Immediately the whole village burst into an uproar; they laughed so hard it upset the hen. Yimshi bared her teeth and sniffed triumphantly.

'You see what I mean? Jaguars do that.'

'*Not* jaguar. Not, not, *not!*' She sprang up, flashed her eyes, and went off, still muttering, '*Not* jaguar. *Not* jaguar.'

The night was pitch black, but the hut fires flickered a soft glow over the village.

Maipuri, at the fireside of his hut, began the singing. He drawled a soft chant, with his arms outstretched to the village. Anarau said he was calling his people to dance. The babies were bundled into the huts, and the children ordered out of their hammocks to watch. The chant was slow and it was a dull sound, so that while everyone sat in silence I heard the night: a low murmuring howl, the river chattering, and the drowsy clucks of the hen.

The men of the village, only five of them, got up from their logs and formed a line, swaying to Maipuri's drone. A woman, like a ghost in the darkness, served up beer to the men, each in turn, putting the gourd to their lips as they listened side by side, facing Maipuri across the yard. After the drink, the men answered Maipuri's song with a slow chorus. They wailed, as if they were in mourning, and their bodies began to arch and writhe, their torsos rippling. I didn't know what the song meant, but it brought tears to the men's eyes. Later Tautau explained it was to do with paying respects to the spirit of the dead tapir, which, after all, had put up the feast.

Five women formed another line, standing to attention facing the men across the fire-sparks and darkness. Maipuri turned aside and led his men off in a shuffle. They encircled the women, who stood rigid with their eyes tightly shut.

The children began drumming a rhythm on the logs, and one of the men in the line blew on a flute. The beat quickened. I tasted the dust in the air and the grit in my mouth. Just as the rhythm began working, seducing the women to open their eyes and look at the men, it stopped. The dancers dispersed and settled back down on their logs. Maipuri shouted that Louco Benedito should now get to his feet.

I got to my feet.

'You tell Maipuri who you choose as guide into forest.'

'What, *now*? I was standing in the centre of the village, where the pig-fight had started and ended, and the same hungry faces were looking me over. Into the darkness and silence, I gulped and said:

'I choose Tautau.'

The darkness and the silence continued. The crowd was waiting to hear the name of the chief's son. I screwed up my eyes and breathed in. The four boys braced themselves in a dim corner.

'And Ak-ak.'

The men whooped, so hard they woke the hen again. The crowd tossed Ak-ak into the air, and Maipuri thumped him in the chest when he landed and paraded him around the village. The other three boys ran off into the night and I never saw them again.

As the fires faded, the dancers became only pale shadows in the dark, and I caught the rhythm from the trembling of the earth. While I watched, humming along, Yimshi's two girlfriends surprised me from behind. One of them wrenched at my hair and tipped back my head, clamping it tight between her bony, hot knees. As I opened my mouth to shout, the other one poured a gourd full of beer down my throat. I might have drowned in it, but they pranced away giggling.

Ak-ak, with fresh red feathers in his ears, was dancing with the men. They were circling, with their hands resting on each other's shoulders. Ak-ak couldn't reach, even on tiptoe; his voice was weak, and it piped clear above the others.

For the first time the women began to sing. They answered the men's chant by throwing back their heads, winding their necks around like courting swans. The men paddled the dust, surrounding the women again. The women lurched off around the other way, facing them.

The dance was a wild reel and the noise at such a pitch that the trees picked it up and it came booming back. The men stopped dancing and faced in on the women, who opened out their circle and, spinning round, came closer and closer to the men. They teased the men by brushing so close with their breasts that the men's heads were swimming. Then – perhaps it was the heavy clouds of incense from the men's paint – the dance pace slackened. The bodies of the women became limp and sleepy. Their heads lolled. The song became a gentle murmur and, with its last breath, almost a sigh of relief. The mass of dancers dissolved into the darkness. The audience of children filed away and a feather, red in the fire glow, dropped softly to the ground.

Even in the gloom of the hut I knew I was not alone. It was the slight whiff I caught of a man's body paint. I saw the faint outline of a hammock. I tapped the hammock cords with my fingers. They were taut, like bow strings. I could swing the hammock with ease, so I guessed it contained a child. Ak-ak, I reckoned, had decided to start his duties as a guide right away. He had curled himself up in my spare clothes, making a nest to keep off the cold, and positioned his hammock alongside mine. I squeezed off my boots and rolled into my hammock. Tomorrow I would be moving on again into the forest, with Indians this time. I would have Tautau and this boy Ak-ak as guides; Maipuri had said Anarau and Cheroobé would be porters. I drifted into a cosy sleep.

My dreams at first were of hunting the tapir. I dreamt *I* had shot the animal dead with a bow and arrow, and was brought back in triumph above the heads of the villagers. Then I dreamt of Yimshi. I didn't want to, but she forced herself into my dream, leering at me through the jungle garden. Then suddenly she was right up against me. The dream was so strong I could feel the warmth of her body against mine, even taste the salt of her sweat and feel the softness of her skin against my lips. Then I began to get uncomfortable. She was too tangible. I opened my eyes with the shock which usually terminates a nightmare, when you think for a second that it has all been real. This time it was: in the dark there was the creak of the empty hammock next to mine, and Yimshi was in mine, hugging my neck. She was heavy, and she purred gently in my ear. Was this a kind gesture from Maipuri, lending me this ravishing girl for the night to please me? More likely, I thought (because she was ravishing mostly in the sense of hungry), it was her way of exercising a claim on Lizbet's tribe, a way of picking up a slice of Lizbet's fortune at the very least. No doubt she wanted the whole lot under her thumb. Or maybe I would just be stuck here in the jungle to raise a family of twelve children with her.

I recalled what a mess of things I'd made with Zorola, accepting her gift of crab. That memory still made me wince. Outside, the men and women were stamping out another dance, howling tunes like lonely dogs.

'Yimshi?' I said. I heard her snuffle and knew it was her laugh.

'Mad White Giant!' she said, tittering. She squirmed a bit closer. Her warm breath in my face smelt of honey. She put her mouth to my neck and it stuck fast, like a limpet.

'Yimshi,' I said quietly in her ear. 'Yimshi must go.' She must have covered her body all over in the perfumed greasepaint very recently. The smell was overwhelming me; I felt so light-headed I smiled when she didn't answer.

'Yimshi must go,' I said again.

'No,' she crooned. 'No. Yimshi not go, Mad White Giant. Yimshi stay to see if you giant all over.' She hissed a laugh.

Her head lifted like a snake about to strike. My face fell in the shadow of her breasts. In one clean sweep she took me in her arms and drew my chest up against her. Her fingernails dug into my shoulders like claws.

'Yimshi, *no*!' I prised her off. You *are* a jaguar, aren't you? I thought, getting my breath back. On my neck I felt Yimshi's mouth slacken; her lips slowly closed together. Her teeth clicked as they met. I felt her warm tears dropping on to my throat. She whimpered in my ear. It was a horrible thing I was doing to her. She would be in disgrace now that she'd been rejected. The whole village was probably pinning its hopes on her. Maipuri wasn't going to be pleased that his gesture had been rejected, either. I tipped Yimshi gently to the floor; she rolled off the hammock limp, in a heap.

'Yimshi?' I called softly. 'Yimshi?'

I heard the unfurling of the empty hammock next to mine, and the creak of the strings as she clambered into it; then a final, soft, mewing whimper.

– 12 –

Secret medicine

When I opened my eyes again, daylight was seeping into the hut and Yimshi was gone. The whole village knew that I hadn't accepted her, and every man, woman and child was smarting. Maipuri wouldn't talk except to say he'd thrown Yimshi into the cage and she'd stay there for as long as he thought fit. He turned his back to me when I said it was no good, I didn't belong here, I had another world waiting for me, and I was not a Wai-wai, a 'forest dweller'.

After a drink of cassava beer he softened and put his arm around me. 'I understanding you.' He talked slowly, looking down at his feet. 'You too good to be Wai-wai.'

I said it wasn't that at all; maybe I wasn't good enough to be a Wai-wai. 'What will you do now, Maipuri?'

'We go hide. We seek place wid no Godmen, no *garumpo*, no guvment. Maybe find more good Injuns. You come back, say hello to Maipuri?'

'But how will I find you?'

'If you find way out of forest, you find me easy, Louco Benedito. You come back wid Lizbet. You tell her Maipuri people dying. You tell all your people that. You promise?'

I promised.

Maipuri said, 'Mmmmmmm', brought out his black hen and said he wanted me to have her. 'Her spirit happy only if you thinking of her when she being eaten.'

I made a nest in my pack for her. Maipuri's wife unstaked the tortoise and presented it to Tautau, who stuffed it into Ak-ak's wicker backpack, ignoring his screams of protest.

Maipuri had forgiven me for leaving, but that didn't make me feel any better. His renegade Indians had been looking to me for hope. They had already looked for it in the missionary who'd left his shotgun, his crucifix and disease, and in the government, which had tried to domesticate them, and now in me, with my woman chief.

'We go hide,' Maipuri had said, but he knew the *garimpeiros* were only the first of the non-Indians to come into the forest; hiding wasn't a hope either.

The pathetic village group lined the riverbank and watched the five of us walk into the forest: the children with dogs nuzzling their faces, and the women huddled in timid groups behind the men, as if I were a stranger again. The women's frightened faces hurt me; so did the sight of Maipuri standing in front of the crowd with his arms folded, and the empty village and Yimshi's cage behind. There was no waving goodbye, or movement of any kind; they had taken on the drained faces of the goldmining Negroes of El Callao, the ones left in the lurch by the miners after the gold rush, with a graveyard in remembrance.

It was a relief to be in the forest, though I hadn't expected it to be. The heat, the sweat and the sodden leaves were refreshing after the empty stares of the Indians. Tautau and Ak-ak went ahead clearing a path; Cheroobé and Anarau grunted along behind, humping loads.

We went on, day after day, sleeping very little. When we did sleep, it was during the daytime, in the hours when the jungle sizzled and snored in the heat. We covered most ground at night, moving with the snakes and frogs. In the dark I tagged behind Tautau, holding his pigtail and with my eyes closed, learning to move using my sense of smell. The leaves had smells, and so did the barks, the flaky-skinned vines, and the water trapped in the pineapple bromeliad leaves.

I had always thought that listening was more important to Indians, but Ak-ak laughed out wildly at this, and Tautau put a fistful of leaves in my face and asked me to smell whether they would be bitter or sweet to taste. I said sweet, and then he asked Ak-ak, who said bitter, then he made me eat the whole lot, and I was sick. 'That why smell more important.'

The Indians scorned my heavy boots, mainly because with their splayed-out toes they could stalk monkeys without cracking twigs, but my boots were what kept me upright. Within them I was waging chemical warfare against skin fungi, and my skin was as weak as blotting paper. What my feet needed was a good airing, but nothing in the jungle got an airing – even by the camp fire my hair was wringing wet. Because one palm splinter through the heel would be enough to cripple me, I never took a step anywhere without the boots.

Resentful frog

Five days on, tunnelling through a deep fence of bamboo, Tautau asked if I could smell anything. The smells of that moment were the raffia-basket smell of the bamboo canes, and the slimy, warm smell of the mossy soil. But there was another and it was of bonfires.

We dropped down into a gully, and by a brookside was a smouldering pile of leaves. The ground had been smoothed by naked feet. There was no one about, just ourselves and the jungle, and the light falling in filtered green seams. Ak-ak tapped my arm and pointed further up the brook. He had spotted a white-and-brown-blotched mongrel on the ground. It was dead, I thought, as we came nearer and it didn't flinch.

Tautau yelled through the trees. There was no answer, but an old man pattered out after a time. He appeared from behind a fig tree which was strangling another fig tree, squeezing it dry with its roots. The man was a Wai-wai, I knew that from the pattern of his loincloth, but he was a wasted-away one. His eyes were yellow, his skin stretched and translucent over his cheekbones, and gnarled like a tree where it sagged around his neck. His hair was black, but in tangles and coming away from the scalp.

'He come here to die,' said Tautau, loudly in the man's face. I blushed, grinned awkwardly at the man, and told him I was sure it wasn't as bad as all that, he'd be better soon but he ought to lie down and take a rest. Maybe later we could carry him back to the village.

'He *come* from village. He come here to die, one moon back. He surprise me he still alive.' He patted the old man's shoulder, winding him. 'Not long now, old man.'

The old man smiled.

I helped him to the pile of smouldering leaves. The skin of his arm was dry, and as rough as a peach stone. The old man warmed to me, clenching his fingers on my fists and peering into my face with syrupy eyes. I sat with him for an hour, while the others dozed. He opened his mouth to speak sometimes, but nothing ever came out. Once I had wondered why there were no old people in the Wai-wai village; now I knew.

While Cheroobé went back into the forest to lug up the supplies we had left further back, Tautau came up and cross-examined the old man to see how long he thought he could last out. It would be bad form for us to be around when his time came, so Tautau asked him whether he thought he would peg out that night. The man shook his head. He thought he could last out that long. Tautau was pleased because we could make our shelter here, without having to move on before nightfall.

Ak-ak was eyeing the old man's neck beads greedily. He couldn't take his eyes off them, even while he was helping us cut palms for a lean-to shelter. Eventually Tautau, saying they were too valuable to waste, untied the beads from the man – who didn't raise a hand to object – and strung them around Ak-ak's neck. Ak-ak rolled the beads over in his little fingers and puffed out his chest for me to see them.

'Dog die also,' Tautau said.

I bent over the mongrel, which after all had a flicker of life left in it. 'But he's only young,' I said.

'He die young, then.'

When it did not touch them personally, as Yakka-yakka's plight had done, the Wai-wai accepted death without emotion; no fear, no ritual. It was as natural as their love-making.

The dog's main sign of life was its eye, which was hazel and swivelled in its socket inspecting us. Its face was barely out of the leaves. I said that perhaps Ak-ak could take the dog back to the village and keep it as a pet. Tautau said no, and pointed to its paws. The toenails had curled around into the pads of its feet, and they oozed a creamy pus. With Jorge's stabbing knife, I sawed through the nails, dipped the pads in disinfectant, and lifted the dog to its feet. It wobbled and fell. Tautau said it was best left in peace to die here with the old man.

Anarau and Cheroobé stumbled into the camp with the remaining supplies while we were cooking up the tortoise into soup. I gave the dog and the old man a leg each. Tautau laughed and said I might as well throw the food to the eagles. The dog accepted it, but the man shied away and wouldn't even take a sip of the soup. Instead he held my hand tightly in his, so tight I thought he wouldn't die for weeks.

At daylight, hardly lighter than night in the thicker forest, but with the leaves wiping our faces with dew, we were walking again. I was the only one to look back at the old man. He was staring into his slow bonfire, breathing in the grey smoke, trying to choke himself to death. The dog was around my neck; I felt like a shepherd lugging home a long-lost sheep. I would take it along to the next village – it had perked up already.

After three more days I was a wreck. 'You too tall,' said Anarau, who carried two pillow-sized rice sacks on his back. 'You Mad White Giant,' he said, ducking under a tree which was across our path.

As I squirmed under it like a toad, he laughed at me through the feathers in his nose, which he had plucked from the hen.

Ahead we heard what sounded like a woodpecker tapping a hollow tree, but it was Tautau signalling to us by thumping his heel against a root buttress. Cheroobé whooped back and beat a tree himself.

'We not far to go.'

'How far?' I said, wheezing.

'When sun is high, we there.' That answer was vague. The sun was hidden in the tree canopy and no one had sighted it since the village, a week ago. I listened to the cicadas, their pitch rising in the heat, and when they were whistling in my ears and the parakeets tucked their heads under their wings to take a nap, I knew it was time.

Tautau slipped his pack off, and dumped it lightly on the forest floor. The headband of bark he used to spread the weight had scored white stripes across his forehead. But he wasn't short of breath, and he lifted my pack down with the thumb and forefinger of one hand. The black hen was roosting on top of my pack.

'What you carry inside here? Feathers?'

We faced a sluggish stream. From what Tautau said it was a southern tributary of the Cafuini. That meant in one week we had come one degree, sixty miles or so eastward, skirting north of the first of my six Amazon tributaries, the Mapuera. We waded through the water without difficulty, but when it came to the turn of Cheroobé and Anarau, their legs got tangled in filaments of hairy weed and they dunked most of my food. Tautau laughed at them floundering and said they were as tired as I was.

Ak-ak scampered ahead up the far bank, and jumped up and down waving. He screamed that he could see village smoke.

The huts were conical, like beehives, and had dingy interiors like caverns. There were only two of them, and only one tree had been felled to open up the tree canopy. The undergrowth that was dying from the shock of light was the same buff colour as the palm hut roofs. If it hadn't been for the smoke I might have passed right by.

No Indians came out to welcome or attack us. Tautau frowned and said, '*Chichibé*', bad, and told us to wait by the river.

Did he mean a bad time to call, or bad Indians? I wanted to know. The others didn't know either, and we backed behind a clump of palms.

Tautau called out to the huts, mentioning Maipuri, but not even a dog trotted out. He beckoned us to come out from our cover. As soon as we showed ourselves, four men trickled out of the huts, squinting in the sun. The men were red with *roucou* fruit dye, their skins looking glossy and wet in the sun; snaky black lines were painted over their bodies from their throats to their ankles. They looked gormless, not hostile, on the whole, and so I decided we had just called at a bad time, and they were not bad Indians.

One of the men shouted at me in Wai-wai, with his head jerking forward like a threatening lizard. He wanted me to go away. Tautau flapped his hands dismissively and was short with the men. They watched us, not sure what to do next. They were as red as poppies, with red aprons which looked drab next to their skin.

They were as short as our Wai-wais, but none of them had pigtails. A woman with shrivelled, exhausted breasts meandered through the men towards us for a better look. When she saw me she upset her bowl of yucca tubers. They spilled over the men's toes, and the men flashed their teeth at her and bumped her with their knees as she stooped to gather them up. They had a brief chat with Tautau, then stomped back into the huts.

In one of the huts there was a woman with a dire illness, and the witchdoctor was busy treating her. Tautau said we shouldn't disturb his magic. For the rest of the afternoon we sat on the edge of the camp, dozing.

Under cover of dark Ak-ak crawled into the village on his stomach to spy out if they had been telling the truth. He came back without being detected and with a spider bite just below his navel. He said he thought they *were* telling the truth. I gathered that there was one woman who was just about to die, and she had two husbands who were fussing over her. The woman we had seen was the only other woman, and she also had two husbands. That just left the sorcerer, who was a failure at his art and had an enormous chip on his shoulder about it. Then Ak-ak fainted from the pain of the spider bite, and Tautau carried him away to be revived in the stream.

We made a fire up-wind of the huts, and enticed the Indians out by cooking up the black hen and singing a song to her memory. The smell of the roasted meat drifting over the huts brought all but the dying woman out. The villagers stood around us and tried to make polite chat, while we cooed over how good the food was. They began to rub their bellies, and moan.

'*Kiriwanhi, mawa jiant?*' they asked me. 'Is it good, Mad White Giant?' They patted their stomachs, and pleaded with whines and smiles.

'*Mawa jiant, mawa jiant. Maaawa jiiiiiaaaannnt!*'

I handed over most of the chicken and they fled with it. Anarau and Cheroobé looked daggers at me. They had not eaten for days, they said. This was the final straw. They would leave tomorrow, and weren't going to carry my stores any further, and that was that. Tautau calmed them down but they were adamant.

Tautau said, 'Unless these Wai-wai help you, you live for ever and ever our men with us in forest, Mad White Benedito Giant.' He went to see how things were coming along in the village. It was now dark, a night of shooting stars. They skated through the sky and faded amongst the fireflies.

Tautau yelled back that I could come forward. His call woke two Powis birds – clumsy, black, turkey-like creatures with white breasts and golden legs – which almost fell from their tree with fright.

The witchdoctor, a sunken-eyed man with disorganized hair and bow legs, appeared and showed me into one of the huts. It reeked of black fire smoke. Tautau said special leaves had been put on the fire to clean the air of bad spirits. The witchdoctor ordered everyone but Tautau and me out of the hut. Through smarting eyes we saw his patient, who lay shivering, bathed in her own sweat, in a hammock. Her face was knotted up with pain and she smelt cheesy. I pinched her leg; she didn't notice. The skin was like polythene, and the crease I'd made didn't disappear. I said I thought on the whole she was dying, but might last the night. The witchdoctor agreed, and so did Tautau. Tautau whispered that the witchdoctor's future wouldn't be much better than hers if he didn't get this patient fixed up. Though most doctors had a rigorous training and knew all the jungle potions, this man didn't have a clue and had had a long run of failures.

I said, 'Good, then maybe we can come to some arrangement.'

Half an hour later we had drawn up an agreement whereby I would try my own magic on the woman (no one else need know), restore her to health, and the witchdoctor would get his Indians to help me to travel further east.

I wasn't left alone with the woman until the middle of the night. Ak-ak was on his feet again by that time, and offered to work as my assistant. I couldn't fathom out why; it was unusually charitable of him. He ran to fetch my medicines and a gourd of cold water. I listened to the other Indians rigging up their hammocks in the next-door hut and to the weak gasps of the woman at my side.

Ak-ak came back. I asked him what he thought. He bit his lip and shrugged. 'Hell!' I said. 'What now?' I opened the woman's mouth and looked at her teeth, as I'd seen people do to horses. She had lost most of them. Apart from being about to die of fever, she looked short of all basic vitamins. Ak-ak asked what I was up to. When I explained her diet was bad, and he wagged his head and said, no, it was definitely *much* more serious than that, I wanted to strike him.

Together we rolled the woman over. She was getting on in years and her back was curved from bending over cooking pots. A bandage of palm had been strapped down her spine. I began to peel it away, but Ak-ak grimaced, and held back my hand. '*Chichibé, chichibé!*' He didn't want me to disturb the witchdoctor's magic. He got up, and peeped from over by the doorway, as I stripped the bandage off. Underneath were tramlines of black bruises along her spine. I looked carefully at the bandage. It was woven with black ants tied on with their stings projecting on the underside. The witchdoctor was hoping to torture the evil out of the woman. I threw the bandage into the fire, and the bodies of the ants spat and crackled like chestnuts. The fire flared up to light the room.

I dressed the woman's spine with calamine lotion, then gave her a general antibiotic, not knowing what would happen.

Ak-ak eased over to me. His face was pale. He was working himself up to tell me something. It looked serious; very serious, from his small pained face. I tried to visualize the sort of evil spirit he thought was going to descend on me for having messed about with the witchdoctor's spells. Ak-ak turned his head away into the darkness and said: 'You think Yimshi beautiful?'

The question took me totally unawares, making me cough. It was not an evil spirit which descended on me but a mental image of Yimshi, in the darkness, her skin smelling of incense and her breath of honey.

'Why you no answer Ak-ak?'

'Er . . . yes, I think Yimshi very beautiful.'

'She not beautiful enough for Mad White Giant?'

'She's plenty beautiful enough for Mad White Giant.'

Ak-ak said he wanted to know the reason why I had turfed her out of my hammock on the night she came to me, because, if I didn't mind of course, he sort of fancied her himself. He could offer her a good future being the headman's son, and if Mad White Giant Benedito ever returned, even if I was married to Lizbet by then, I could have Yimshi during my stay at the village. That would make Yimshi very happy and of course Lizbet would have a say in the arrangement. Why was I laughing? Didn't I think he was strong enough to satisfy Yimshi? He was stronger than any of his friends, and very nearly a man. *Please* would I stop laughing.

Outside, it was raining. The patter of the rain on the roof soothed the woman, and her breathing slowed and deepened. We stayed the night in the hut, taking it in turns to douse her with cool river water.

Finally I dropped off to sleep in my hammock, but at five-minute intervals Ak-ak would shout progress reports into my face – '*Kiriwanhi! Kiriwanhi!*' Good! Good! – or else tell me what he was going to get up to with Yimshi when he got back to the village.

The ill woman's progress was remarkable. At daybreak whatever illness she'd had before the witchdoctor treated her was well under control, and even his medicine was wearing off. She tried to smile.

The rain gave the air a fruity smell. The leaves paled and softened to a lighter shade of green, and the palm fronds of the hut roof swelled and looked like corn.

The witchdoctor had the goaty, thin-lipped sort of face I had learnt to distrust even at kindergarten age. In addition he spent most of his daylight hours plucking stray hairs from his cheek, and spewed saliva from his mouth while talking. He also hated me for delivering his patient from the jaws of death. Tautau, in a moment of absent-mindedness, compounded the situation by announcing that I had already worked a miracle on his son Yakka-yakka. The witchdoctor left under a stormcloud, spitting like an angry cat. Tautau made amends by saying he would help me force the witchdoctor to fulfil his side of the bargain. He would even come with me, further into the forest. So we arranged for him to stay on with me until the next village. It was time for the others to go.

Anarau and Cheroobé led off across the river, back to the village with Ak-ak. They began trotting with the thought of getting home; I caught a look of sadness in Tautau's face and knew he wanted to get back and see Yakka-yakka. Ak-ak was cheerful and said he would kiss Yimshi thoroughly on my behalf. He waved for some time through the green beams of light before the party was invisible.

'Right, let's get these people into action,' I said to Tautau in English.

'Into action,' he said, and nodded gravely. He walked back into the hut ahead of me. You're a real stalwart, Tautau, I thought. He was as staunch a friend to me as Pablo had been, but more civilized.

I spent the day telling the witchdoctor how he should complete the woman's course of antibiotics, but he refused to understand,

and only harped on about the power of the ants he had administered. Tautau and I ended up staying another whole day, so that the woman was strong enough to stave the witchdoctor off.

The remaining Indians worked together in completing a dugout canoe. It was a graceful craft, as straight as a pencil, light but not frail. The Indians roasted it on a fire to harden the wood and covered it in black pitch. We launched the canoe into the river, and it was sound.

Choosing a new eating-bowl from the gourd tree.

Tautau made the decision about which guides to take. They were all equally unwilling. I had to proffer a third of my gold to raise any enthusiasm at all, and none of the men looked worth it. They were lethargic, measly Indians. Their mouths were like muzzles and their teeth fawn-coloured gravel chips, sunk in grey, spongy gums. Fritz would have said it was because Indians were savages and, like any animal, didn't have 'ze common senses to fortify zemselves vith ze vitamins'. Tautau said it was because these Indians were part of their tribe that had come from Guyana, and like most Indians who had seen 'Godmen or guvment' they became lazy, and didn't grow the right food, or drink good cassava beer.

Tautau ran into difficulties picking out the guides. He couldn't stop them bickering with each other.

'Can they all paddle?' I asked.

He said it was an insult to ask a Wai-wai if he could paddle.

'Well, can they?'

He said he didn't know.

'Look, Tautau, just tell these men I want someone who can paddle.' I went away to load the stores into the canoe, and came back an hour later to find Tautau still standing around with the other men.

'Right. All settled then, Tautau?' It obviously wasn't. Tautau had not plucked up enough courage to ask. 'I cannot have a guide who can't even paddle. That is a basic requirement.' I felt my temper fraying.

'Is what?'

'A *basic necessity*! Got it?'

Tautau put his hand over his eyes.

'Sorry, Tautau, I didn't mean to shout. Just ask these people if they can paddle.'

The men said of course they could paddle. Anyone could paddle. They claimed that, though they were all exceptional paddlers, each of their friends was actually even better.

'What do you think they're up to, Tautau?' I said. 'Why don't they want to come?'

'Benedito Mad White Giant, I not know. I sorry. I think your journey end here. I sorry. You stay marry Yimshi. Maybe share with Ak-ak. He tell me you not mind, and she like it. She powerful lady. And if you not like her now, she *make* you like her. She very clever.'

'I'm sure she has her ways and means.'

'Yes, and maybe Lizbet not mind you stay in forest, and not bring gold home.' Tautau was desperate to cheer me up, and had an anxious grin on his face. '*Maybe* Lizbet come out and live with Mad White Giant and Yimshi.'

I thought I was about to faint. 'Please, Tautau, just find out what will satisfy these people. I don't care how you do it. Get them drunk or something. I want to know why they don't want to come.' I stormed away, bitterly sorry I was putting so much pressure on Tautau. He was only trying his best. I went and talked to the dog, who was snoozing in the canoe. Today he even had the strength to stand, but he was not yet strong enough to cope with the witchdoctor's medicine and I'd have to take him on to another village.

Because he didn't have a name, I called him Cashoe, to simplify things. It meant 'dog'.

I wondered if it wasn't too bad an idea to marry Yimshi after all. She couldn't be more physically tiring than this expedition, surely.

Tautau came over. He had cracked the problem. It appeared that each of the men had thought the husband with whom he shared a wife would maltreat her or wear her out. They each wanted to stay and keep an eye on things.

'Good grief. All right, I'll take the two husbands of the sick woman, and get the witchdoctor to see she is safe. The men will trust the doctor?'

'Everyone trust doctor. Life not worth living if not trust doctor.'

'I can imagine.'

The jungle is an eternal prison, Pablo had said. I marched to the canoe half in triumph, because so far the jungle was not proving a prison, and half in fear, because it had almost been a prison several times, and now I was about to go deeper into it than ever.

The witchdoctor did not stand on ceremony. There was no farewell. We tugged the canoe downstream, through a mass of water plants that wrapped round our legs like seaweed. The last we saw of the settlement was the woman spilling her bucket of yuccas again when she saw me; she stood gaping, while her two husbands biffed her.

'He the same witchdoctor our village had many, many moons ago, in land of Guyana,' said Tautau. 'Godman sent him away.'

'Not surprised,' I said.

– 13 –

In the jungle deep

Haimarha and Sipu were bad guides. Their hearts were not in the journey, and I had to give them a pinch of gold a day just to keep them from fighting. After a while I learnt that what they yearned for more than anything else was Western clothes. They were much happier once they had stolen all my underpants and were wearing them over their loincloths. But, as Tautau said, 'Mad White Giant, problem is they bad Wai-wai. They seen too much Godmen and guvment.'

About a week after setting out from the witchdoctor's village, pulling the canoe like a sledge through dark backwaters of the Cafuini, we hit a fast stretch and climbed aboard. This was a chance for the two new guides to prove they could paddle. So far the water had been sleepy.

In the prow, Tautau pointed left with his finger. He was signalling us to cut across through two boulders which were shooting out spumes of white water.

'Left!' I shouted, from half-way up the canoe.

'Left?' said Sipu, the Indian paddling in front. 'Why not right?'

'No, left,' I said.

'Left, then,' said Sipu.

'Left,' agreed Haimarha, behind, and dug the paddle to swing us right.

'Left, not right, you fool. Keep hanging on, Tautau!'

Before we had properly sorted that out, the first white lip of the rapids was tickling the front of the canoe, jockeying Tautau even more.

'More speed,' said Tautau.

'More speed,' I ordered.

'Left,' said Sipu.

'More speed, I said, not left.'

'You said left last time.'

'What was that? Left?' said Haimarha, at the helm, and started paddling us right again.

'Maybe more speed not good idea,' said Sipu, and dabbled about with his paddle vaguely.

Haimarha had steered us into the worst of the rapids, and more speed *wasn't* a good idea any more. I leapt forward and snatched Sipu's paddle. The rapids were licking over the sides of the canoe and water was splashing into our faces. It was a battle just to keep off the rocks.

'Give me back,' said Sipu, reaching for my paddle.

'Right turn,' said Tautau. His voice was weak. He was spitting out water, and his eyes were desperate. 'What you doing back there?'

'I been here before,' said Sipu. 'I know river, I want go left.'

'Are you blind? Look at that rock over there.'

I was the only one paddling and the current swept us on to Sipu's rock, which bit hard. The front of the canoe dipped, scooping froth over Tautau.

'Help!' said Tautau. 'I drinking too much water. I get out of here.' He threw himself overboard.

The rapids were now behind us. I steered to the bank, where Tautau was spouting water out from his mouth. Once we were on dry land my temper boiled over. Why had Tautau deserted the canoe?

'I swim for my life. I think we all going to bottom of river for ever and ever our men.'

Why had Sipu questioned the orders?

'Me a think-man, not do-man.'

'And you, Haimarha, can't you tell the difference between left and right?'

'No.'

That was the day we worked out most of our problems. My job was to navigate and make corrections to the maps; the Indians were to paddle without querying all the time; Cashoe, the dog, guarded the stores at night in the canoe. We cooked and hunted together.

A moon waxed and waned, and rapids came and went. Sometimes they were white mashed-up water, other times gentle furrows as clear as glass. We went deeper into the interior. It got no darker or danker, or thicker. It didn't change. The forest had a black canopy roof, so high the pinpricks of light in it might have been stars. And the air between the ground shrubs, on the floor where we lived, was the green colour of stagnant ponds.

The Acarai hills loomed up on the left, the north; green ranges with jets of snowy white cloud streaming over the lowland in the wind. Then, one afternoon, we rounded a tight river bend. When we looked up to see the hills again after the river unbuckled, they were not there.

Soon I forgot I was beyond reach of the outside world of *racionales*, and lived from day to day like the others. I let myself go, and lived as part of the forest. We ran through the trees below the monkey troops, sprinting on and on until we were ahead; then we lay in ambush ready to shoot them down; we went nut gathering; we harpooned fish, or whistled mating songs at birds to lure them.

Only when I was weak with fever did I know the real strength of the jungle, and then I almost cried if I had to resort to using the medicines I had brought along with me from the 'outside'.

There were days when I was taken with fevers. They were mysterious, whimsical diseases which could bring me to my knees within hours. When I was ill I had one recurrent dream – that I was being flushed down a drain. 'That drain is my future,' I would say as I woke, burning all over, still with the image in front of my eyes. I would be stuck to my hammock with sweat, and think of myself swirling down the black drain hole. The dream was the expression of my fear that I would never escape the jungle. Then, as always, Tautau was there as my source of strength. I came to see him as my only hope of ever getting out.

Tautau had to turn back shortly, I knew. I dreaded being stuck with the other two Indians. They spent most of their spare time preening themselves, stroking the feathers in their hair, or daubing paint over their chests and legs. Tautau said that once these had been bold, perky men. The Godman had told them they sinned in sharing a wife, and ever since then they had lost their love of life, and even forgotten how to laugh like a Wai-wai.

Tautau and I lay in ambush for some ring-tailed capuchin monkeys. We were side by side, and Tautau had plotted their course through the trees. It cropped up in conversation that he had killed his only brother. They had gone hunting together as little

On the Move

boys, during an initiation test, and they were stalking this fat peccary, an old boar which had already mauled several members of the tribe. One of the boys had loosed off an arrow tipped with curare poison. It had bounced off the leathery old pig, and driven straight in and out the other side of the neck of Tautau's brother.

The boy had keeled over, half-paralysed with nerve toxin, half thrashing with pain. There was only one thing to do. Two boys held him up by the arms in a crucifix position, another boy covered the brother's eyes, another his mouth to stop the screams, and Tautau got out a fresh arrow, and shot him clean through the heart.

Tautau said he'd not been happy about doing it – he ran his fingers down his face and chest to show how he'd wept – but his brother would be pleased with him in the afterlife. I asked him if bad people had an afterlife. When he had stopped laughing, he said of course they did: 'We meet all friends and enemies after dying. We go drinking together, and live happily again. If you bad man, then you have many enemies waiting for you. You have hell life afterwards. That why Wai-wai so good people when alive.'

Tautau said that what the Godmen didn't understand was that everything went to the Creator. Pebbles in the rivers, ants on the forest leaves, even the fat old boar. Everything went to the Creator, because everything had a spirit. The forest spirits weren't good or evil – unless, of course, the witchdoctor worked magic on them. So the world was as nice a place as we made it. It was up to everyone to make it as happy a place as possible by sharing all things. God did not bother to listen to our prayers, because he hadn't asked for them in the first place. Why should he? What marked man out from all the other spirits? God didn't look like a man anyway. Saying that was an insult to the other spirits. 'What make us so special?' Yes, said Tautau, everything the Godmen said was silly when you came to think about it.

The jungle was neutral, Tautau told me, tough but rarely with evil intent; and I felt more content in the forest than ever before.

A day or two later, on a stormy night, rain lashed the treetops above our palm shelter and caused the camp fire to hiss and splutter. I asked Tautau what the peals of thunder were.

Didn't I honestly know? he wondered. He said it was an Indian rolling a log through the heavens.

How was he certain that spirits existed? Where was his proof?

'Ploooof! Louco Benedito need ploooof!' He called to Sipu and Haimarha to come over. They were grilling a capybara, a ratty animal the size of Cashoe, and probably going to undercook it as usual. (Instead, they left it unattended so long it burst into flames.)

Tautau asked if I dreamt at night. I said yes, of course I did. He gritted his teeth to stop himself laughing at my stupidity. 'Well, dreams is spirits. When someone die, spirit still live, and sometime walk down from heaven.' That was why last night he had dreamt about his brother, and he knew he was dead because he had killed him himself.

For a few days now we had been trying a short cut east from the Poana river overland through the forest to the Curiau, though two of us could hardly raise the canoe from the water surface even when empty. We were making for two villages, Maloca Aroni and Maraxó Patá, on an eastern reach of the Anamu. That night, however, we decided to beat a retreat and continue south on to the Trombetas, before cutting further east. The river ahead was barricaded with fallen trees from flooding. During the day it had rained so hard that the river exploded its banks and the current swelled and churned with clouds of red clay. The water was choked with straw-coloured leaves, bugs with black spiny hairs, caterpillars of all sorts, and crumpled leaves and saplings. Hundreds of spiky black ants skated on the floodwater towards us and grappled with each other for a hold on the canoe.

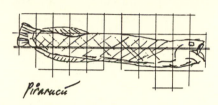

Pirarucú

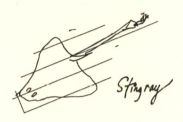

Stingray

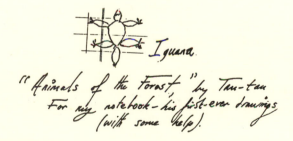

Iguana

"Animals of the Forest" by Tau-tau For my notebook – his first-ever drawings (with some help).

Sipu and Haimarha almost capsized us trying to stamp out the would-be boarders.

'They no good Wai-wais,' said Tautau, tutting. 'Even *you* better, Louco Benedito.'

South we went down the easy northern Trombetas, where Sipu and Haimarha wore through two perfectly good paddles, east another fifty miles up the Ventura tributary. Afterwards, there was a gruelling march overland on to the Marapi, during which, as we heaved the canoe between the trees, Haimarha dived for a tortoise that was plodding by and dropped the stern, cracking it on a tree root. It made the same sound as a breaking egg.

Poling north up the Marapi we were in a dire state. I knew I had pushed everyone too hard, and Tautau's skin was greying and flaking. In the old days Sipu and Haimarha had spent much of the sunshine lying back decorating themselves with feathers and paint. Now they slept.

'Mad White Giant Benedito?' said Tautau paddling behind me one bitterly cold dawn.

'Yes?' I knew what it was.

'Mad White Giant, Tautau think he cannot go paddling much further with you. I been good. I come two moons with you. But time coming for me to leave. When I leave I cry much.' He rubbed his eyes. 'Maybe Yakka-yakka need my help.'

'You have been very good to me, Tautau.'

'You have been very good to Wai-wai, Benedito.'

The village was on the Marapi. Sipu said they were Kuxúyana Indians. They were good people – but not as good as Wai-wais, and they didn't wear clothes.

We paddled up slowly, half asleep under the morning sun.

'I going back as soon as we arrive,' said Sipu.

'I going too. Soon as we arrive,' said Haimarha.

Good! I said to myself. Tautau knew what I was thinking and giggled. I said what we all needed was a good feast, lots of alcohol and dancing; and we all cheered up.

We saw a dog first. It was sneaking up on a collection of butter-flies, which were like violets on the river mud. Cashoe yapped at it, making it bolt into a thicket, howling and with its tail between its legs. The dog meant that Indians were near, but there were none to be seen. I spotted a fish trap: two walls of reeds in the water shallows, which funnelled the fish up a one-way lane. Haimarha and Sipu shrieked out that they'd seen it, when we were only a paddle stroke away, and Tautau tried to wink at me as he'd seen me do.

We got Cashoe to track the dog, and ran along behind him.

'He damn good friend,' said Tautau. 'He not afraid of danger.'

The Indians did not attack Cashoe. No one at the village was going to attack anything ever. 'Godmen been here,' said Tautau. His face went cloudy.

'How do you know?' I asked, because the Indians looked normal to me. All we could see so far were a bunch of tidy huts and the standard naked children running in the sunlight, some of them red with dye.

'Because people not happy.'

'Why no one welcome us?' said Sipu.

'Why that hut stupid shape?' said Haimarha. He was looking at a hut that was square, with a barn-like roof.

We walked up quietly behind Cashoe, who was being sniffed at by a pack of overweight dogs. We could see shadowy figures in the huts, and the profile of a few naked bosoms and bottoms. One woman looked up – I saw the white of her eyes – then carried on cooking. It was so very quiet I could hear the pot bubbling.

This was like the silence that had welcomed us at the witch-doctor's village. But here it wasn't because anyone was ill. It was because they weren't interested in us. The silence was unnatural in the middle of the hectic forest.

Sipu ploughed his fingers through his hair and said, 'These people funny in the head.'

I heard the dial of a transistor being tuned. SSSSSHHH-ZZZZZIIIZZZXXX. When it hit a rock-and-roll station, Tautau jumped. ZZZZZMMMMXSSSSXXXXSSHH

MEIA NOITE NO MEU QUARTO

ELA VAI SUBIR

OUÇO PASSOS NA ESCADA

VEJO A PORTA ABRIR

O ABAJUR COR DE CARNE

O LENÇOL AZUL

CORTINAS DE SEDAZZMMMEIISSSZZZ....

The signal faded, and was lost.

A little Indian girl in a freshly laundered, clean white frock, her hair in bunches, ran up to me. Seeing her bright red squeaky shoes, Tautau gasped. Sipu and Haimarha ran back into the forest.

She stuck her hands out in front of my chest and said in broken Portuguese that she wanted some sweets. Tautau leapt back from her. Then when she didn't go away he whacked her on the cheek

---

* These words from a song popular in Brazil at the time translate into English roughly as follows: *Midnight in my room,/Soon she will come up./I hear footsteps on the stair,/I see the door opening,/The flesh-coloured lampshade,/The blue sheet,/Curtains of silk. . . .*

with the back of his hand. The child put her hand to her face, then stamped away to a podgy woman behind and began screaming.

'What was that for, Tautau?'

'She bad Injun. How she know you not enemy? Maybe you want kill her. Mmmmmmmm. Good Injun let man talk first. She bad, bad Injun.'

The girl's screams brought the place alive. It was as if we had set fire to all the huts. Indians ran all over the place, tipping through their possessions and digging out Western-style clothes. Then they began squeezing into them. 'They think you are angry Godman,' said Tautau.

Tautau was right; that was exactly what they thought. They flooded out of the huts, the women pulling dazed men out into the open behind them. The men already had baggy blue jeans on. A congregation was assembling in front of us. Some Indians thought they should kneel, others thought they shouldn't. So they crouched at our feet instead and crossed themselves. They all wore Sunday best, but whoever had dished out the clothes – they were uniforms – had forgotten that the tropical heat and moisture make new material shrink. The clothes were still being pulled on; one girl had an arm through the head-hole, and another was guiltily smearing off her red body-paint on to her neighbour's shirt. The singing started, but it was more than a hymn, it was a hysterical wail for mercy.

'*GLORIA, GLORIA ALELUIA! GLORIA, GLORIA, GLORIA ALELUIA! LOUVEMOS AO SENHOR!*'

That was the chorus; now they were looking for a leader to prompt the words of the first verse.

'Mad White Giant?' said Tautau, backing away from the din.

'Yes? Speak up, I can't hear.'

'Is horrible!' He was staring at the prostrate Indians. It wasn't the racket he found distasteful, it was the hideousness of the people; the women with bottoms squelched into white skirts with rolls of fat hanging over the belts; the men with their groins pinched by seized-up zips, and the rust-stain smears down their legs.

They started up. '*Jesus Cristo é amor, da vitória sobre a morte. . . .*'

'I am going home, Mad White Giant. I sorry. I come long way. Now I go.'

He ran off down towards the river. Cashoe went after him.

I looked at the bellowing Indians at my feet.

'*GLORIA, GLORIA, ALELUIA!*'

I shouted, 'Tautau, wait for me!'

Sipu and Haimarha were waiting for us, but they were not alone.

'Gee! Where did *you* spring from?'

The man was pale, dressed in chain-store clothes, and had a straw hat like mine. He had a button nose, crewcut, freckles and evidently ate too much; he looked as if the heat was torturing him. His grey cotton shirt was blotched with sweat everywhere except along the buttonhole line, and he wore black lace-ups. He didn't seem to like the wobble of the dugout in which he was standing, and he was clutching a leather-bound book in his hand.

I had forgotten how to greet a non-Indian. Should I smile? I felt like backing away slowly, as Tautau was doing. The man held out a fat white hand with black tufts of hair on the knuckles. I shook the hand – it was soft and unhealthy after the Indian ones. The man was smiling but his eyes were on my machete.

'What are you doing here?' I said, before he could ask me. Tautau stood at the end of his canoe, keeping the man from getting to land. Tautau was grinning at the man's frightened look as the canoe rocked.

Through the trees I heard the quivering notes, '*Glória, glória, aleluia!*' The man raised his hand to his ear, flapping the other arm as the canoe almost went from under his feet. He smiled at the sound.

'*That's* why I'm here. "Yea, so have I strived to preach the gospel, not where Christ was named." Comes from Romans – like it?' He smiled again at the soft Indian voices in the wind. 'Here's another reason. "Repentance and remission of sins should be preached in His name among all nations."'

'Luke 24:47,' I said, and smiled at his astonished face. 'Heard it somewhere else.'

'Wanna can of Coke? I got plenty in the freezer. How about a burger? Er. . . .' he was examining the skin flaking off my nose. 'Hey! Bet you ain't seen a can of beans in years, have you, now? We could have ourselves a real good party!'

'He say party!' Sipu said.

Tautau said: 'I not like dis man.'

'Hey, you speak English, son?'

'I not your son.'

'Hey, how d'you feel 'bout hanging on around here, huh? We do singing and dancing, and this 'n' that. Nothing elaborate, mind you. You boys'd love it. Guess you can hear them singing now.' He touched his index finger to the hat brim and concentrated on listening. 'What d'you think, boys?'

'I am man, not boy.'

'Good music though, huh?'

'Bad.'

'Real nice bunch of friends you got,' the man said to me quietly, and gave me a sympathetic smile.

'How about me dressing you up in some nice wholesome clothes? Fresh off the peg. You could sure do with some.'

Sipu asked what the man was talking about. He said if there were any clothes going, he was interested.

'We go,' said Tautau. He picked up Cashoe and placed him in our canoe, knocking the other man's so that it see-sawed.

The man almost lost his book overboard. He thought it was an accident. He said: 'Cute pet you got, son. What's his name?'

I missed the face that Tautau gave him, but it sent the fat man bounding up the riverbank.

'I think we ought to be going,' I said.

'Going?' he called, as we undid the mooring line. 'Are you kidding? Where to?'

'Bye! Thanks for the offers.'

'So long.' The man blinked in disbelief as he watched us slip into the trees.

We had spoken to the missionary for only five minutes, and had a very brief glimpse of his parish, but for the rest of the day the Indians paddled without saying a word. Tautau looked as if he had stared death in the face, and Sipu and Haimarha were perhaps worried in case the man knew they had only one wife between them, and looked over their shoulders to see if he was following.

But the memory of the Godman had faded the next day. Tautau said it might have been a bad dream we had shared, and the others said they'd wished they had taken off the man's clothes to bring with us.

Not much further up the Marapi we took a right turn east up an unnamed tributary, and came to Tirió territory. We knew only because we happened across them unexpectedly, while harpooning fish with arrows. Tautau and I were spearing at a pike-like fish which had banks of needle teeth. Tautau was saying that this kind of fish had once eaten up a dog he was swimming with. This one was lurking in a sward of weed, keeping in the canoe's shadow, and passing time while a gentle *paku* fish, fat and round and the colour of tomato ketchup, swam dreamily into range.

Haimarha had been named after the pike fish, but as a joke, because he was never able to get his jaws into anything.

'We being watched,' Tautau said softly in my ear. I looked up. I couldn't see anyone; only brittle ranks of sepia grass and bottle-green trees which cloaked us like parachutes. One of the Indians moved his eyes, a glint of white that was enough to give him away. I saw curved twigs – they were bows – and next I saw their bodies, as dark as the tree trunks.

'Tirió,' said Sipu.

'Why are they hiding?' I said.

'Maybe they not want to be seen,' said Haimarha.

'They so scared they dangerous,' said Tautau. 'You got presents?'

'Yes.'

'Now is time for presents.'

I decked the canoe with beads, and my last postcards. The two Indians came out of cover. From the riverbank they were just like Wai-wais, but once Tautau was near them he looked like a child. They were taller, their skin auburn, and ruddier, as if they lived out in the sunshine. They had no feathers, but red armbands which Haimarha wanted to swop for his paddle, and red loincloths like the Wai-wais.

I couldn't make the men understand my version of Wai-wai, but Tautau could with some sign language. He said the Indians had never seen someone with a long nose and so many clothes before – they were looking at me – and this was what had upset them.

The two Tirió Indians took us along to their village, and we left the canoe to be guarded by Cashoe. But it wasn't a village. The Tirió were on the move, searching for a new hunting ground. We found the group raising shelters and adjusting hammocks under them. A woman had black ink lines in intricate spiderweb patterns over her face, and while Sipu was getting one of the men to decorate him like that I handed out postcards. The children grabbed eagerly at them, but a man with white streaks in his hair,

no eyebrows and a stoop confiscated them and fed them to the fire
as kindling. Tautau said they didn't want to be burdened with too
much clobber, and food would go down better.

Haimarha was sent back to our canoe, and brought back a
tortoise we had bumped into in the river that day. We had saved it
in the nick of time, because its legs were being chewed off by
piranha fish. The Indians jumped for joy when they saw it, and
cracked it apart with two chops of a machete. They drew up some
logs and invited us to take a seat. Sipu rubbed his hands. He said if
this was going to be a feast he wanted to know because he would
dress up for it properly. Tautau said, yes, it was probably going to
be a proper feast.

While the tortoise spun round and round on a spit, steaming in
the flames, Sipu and Haimarha took it in turns to paint each other.
The Tirió men, five of them, said they could do better than Wai-
wai Indians, swiped our pat of red dye, and plastered it over their
chests as a background to more black spiderwebs. Tautau spotted
a small boy's pet macaw and plucked some puce wing feathers
from it, which he plaited into his pigtail. The Tiriós put showers of
the feathers into their armbands and by nightfall the bird was bald
and miserable.

We drank and drank a sticky type of cassava beer, which was
stronger than the Wai-wai brew. The man with the stoop was the
headman. He had a drum of furry tapir skin which he held to his
ear and knocked with his fingers until he gave the men either side
of him a headache. We ate the tortoise around one deep red fire.
My neighbour was an aged woman with a pitted face; her flesh
smelt of decay and hung in dry bags from the bones. She droned on
and on at me for hours, not caring that I didn't pick up a word.
Tautau said he thought she had a lot of problems. He was still
nattering to the two youths who had brought us to the camp, and
Sipu and Haimarha were flirting with two girls who had cropped
hair and only just hummocky chests. I noticed the narrow-eyed
glances of the Tirió men and knew Sipu and Haimarha shouldn't
be talking to them; they were coming of age.

But the girls were finding the Wai-wais fascinating, and twid-
dled their feathers and earrings. The chief stopped drumming and
told two men to prise them apart, which they did, roughly.

Tautau came over and said there was going to be an argument.

'Surely we can do something about it?'

'No. Soon there be argument. Golly God, yes. That certain.' He shook his head.

I said I thought it would simmer down soon if we pulled Sipu and Haimarha away. I joked that it would be a pity if Cashoe had no home to go to if we all got killed.

'That not funny, Mad White Giant. That not funny one bit at all. If there be argument we all wiped out with bows and arrows.'

'Oh, I see. *That* sort of argument.'

'Yes. I go to meet my brother in the sky. Cashoe get us for food.'

I went over to Sipu and Haimarha and told them that Tautau wanted the two girls for himself and that if he didn't get them he was going to leave both men stranded in the jungle, and they would never get back to decent Wai-wai country again. The atmosphere changed in a matter of minutes. Tautau cooled things further by dousing the fire with water, and the fight was to get it alive again.

We talked until the bats went to sleep, and Tautau said he had found me two good men who wanted to be my guides.

'They say they take you on towards where the sun comes up. Oyampi Injun country. Rest of the Tirió go to guvment home soon. They say they want easy life there. These two men say they want Tirió life. They want be happy still.'

'Can I trust them?'

'Mmmmmmm. They *kiriwanhi*. They good. They say, "Can we trust Mad White Giant?" One of Tirió say he want go furder wid you. He want see where de sun come up. He say he hear from witchdoctor it come from endless lake.'

The endless lake was the sea; the mouth of the Amazon. I leaped up and down hugging Tautau. He had found someone to take me to the end of my journey. He started to hug me as well, and his grip was so strong my ribs nearly buckled up.

'Mad White Giant! Mad White Giant! You pleased wid me! Mmmmmmmmm! Tautau very happy! Mmmmmmmmm. Louco White Benedito Giant! Tautau happy for ever and ever our men.' We danced around the fire holding hands. Tautau burnt his toes but said he didn't care. 'Benedito happy, mmmmmmmmm!'

– 14 –

The fire dance

The mists were thick in the trees the next dawn. The Tirió said goodbye at the riverside and left us. I split the supplies into two heaps. Tautau heaved my share to me from the canoe sack by sack, while Sipu and Haimarha lay around talking about how disgracefully the Tirió Indians had decorated themselves last night.

'Maybe you come back to Wai-wais in many moons?' said Tautau.

'I hope so.'

'Tell Lizbet I think she beautiful. Mmmmmm. Tell her I kiss her when she come.'

'Tautau, tell Maipuri that Pablo the *garimpeiro* is a good man. Will you do that? He is tough and fights more than a Wai-wai, but he is on your side. Ask Maipuri to make friends with him. Please.'

'Tautau try.' He scooped Cashoe from the canoe and snuggled him into my arms, patting his head. 'He good friend to you. Keep him till you out of forest. He Wai-wai. He good friend.'

I said I would do that. Sipu and Haimarha said they didn't want the gold I owed them. We had been friends and only non-Indians had to have money. So I kept it. We wished each other luck and the canoe swung into the mist, cutting through it. Sipu and Haimarha paddled, and Tautau, riding in the bow, stared back in my direction long after he must have lost sight of me standing in the trees. As the canoe blurred into the mist, there was only the slopping sound of paddles. That sound fading was the loneliest sound in the world in the stillness of the early morning, and I ran off into the forest so as not to hear it slowly die.

It was a new day, and I had completed another link in the journey. I made myself think of that. On my way back to the Tirió camp I watched the skipping parrots and silent flutter of golden butterflies, which were like autumn leaves. The large metallic-blue morpho butterflies were always bolder. They flew alone and haphazardly, like wounded birds. That morning I saw some perched on shelves of leaves, waiting for the damp to lift from their wings, and they were like scraps of wind-scattered satin.

The Tiriós were packing up and about to march on. The only two who were not standing with their legs wide apart to support loads were my guides. They squatted beside the dead fire, dragging on smouldering rolls of tobacco. I sat on my haunches next to them. We waited without a word, while the others got organized and the men led them away into the forest. I watched them go. Bananas and yuccas bounced in their packs; the clanging of pots and knives, and the chatter of their voices, at last grew faint.

Pimi's offer of friendship

The two Indians smiled coyly. They looked me over. I looked them over. They handed me their cigarettes in turn. I drew on each and handed them back. I lit up my pipe, and they sucked on that. It made them cough raucously, and they hated it.

'Benedito,' I said, patting my shirt. They said their names were Pimi and Toeleu.

I spread out my maps and asked them about the local geography. '*Dicta?* Hills?' I said, pointing east. '*Gashin?* Rapids? *Atchi wau?* What do you call that river?'

The Indians were polite, intelligent and honest. Toeleu was a quiet, ponderous sort, who smoked his cigarettes right up to his lips. His eyes were as round as an owl's and his neck could revolve to the same extent if necessary. Pimi – Pim for short – was bouncy and mischievous, about sixteen years old. He was the one with the ambition to see the sun come up out of the sea. Most things made him laugh; so much so that he was dangerous if he wasn't watched. He gave the stubs of his cigarettes to Toeleu to smoke, pretending each time that his fingers had been set on fire, blowing on them and licking them like a cat.

We spent the day in a hard march through a scrubby open forest with grass lawns, more crickets, fewer cicadas and even patches of burning white sky. At nightfall we were at the Borboletas stream where the Tirió group had abandoned their dugout. We then had to tramp back again for the remainder of the supplies.

'Why you cover your body in clothes?' asked Pim, two days on, when we were waterborne. We communicated in a clumsy Tirió/ Wai-wai patois.

'My skin is weak and white. My skin hates the forest.'

Tautau had told Pim I was a kind of lesser Indian, I discovered. So Pim split his sides laughing each time I said I needed my hat to deflect the showers of tree ants, or boots to keep out the poisonous thorns.

Those thorns littered the ground like pine needles some days. Other days, when the rivers were dried up into silent puddles, and we had to hop overboard to drag the canoe, stingrays flapped through the sands between our feet. A slash from one of those, or a nip from an electric eel, would have made life not worth living. These things, and a few animals like crocodiles – the black cayman – made the Indians more cautious of the rivers than of the land. But theirs was not a real fear; when they talked of snakes they thought of food, not bites.

Pim was convinced that I had no worries in the jungle. After all, I could smell rain coming as well as them, and seemed to be as good at stalking game birds. It was time to put me to the test.

I was swimming naked with the others in a rivulet of frilly green weed. We had had a bad day's hunting and had come a full day from the canoe. Pim and Toeleu suddenly ran whooping from the river, and left me behind, waist deep. They had surged to get out as quickly as possible, then pointed at what had scared them. I looked over my shoulder and saw nothing, and said so. When I looked back, Pim was streaking into the forest with my clothes, and Toeleu was on his tail clutching my boots.

I gave chase. 'Oi! Come back!' But they were soon out of sight. I tracked them as Tautau had taught me to track pigs. I searched for bruised leaves, smelt the air for fresh leaf sap and raised dust. I looked out for flipped-up earth. Their tracks divided – which meant they knew I was trying to follow – and I gave up.

It would be a day's walk back through the forest, even with machete and clothes. I had my survival belt, and Cashoe, and nothing else. We sat on the water's edge and stared into the water. I knew it was one of Pim's little games. He wanted to see if I could survive without clothes, like any normal Indian.

What do we do now?

If I ever saw him again, I'd wring his little neck.

The light dimmed. The mosquitoes were hounding me. I avoided them by lying in the water up to my neck. Then, as the night chilled, I caked myself in mud and lit a fire. The heat baked the mud, which cocooned me in a protective layer. I tore up palm leaves, made a bed, and lay deep within it. I snuggled up with the dog to keep the cold off. At first light I filled my stomach with river water, got the dog to drink as well, bound my feet in spongy leaves and marched back through the forest to the north. Once I hit the river five miles on, all I had to do was follow its course to where we had left the canoe. The forest cut me to ribbons, but I hardly paused for breath. I couldn't wait to get my hands on those two Indians.

'You take long time,' said Pim when I stormed up to him.

'We almost leave without you,' said Toeleu.

'Why you not travel in dark like *good* Indian?' Pim asked.

I didn't know what to say. They were leaning on the lip of the canoe, side by side, and they looked bored. 'Where are my clothes?'

'Hey. You bleed all over, Benedito.' Toeleu was looking aghast at my thighs, which had been ripped raw by the forest. Some leaves were like hacksaw blades, others had edges as fine as razors.

'Where are my clothes?'

Toeleu shuffled his bottom along the canoe uneasily. 'You almost *die*.'

'I know,' I said. 'My clothes, please.'

'If you die, *I* not sorry. You not good Indian if you die, and so death no problem.'

'Thanks.'

There was a bad scene about the clothes. They had been scattered through the jungle and Pim had saved only the boots and hat, which he wanted for himself. The bootlaces would be excellent for stringing beads on, and the hat good for handling freshly caught piranha fish. (He said he had a friend who had lost a handful of fingers in their teeth while gaffing one.)

Deserting me like that had been an initiation test, as the pig killing had been to the Wai-wais. I couldn't be too angry. I had passed and I would rise in the Indians' esteem.

Our dribbling stream, the Borboletas, joined up with the Cumina, and we arrived there at the turn of another moon. It was hard for me to think in days or months now. It was about mid-June, and I was journeying not so much east, but to where the sun rose each day. I had almost forgotten why.

On the Cumina we paddled south, then forced the canoe through the trees to bypass a sequence of rapids. That brought us to the Santo Antônio, a stream which petered out into gravy-like mud numerous times, and twisted so much Pim said it made him dizzy. We took to the land again, harnessing ourselves to the canoe and tugging it to another backwater, which was the upper reaches of another unnamed tributary. There the air hung with white gnats. Our faces had already been peppered with wasp bites from the forest hike. That tributary led to a stream, and the stream to the Citaré. We began to grow tired of always heading to where the dawn sun came up. We never saw it, and Toeleu said he was going to die if we went on like this much longer. 'Too much paddle paddle not enough hunt hunt.'

Pim had a festering ant bite on his left kneecap, and I had swabs of herbal leaves over both of mine to lower the swelling from an incident when the canoe had gone 'rogue'. I announced that it was time for a holiday, and we fixed up a shelter, mixed medicines for each other and snoozed flat out in our hammocks for two days.

It was on the second night that we met the Indians. Pim and I were hunting, gliding our canoe on the river current like a crocodile, to come within reach of a paca, a beefy rodent. We often found pacas hunting like this, as they were sipping water under cover of night. We could hear their lapping in the dark, and though we could not see them when we shot, Pim never missed with an arrow. They tasted best roasted.

Just as we were drifting near, not daring to disturb the water with the paddles, I reached out to Pim in the dark and touched my finger to his ear. That was the signal for him to listen out. The noise was distant and upriver. It might have been a crocodile but was too regular, like someone smacking their lips again and again. The paca heard it and darted away. We knew the rhythm was of dipping paddles.

Pim called out, and a man's voice yelled back with the same twang. He was also a Tirió. Pim's call had been aggressive, and the answering voice sounded scared; a man with a lot to lose.

I told Pim I wasn't going to stand for trouble, and if these were a rival group of Tirió Indians he must let them go on by. The scared voice called again, and shimmered weakly on the water. I heard the muffled jibbering of a baby monkey from the canoe. As they had pets, they probably had children aboard as well.

Pim said it was all right, he knew one of the men. Then he took hold of our shotgun and changed the cartridge for a heavier gauge. I told him to put it away, but he slipped off the safety catch.

The canoe came up, as black as the water. We heard it parting waves, then it knocked against our dugout. It ploughed us back with the weight of its load, and I smelt tobacco, meat, and the monkey. Possibly five adults, I thought, and heard the light breath of children. They were hiding in the bottom of the canoe; they sounded cramped and were probably getting wet lying in shipped water. The man who had spoken reached out and placed a gourd in my hand. I smelt what he was offering, and dabbed some on my tongue. It was a cassava beer. I took a swig, then finished it.

While Pim was being presented with his drink, all I could hear was the zinging of the bats, the whining of mosquitoes and the grinding of the kissing canoes. The children were holding their breath. Pim said the drink was good stuff. A cheer went up and the other canoe sloshed in the water while the children squirmed up from out of hiding.

We had not yet seen each other and we received a first glimpse only in the glow of the fire we lit on the riverbank. They were four women, three husbands, one older bachelor and three waist-high children, two of them boys. I demanded presents from them. Pim said this was what was expected; I was to insist on the meat they were carrying and mustn't be fobbed off with silly bits of jewellery.

We managed to get the meat. Pim put the gun away, and we huddled around the fire. The older man had heavier bones, a long jaw and hair with a centre parting. The hair extended the length of his rib cage and was frizzy at the ends like wool. I thought he was a freak, but Toeleu said he wasn't a Tirió at all but a Wayana Indian. He called the Tirió loincloth a *kamisa*, which was the word the Wai-wais used, but his own was longer, almost to his knees, which were knobbly.

The Indian group weren't sure where they were going. They just wanted to get away from their village, where people with white skins had put metal sheets on top of their huts and others came to gawp at them by the plane-load. They had started out right up north, in the Tumucumaque hills, east of Tirió land, where the Wayana Indian came from. Two moons ago they said they had seen other Indians at a village called Akotipa, and coming on down the Citaré they had been watching our smoke since two sunrises ago.

Another canoe, full of their children, was two days behind them. We drank more of the cassava beer as the night wore on. It was called *kasila*, a Wayana Indian recipe, and was too well fermented, because it put us to sleep before we could get down to a proper feast.

The sun was up before the Indians the next day. When I clambered out of my hammock the forest was rattling with snores. The men, women and children were lying in untidy piles under the food store tarpaulin. The women had the first right to bathe. They wiped themselves over with roucou dye (another Wayana Indian import) and came out of the water bright red. I went for my wash, and Pim stole my clothes again. I was forced to wear a *kalimbe*, the red Wayana loincloth. We also covered ourselves in red dye, and I dipped Cashoe in a trough full of it, as the Wai-wais would have done.

Whilst most of the Indians were away all day shooting arrows at fish, Pim walked around the camp saying I was a good Indian now that I was as naked as they were. True, I was an Indian who had blue eyes, but I was still an Indian. The three children said I couldn't possibly be. But after fingering my hands to see if they were as rough as theirs and making me warble like a song bird, they said they had to agree, I *was* sort of one of them. 'Yes, he Indian,' confirmed Pim, and said he would pierce my ears, by force if necessary. It was the greatest compliment these people could offer me, but it made me sad, because they were almost desperate to change me into one of them. They wanted reassurance, because their future was a choice of joining the parish of a Godman, being a zoo specimen in a 'guvment' reserve or, if they were determined to retain their pride, living on the run like Maipuri's Wai-wais. I was sad because being called an Indian was like being called a dodo.

Pim and the Wayana Indian called Yepe, whose name he said meant 'friend', forced me to the ground and trimmed my hair at the front into a fringe. Pim said he had tried to do that himself the night before with a knife but had accidentally almost cut my throat.

'But my throat's nowhere near my hair!'

'I very drunk.'

He was still very drunk. When Toeleu announced he wanted to leave my expedition and join these people, Pim went on drinking to cheer himself up, right through the dusty afternoon heat.

That night we never cooled down. As the heat of the day passed we sat in close to the fire, passing around the fish meat and *kasila*. The fire shot sparks at us, and took so much of the air in the clearing that we were lightheaded. I wanted to widen the circle so we were further back – the flames were high and were making the leaves of the trees above crackle.

'No. You start dance.'

I knew I should not have shown weakness. 'Why me?'

The women were already applauding the idea. While I jogged a few circuits around the fire Pim stuck out his feet, so that to avoid tripping I had to swerve even closer to the flames. I collapsed back on my log and drank so much *kasila* to cool down I became as drunk as the others.

Every visible object was tinged red in the fire-glow: the moths, the tubular roots, even our eyes. Our clothes and skin were an even deeper red from the dye. The leaves curtaining us trapped the sparks and smoke as if we were in a cave. The Indians looked into the flames with vacant expressions and seemed to relish the scorching heat, as if wanting to forget the cold world outside, as if they believed it was against them.

As the men wheeled around the fireside in the first major dance, the four women stared into the flames through the gaps made by their legs. Then they slipped inside the men's circle and formed their own, on the very edge of the fire. This was a very different dance from the Wai-wai one. The women were loose-limbed and raring to go. They spun holding hands, so near the fire the sparks were zipping through their hair. The men stood still and watched in an outer circle. For the first time ever I was entreated to stand with the men to dance.

The women closed their eyes, upturned their heads and let their hair fall back down their shoulders. The men were beating a rhythm with their feet, but their eyes were glazed and fixed on the heart of the fire. The women seemed to be melting in the flames in front of my eyes. They strutted round with their backs to us, their toes brushing the embers. This was a fire dance. The women were worshipping the fire with their bodies. They stopped skipping and took a stance with their feet wide apart. They let the flames lick over their skin and wriggled their hips at the fire, wailing. We watched and chanted as they bent forward, almost straddling the fire core. I thought they must be in terrible agony; they sang in high, convulsive screams, like gulls, above the furnace roar. Through the flames I saw tears running down the women's cheeks, spilling over their breasts. I winced at their pain.

Then I knew there was no pain. We men were all now pressed in there amongst them. The women's skin seared mine at first contact, then we were intertwined. We were clinched together, our arms fastened in a tight circle. We began moving in a solid ring around the fire. A moment before I would never have dared approach a fire this close, but now the circle was tightening and shrinking. We were coming in closer still. I couldn't get away, and I didn't want to.

We were fused together, smelted by the fire, and this was complete unity: acceptance by the Carib Indians. I felt tears brimming in my eyes and saw them trickling down my chest and dropping into the fire. The teardrops, like everything else, were bright red.

Yepe came away with Pim and me as Toeleu's replacement, on the second sunrise after the dance. We were still red from the dye and left streaks of it behind in the water.

With Pim and Yepe

We were perfectly at ease. The water was quiet and wide and had a golden-corn glow in the sun. A haze of rain came in the morning, and a torrent in the afternoon, which flicked up the water and slashed the leaves in the trees, sending the monkeys clattering through the branches for cover. Afterwards, because the dust had been sponged from the air, the forest had a fresh tang, and the leaves looked varnished and were swollen and soft.

We joined the Paru river, with only the Jari river system still to confront before we reached our goal. Almost immediately there were signs that we were coming out of the interior. The first was a non-Indian's hut. Pim and Yepe saw it was square, not round, and sat bolt upright in their seats. The owner was a lone trapper. His face was cross-hatched with scars and his teeth were black.

He sat in the sunlight with a crumpled bachelor's palm shack behind. Around him was a flock of vultures. They were wrenching at carcasses lying between jaguar hides which were staked out in the sun. The sight of us – red skins, bows and arrows – terrified him into his hut, but we got on well once we were properly introduced. The skin trade was illegal, but he, like the *seringueiros*, the rubber-latex gatherers, held the forest in esteem. The Indians could understand this and shared his disrespect for the outside world.

The trapper warned us away from the nearby village of Aldeia Bona, where, he said, the Brazilian government were busy 'integrating' Indians.

We descended the Paru, leap-frogging from hut to hut, and stopping for chats with empty-headed Indians in rags. They stood by their huts with *cachaça* bottles, taking slugs of it while gutting fish. The commonest fish they called *pashina*, which had large shiny scales like shillings. When the smell of blood drew the piranhas in close, and they were snapping at the gutted entrails, we bathed amongst them as if they were not there, and laughed at the faces of the Brazilians who'd been taught to fear them. Yepe said piranhas were dangerous, like *haimarha*, only when trapped in small pools during the dry season, and even then they had to be more than peckish before they started to shred you to pieces.

The Brazilians were a curiosity at first: real white men. We gaped at them as much as they gaped at us. But they were scared out of their wits, whereas we were just curious. We met them more and more frequently downriver. We had a growing excitement, a trembling in the pit of our stomachs, as the outside world came within reach. We were paddling towards our future. The Indians didn't know what to expect of it. They just marvelled at each Coke bottle and twist of sweet wrapper that floated by as we canoed on. My excitement was the achievement of my goal, the end of my journey. The completion was all the more sweet because Peña's advice had been to keep looking ahead. He said if I did that I would find my gold waiting for me as he had done at the end of his trek. Now his metaphor made me laugh, because the Brazilians we saw along the riverside in their slum shacks were goldminers.

Yepe and Pim were not able to resist a closer look. We never saw the gold, only the men and their piled-up bottles – all empties. Yepe and Pim developed the habit of sifting through the junk heaps and pilfering what they could. After three or four calls –

Porto Jarocomano, Tiui, Nauari – went by, both Indians had hacked off their hair with some scissors (bartered for an arrow), given away their bangles, necklaces and armbands, and dressed up in T-shirts and shorts. 'Is wonderful,' said Pim, dancing with glee, having just swopped his earrings for a deck of playing cards.

Pim and Yepe were never as pleased as the goldminers with the deals. 'Ask that boy if he wants to flog those bows and arrows – or, come to that, any other nice little trinkets he's got. These earrings are going to fetch a packet in Santarém market. Some gringo is bound to snap them up. Pretty, eh?'

Another *garimpeiro* with pockmarked cheeks said I should let my Indians know that there would be good money for them if they went back into the interior and fetched back some healthy Indian women. 'Higher prices for virgins, of course.'

I said I wouldn't and he spat in my face.

Alcohol flowed at every port of call. The goldminers paid the Indians to throw off their clothes and dance naked holding hands together on the tables. They jigged to the miners' whistles and handclaps and kept on until they keeled over. This happened at least twice, but they resented my icy glares.

'Why you not dance with us last night, Benedito?' asked Pim, as we paddled on further downriver.

'You once danced good,' said Yepe. 'Now you not even singing praise when we dance.'

'Can you not see that they're laughing at you?'

'*No one* laugh at Pim and Yepe,' said Pim. He stood up in the canoe, and put his knuckles on his hips.

'They laugh when you're not looking,' I said. 'They think you're like children.'

What I said hurt them. They hated any suggestion that they were not adult. For a while they held back on the *cachaça*, and paddled with extra fervour to show they were men.

We abandoned the canoe. Pim, Cashoe, Yepe and I walked east through the forest to the river Jari.

We passed through a mining camp, Santa Cruz, which had its own airstrip and a plane which had failed to clear the trees. Some pieces were still up there. Neither of the Indians had seen aeroplanes, except as silvery specks in the sky, and they asked me to patch the remains of the wreckage together so that they could have a go.

Goldmining

Drink had been banned from the camp after two fights which had been more passionate than usual. I was shown the guns behind the bar counter and where the bodies fell. The sky still shone through bullet holes in the roof.

'There's real gold fever here, is there?' I asked a miner.

He was a stocky, city-bred man with a molten nugget on a gold chain round his neck. He hated every leaf in the jungle and was here only because it was a family business.

'You wait till you see what they're up to where you're heading.' He told me that most of the fighting had been stamped out nowadays because the forest had been divided up by powerful families, and anyone who came scratching in the soil on those plots was in big trouble.

'Big trouble?'

'Big trouble.'

At the river Jari, they told me what kind of big trouble. The Mafia family who owned the patch at Santa Cruz had machine-gunned down a dozen goldminers, they said, but they had had three warnings to move on.

'Well, I suppose they should have known better, then,' I said to one of the men.

'Not really. This was on no-man's-land. Anyone had a right to it.'

I smiled and said it was probably just one of those colourful stories that gets around.

'This one's true.'

'Ah . . . but where's your proof?'

'I was the only survivor.' This man said the stocky man with the gold nugget I'd spoken to earlier was the head of that family, and there was a fat thug with pebble-lens glasses and a neck like bacon rind who hung around with him and was his arch hitman.

On the river Jari, near the mouth of the Ipitinga tributary, where we bought a new dugout, the miners were all yellow with malaria. 'No one escapes here without a taste of it,' they said, and gave me a list of unfavourable statistics. They also said the malaria parasite had grown accustomed to their medicines, and they drank Dr Bittencourt's Licor Amazonia all day. One man was green, not yellow. He was also skeleton-like, and counting the days to his end. He said the malaria had developed a taste for Dr Bittencourt's medicine and thrived on it.

The sight of the decaying men changed Pim and Yepe. They became sullen. They had been led to believe that white men were strong; invincible almost. They stepped out of their aeroplanes, the Indian stories went, with their arms stacked with medicines. And here the men groaned all day from their hammocks, and then died.

Was this the future I had brought them to? they asked. Was this it? A white man's graveyard?

'Why you bring us here?' Pim asked me. Tears gushed down his face.

'Let us return to happy miners,' said Yepe. 'Where we plenty dance and drink.'

'Is that how you want to die?' I said. 'You go there and you live like pets of goldminers. Like Cashoe. He's our friend but he's also our pet. Is that how you want to be? A pet?'

Pim's eyes blackened, and he got so worked up Yepe had to hold him back from me.

'Do you really want to hit me? Your friend?'

He pouted, knocked Yepe to the ground, and chucked one of our brand-new paddles into the fire.

That same day they both said they were sorry, and would come with me to where the sun came out of the never-ending lake, if that was what would please me. I wasn't sure if it *would* please me any more, bringing them even closer to the edge of the forest, but whatever was just around the corner it had to be no worse than anything here.

We inched to the end of the jungle, continuing south on the Jari. For the first time a few of the men gaping at us from the trees as they leant on their spades wore revolvers at their hips. Their guns sparked off the memory of what the goldminer had said: *You wait to see what they're up to where you're heading.* I remembered that I had made a promise to the Sicilian cobbler far away in El Callao. I was sad because I'd broken my word. I'd sworn never to set foot where there was gold fever.

I was the only one of our party to notice the guns. The Indians' eyes were glazed over and dopey. I kept what I feared to myself, and chewed it over in the back of my mind.

Part Three

The Test

– 15 –

Seduction

The Indians were looking for a future, for their destiny. Finding a decent one was the hope that kept them with me. They looked into the huts for it, squinting through the dark at fat men totting up their nuggets of gold. They looked for it in the weedy men who were thigh-deep in water, digging about for the fat men's fortunes.

'Here?' asked Pim, pointing with his paddle at a toothless man who was panning the silts. The waves he made caused the bow of our canoe to bob up and down. The man's hair had gone and the only red in his face was in his bloodshot eyes.

I said, 'No. This not your destiny.' It was true. Their destiny was even worse, and we all knew it.

Sometimes they even stared their destiny in the face. Then I would have to lie. Their future was with the Indians who stomped around the forest in dank misfit clothes, smelling of *cachaça*. They did all the backbreaking digging for the *garimpeiros*. Once they had been called Oyampi Indians; now they were nicknamed *burros*, asses. Pim and Yepe, so clean in the interior, had abandoned washing. When they stood next to the *burros*, I could not tell them apart.

'This our dess-tinny, Benedito?'

'No. Your destiny coming soon.' But they knew it was here. They were fascinated by what they saw of these Indians, because it was like looking into a mirror. The *burros*, fluffy-brained lacklustre people, were now kindred spirits.

A cloud of noxious-smelling sweat always hung over these people when they clustered together. Mixed up with that was a reek I had come across before. The smell sent me back to the haunted-faced Indians of Tucupita in the Orinoco delta, the puny ones who stewed in the riverside muck. Here in the forest camps

was the same putrid smell of decaying fish washed up on the beach
by the tide. Now I knew it wasn't the fish but the Indians I had
been smelling.

The expedition had come full circle. It was back to the squalor.
This thought took away any feeling of achievement which lingered
on. Pim, Yepe, Cashoe and I moped together.

I forced Pim and Yepe on down the river in the canoe. They didn't
know why they were coming, or where they were going to. They
paddled hopelessly as if stirring soup, slowing to gawp when we
passed more of the sickly Indians. I hoped Pim and Yepe were
mourning the life that they'd left behind in the interior.

'Pim,' I said. 'Let's leave these people. Just look at them! Look
at the rubbish heaps! Let's get away from all the junky smells!'

'What smells?'

'When did you last go hunting, Pim?'

'Half moon back,' he said.

'And you, Yepe?'

'You remember, Benedito. Half moon back also.'

'Come on, then. Let's go.'

We tied up the canoe, and I led them off into the forest. At first
they walked muttering far behind me and dragged their feet in
their pinching fake-leather shoes. Further on, brushing through
the leaves, they pricked up their ears and stalked with me, as we
had done together in the old days. The Indians had sold off all our
weapons to the goldminers, but the spirit of the hunt was there.

We moved in and out of the spreads of palms, part of the forest
again. While Pim was chasing butterflies, trying to clasp his hands
around them, Yepe was talking about the jungle spirits, how he
could hardly feel any here at all, and how it was much better in the
forest we had come from. Could I hear any jaguars coughing? No.
And what about the crocodiles? Not a single one to be seen here.

'Yepe, I want you take my canoe and leave me. Go up river
again. Travel away for two moons, until you find somewhere you
can live quietly with the forest.'

'Where spirits live?'

'Where spirits live, yes.'

'You not want Yepe any more?'

'I can manage. I can find someone to help. But gold men are bad
people. They give you a bad future. Yepe must go a long way away,

and take Pim with you. Go when this sun falls low. Will you do that?'

'You good friend. I do this for you. I go long way away.'

'With Pim?'

'I take Pim. We find forest with spirits.'

We took a different route back to the river, and bumped into a settlement of miners on the way. I saw the signs of it long before: *cachaça* bottles bobbing in the streams, cigarette packets bedded in fallen leaves.

'Let's go another way,' I said, veering to the left, but Pim had dashed forward, and was already mingling with a bunch of silent Indians. The stench of the village, two palm huts with tumble-down roofs, made me queasy.

Hens were pecking insects from an Indian's scaly feet. Some of these Indians' feet were like those of lizards. The earth around the huts was red, and it was splattered over everything: the soggy walls, the man who was slumped against a log digging at his footsores with a machete tip, the bony Indians bunched around Pim, and the dogs. The dogs came at us with their mouths open, their teeth out and their gums showing. Yepe kicked one clear without glancing down – he was ogling a *cachaça* bottle tipped over in the dirt. A dog darted for my ankle with its head low, and I had to swipe at it with my toecap. The dog flew; the others stopped snapping and went back to licking at another dog's protruding entrails.

'Let's move on back to the canoe,' I said to Yepe, and tugged Pim's arm.

He might have come away, but then Yepe said, 'Look. They got women with skin as white as yours, Benedito.'

The thought hadn't crossed my mind. Neither of my Indians had seen a white woman before. I looked, but the only woman here was Indian, with an armful of babies – one not getting enough air and going scarlet, and another puking over her fat arm. Yepe meant the nude on a poster stapled to an acacia tree. Pim said he wanted to keep her. He pulled her away and she ripped in two. The pin-up was soaking wet from the rain and like blotting paper.

The other woman, the real one, crackled at Pim, then limped away into the trees. 'What a dump,' I said to Yepe, but he was too occupied trying to patch up the poster.

Pim toured the camp, running his fingers over everything he admired, which was most of the objects here. I called him back. He ran to me and grabbed my hand. 'Come look what I find!' He pulled me over to a square, tin-roofed shack. 'Pretty!' He ran his hands over the corrugations, then jerked me inside.

Our entry disturbed the flies. They pounced on us from the walls. I had to close my mouth to keep them out.

'Look what I find.'

There was a bench with green slime creeping up its sides, and on top of the bench was the thing that Pim wanted me to play with. It was made of fine metal. He flicked it with his fingernail. *Ding!* the object sang.

'Better leave this alone, Pim. This is what the gold men use for measuring gold.' He was smiling at the scales tipping up and down. 'This belongs to a goldminer man. He's not going to be pleased to find us here. Remember: only Indians share all they have.' But it was too late to escape. A big man was blocking the doorway. Outside, everything had gone silent.

'And what have we got here?'

The voice came from a frog-faced man with a pale white skin, and greased-back black hair. He walked us out of the hut. He was smiling but I didn't like his eyes. They were green and so expressionless they were like balls of jelly. His leather boots squeaked. The Indians in the village kept at arm's length from him and backed off when he looked their way.

'I've already met your chum here.' He pointed a finger at Yepe, who crept up and hid behind me.

'What this man say?'

'I find you have to treat them like children, don't you?' the man went on. 'I mean, that Indian skulking behind you, the tall one with the creepy face. He took me on a guided tour of my camp while you were snooping about in my hut. He took me up to the timbers and began rapping them, and jabbering away in some funny language.'

'He doesn't understand why you use softwood timbers for your huts. He was saying they are about to take a tumble.'

'Was he, now? How interesting. Well, can you get it into his thick skull that I came here to make my fortune, not to build a village.'

The man fattened his frog face by pulling his chin in.

'And if he lays a finger on anything else here, I'll thump him even harder.'

I was thinking: Yepe let you *hit* him? If the miner had struck him a month ago he would have been laid out at Pim's feet by now. The miner rolled his marbly eyes and said: 'It's the only way they learn.'

'What this man saying?' said Yepe. 'He good man? I not like his face.'

Pim wasn't listening. He was slinking back to the hut to play with the scales. The miner went up behind him, and grabbed him by the scruff of the neck. 'Oh no you don't!' he shouted, and beat him over both ears.

Yepe, his best friend, didn't even blink.

'Does that answer your question?' I said to Yepe.

'Which brings me back to what I asked originally,' the miner said.

'Does it?'

'Who are you?'

I told him my name, the names of the others, and that we were just passing through to the mouth of the Amazon. I said the Indians were my friends, and I objected to him messing them about.

The miner said his name was Mendez. 'You know where you are going on to from here?'

'Continuing south, then, up the Iratapuru tributary, then walking east through the forest to the road to Macapá, on the Amazon mouth.'

'I know the track through that forest. I could be your guide for a small consideration.'

'Is the river easy?'

'Easy? No.' Mendez went on to list a dozen rapids, all of which tallied with those I'd heard about. I was astounded: he really *did* know the river.

'And what is the "small consideration"?'

'That you get your two Indians to stay on and work for me. I'm on the lookout for fresh labour. These days you just can't get good workers.'

'No. Not possible. They're leaving today for the interior. Besides, you don't even know them. How do you know they are any good?'

'As long as they've got plenty of muscle, that's all that counts. Tell them to strip. Then we'll have a really good look.'

'You're talking about them as if they are cattle.'

That made him laugh. 'See those children over there?' His eyes were on two Indian boys dressed in canvas sacking. They had Cashoe in their arms, and were parading about, showing him off to other children who all reached out to hold part of him. 'Well, those children are what we call flies. They do the simple work. If your Indians aren't up to much they will work with them. It's quite simple.'

'If you did that they'd die. Being adult is their great pride.'

'Your Indians still have *pride*?'

'Yes. Which means they don't like it here.'

'Are you sure? Ask them for me.'

'I'm sure.'

Yepe sprinted over to us. 'This man got plenty things. Here is wonderful. You seen one these before?' It was a can-opener. 'What it do?'

'Nothing much. Just rips open those.' I kicked at a jagged can.

Yepe picked it up and banged them together. 'Pretty sound.'

'Here, let me show you.' Mendez took the can and opener, and Yepe watched as he peeled back the bottom side of the can. 'Tell him he can keep it.'

'I'm sure he doesn't want it that much.'

'Here.' He put it in Yepe's hands. 'It's all yours. And what strong hands you've got. You're quite a savage, aren't you?'

'It's all the swinging in the trees,' I said.

'Why don't you keep out of this?'

'Ever seen real gold, Yetty?' He tickled Yepe under the chin. 'Seen how it burns like a fire in your hand? *Gorge-ee-ous!*'

Pim trotted up with his hands around the neck of a *cachaça* bottle. He tossed it to Yepe, who took an over-ambitious swig, and coughed and spluttered it out all over the ground.

'That drink doesn't belong to you,' I said. 'Put it back where you found it.' I apologized to the miner. 'In their society they share everything. Possessions don't mean so much.'

'Don't preach to me about Indians. There's nothing new I need to know about them. But go ahead, boy,' he said to Pim. 'Let's see if you can finish it off between you.'

'Leave it alone, Pim.' I told the miner that half a bottle each might easily kill them.

'Doubt it. Ever heard of an Indian who can't take his drink?' He helped the bottle to Pim's lips. 'That's right, tip it right back. Now your turn, Yetty.'

'Yepe,' I said. 'His name's Yepe.'

'You know what? You're beginning to get on my nerves.'

'Perhaps we'd best be off, then.'

'You American?'

'English.'

'Well, gringo, I suggest you stay out of my way.' Mendez clenched his hands around the buckle of his gun belt. 'And keep your mouth shut when I get out the gold.'

When the Indians were wheeling and spewing because of the *cachaça*, they were led off to the tin hut for a display of gold dust. I sauntered after them, but the miner barred my entrance through his doorway.

'Sorry, this is private business.'

Pim shrugged his shoulders in sympathy, then went in. Sitting on the steaming red mud, I could hear Yepe's sighs, and yelps of excitement from Pim. I was sad and angry, because I knew I had lost them.

'Sounds like they know a fair bit about gold already,' said Mendez, strolling out.

'Oh? And what are they thinking now?'

'They are thinking how rich they're going to be.'

'And *are* they going to be rich?'

'Who knows? Have you ever seen a rich Indian?'

'Only in the forest.'

'Ha! We've got ourselves a romantic.' He slumped down beside me in the mud. 'It seems that you've been paying your Indians in gold.'

'So what?'

'They're not as stupid as you think. Unless you haven't noticed, this is goldmining country. Gold is as cheap as tobacco. In short, your payment's worthless.'

'Well, they aren't going on with me any more.'

'You're wrong there. You're going to need them as guides. There's no one else who can help you lug your equipment through the forest. And they say they're angry with you.'

'That's not true!'

'They say you've been paying them a pittance. They say here they could get in one day what you've been paying each month.'

'Ah. So that's what you've been telling them.'

'It's the truth.'

'It was their idea to come with me in the first place. The gold was nothing to them. They are friends.'

'Are they? I think you'd better be careful, gringo!' Mendez got to his feet and kicked mud from his boots. 'Italian. Best leather money can buy.'

Whether Mendez had spoken any truth or not (how had he been able to communicate with the Indians?), I could not tell. They came away still rolling drunk, hiccuping and idiotic. I pulled them back to the canoe behind Cashoe, taking both their hands. They were very confused. It took a few hundred paces before I could shake off Mendez, but he was scared of the dark: the rustlings of mice and the snakes of the night, tree roots to trip over.

We slept in the canoe, the hull nuzzling the water reeds through the night.

It was the *creak, creak* of the leather boots which woke me. Mendez came up to the canoe and peered over from the riverbank. 'Feeling better this morning, are we?'

'What are you doing here, Mendez?'

'Haven't your Indian friends told you? I'm joining your expedition. We start off together, I show you where the track through the forest is. That gets you to the mouth of the Amazon eventually, and the Indians come back and go off digging with a friend of mine called Edwardio, on the Irataparu. We should make a good team. *Bom dia*, Pim! *Bom dia*, Yetty!'

'*Bommy geear*,' said Pim, bleary eyed. He kicked Yepe, who uncurled in his blanket, wet with the dew. He also tried to say 'good morning' in Portuguese.

'Don't look so surprised, gringo. I taught them a few words last night. They're not too stupid as primitives go. Are you, Yetty?'

'This man good,' Yepe said. 'Tell him I think he good.'

'Yepe, I thought you were going to leave here. You *promised* you would. What happened?'

'We find this man. He good. And Benedito . . . we going to be *rich*! We buy plenty these.' He whirled the can-opener in my face.

'But you are coming with me to the end of my journey?'

'Yes. You a friend. We help you. The gold man he say you cheat with gold money, but we know you a friend. Is a mistake.'

'Congratulations, Mendez. You seem to have won them round.'

'Move over, gringo, I'm coming aboard.'

'*Now?* What about your Indians back there?'

'Let them stew. They do nothing but drink. You can get only a couple of years' productivity out of these people as a rule, and I want to move on and start afresh.'

'What about the children?'

'The flies? As I said, let them stew here.'

All the way down the Jari, Mendez kept flashing his gold at Yepe and Pim, nurturing their desire for it. Over the man's gun belt flopped two thick loops of fat. His weight slowed us down. He had a fear of noisy water and he couldn't handle a paddle.

Just as we were reaching the first major outpost of Westernization, the Jari Project – systematic cropping of the forest for a pulp-mill floated here from Japan – we turned away into the interior again, up the Iratapuru. Before we were away we heard the buzz of chainsaws and the heavy crash of a falling tree. Then we saw a logging crew who wore T-shirts with the slogan '*Plante amor*' ('Plant love').

The river mouth was a bottleneck of rapids. There were more Indians who were yellow with malaria, and rubber trees with notches where they were bleeding latex. There was a man whose ears and nose had been chewed away by a parasite. He made us understand that he had Leishmaniasis and would waste to death within a couple of months; could we suggest anything? 'Yes. Say your prayers,' said Mendez, and we shipped several gourdfuls of water as he rolled about laughing.

Well into the interior again, a week upstream of other human habitation, and Mendez had Pim and Yepe eating out of his hand.

'We going be rich, Benedito,' said Yepe, as we glided up to Edwardio's shack. Edwardio, Mendez's friend, would be the fourth miner in the partnership.

'Yes, we going be rich!' screamed Pim. He bounced up and down with Yepe and the canoe almost scuttled.

Edwardio wasn't in. We knew this because his canoe wasn't moored up. We pushed through the forest and came to a primitive hut: no smell of cooking, only a pigsty reek of urine from the clearing at the back. Edwardio came later with a repeater rifle, after Mendez had discovered a store of tinned sardines concealed in the roof. He had woken a colony of vampires getting them down.

Edwardio was lean, and had black eyes – darker than the Indians' – a gaunt face, a high smooth forehead and dry skin. And – it couldn't be true! – he looked as much like a lizard as Mendez did a toad. His eyes were cold and hooded. He blinked slowly and often. He said he wanted some cash for the sardines, but was very happy that Mendez had at last got hold of two strong Indians to work for them. But what was the other stranger doing here? He said he didn't like strangers this far up the Iratapuru one little bit. This was his stretch of mining country.

'I've already warned him not to come,' said Mendez.

'You did nothing of the kind.' I turned to Edwardio. 'He said he would show me the track through to the end of the forest, going east, across the river. These are my guides. Mendez wants them to stay on and work for you, after my expedition's over.'

'That true?'

Mendez grunted. He said he supposed it was vaguely true, but it would be better for everyone if I ended my expedition here and now. It was ruining everyone's plans.

'Why not start tomorrow?' he said to Edwardio. 'I don't see the problem. Forget about this Benedito person. He can paddle back down the river again by himself.'

'He'd never make it.'

'That's not our problem, now, is it?'

'Yepe, I must talk to you,' I said.

'Benedito, what Edwardio say?' Yepe asked. 'He good man too?'

'No. These men bad.'

'Can I have shoot with Edwardio's gun, Benedito?' said Pim.

'Mendez,' said Edwardio. 'Tell these dumb Indians to talk Portuguese. I can't understand a word they say.'

I was never again able to get a word through to Pim or Yepe.

The night fell. It was an inky black one, and we sat in the living quarters of the hut under the soft light of the oil lamp. *Cachaça* was brought out, not a bottle but a crate.

From the goldminers' point of view, the *cachaça* worked a treat on the Indians. They had bottles to their lips for so much of the early part of the evening that I couldn't get a word in edgeways. Later, the Indians' heads crashed down on to the table, drooling rum from their mouths. They smiled at me cross-eyed when I shook them. Yepe tried to say that he was sorry, but his lips were like rubber and no words came out.

'You'd better go to bed, Benedito. You've got a lot of canoeing to do over the next few days. You should reach a settlement in a week or two if you're lucky.'

I hated Mendez – his frog face, squeaky Italian leather boots, bloated throat and stomach. But I hated him more because of what he was doing to these Indians than because of what he was doing to me.

'And one more thing. You can leave that dog. I've taken a fancy to it.'

I woke abruptly in the darkness with the feeling that something was wrong; the sensation was strong enough to make me lift my head from the cotton of the hammock to listen to the night. It was not that I knew what had disturbed me, it was just that the jungle had taught me to use my senses to the full, and I trusted them. Now they had woken me out of my sleep. I would have got up to investigate even if at that moment I had not remembered the miners.

The night was black. The air was heavy. I knew there was going to be a downpour soon. It hadn't rained for three days. The palm walls to the hut were so swollen and soft with water soaked up from the air that they no longer crackled in the breeze.

I lifted up the mosquito net, reached down for my boots, flicked them in the air to empty out scorpions, and slipped them on. I heard the two Indians breathing. I knew, though I had seen nothing yet, that the room was too empty and the miners were still up.

Still in only my loose shirt and trousers, I tiptoed through the dark to the doorway. Then I was outside standing in the dusty clearing with the scratching insects. They were quieter this night. Most were waiting for the rains. Then the frogs would come for them, the snakes would wake up to dine out on the frogs, and larger snakes rouse themselves to swallow the smaller ones.

Here I was dwarfed by the trees. To see the stars I had to lift my head right back. But what I had thought were stars were in fact fireflies, skipping against the black sky. The moon was a pale streaky smear behind the cloud, and the air smelt of the dust crumbs and leaves breaking open under my feet. I listened again and took in the bats whistling in mobs around my head. They swirled in the space of the clearing, round and round in waves; several squeaking baby bats were caught up in the rafters of the hut.

The track led away through the forest to the water. I headed along it to check if my stores had been disturbed in the canoe, down by the riverside. Dry leaves slapped my face along the path. The night was all blackness. Six months ago this jungle would have terrified me – the dry spindly legs of knuckle-sized ants running through my hair, the spider's threads snapping across my outstretched hands, the snuffling of rats in the leaf mould. Now none of this worried me. I was able to walk along a path I couldn't even see.

Then the branches weren't tugging at my clothes any more. The leaves shrank away and I knew I was at the river's edge. There was a smell of oozing mud and algae. The water was silent, but crabs were scuttling the length of the riverbank and there was the clicking of their legs on the tree roots. A large one ran across my foot.

The canoe was undisturbed. I knew because Cashoe lay across the canvas sheeting. He was guarding the stores in the canoe, as he had been taught. The bean sacks, coffee bags, rope coils, sugar, everything lay underneath. Hearing my approach he wagged his tail and it thumped on the canoe side. He knew my stride. I said a few comforting words to him and started back. The forest looked darker than ever before. I glanced at it as I was getting myself free from the river mud which was sucking my boots down. Then I stopped. I thought I had heard a voice from the hut.

The track seemed longer on the return journey. I had a natural craving to know more about what I had heard, but now the only sounds were the flapping leaves and snapping branches. I began to trot, let my hands drop from in front of my eyes, and hardly flustered when a spiderweb netted my face.

In the clearing I heard the voices again. They were speaking in Portuguese: the goldminers. They must have been in the living quarters of the hut, dragging on cigarettes. I saw the orange tips flare up, the light filter through chinks in the walls.

Up against the palm with my nose in against a crack, I smelt the rich smoke. And there, stamping my feet like a horse to clear the mosquitoes, I heard the goldminers say that they were going to cut my throat. All I could do was stand there in my shirt and boots and listen. Was the Englishman armed? Yes, but no problem. He only kept a dagger in his boot. Did the Englishman's Indian friends mind? No, they couldn't care less. And let's face it, who did anyway?

The words rattled about in my brain. Then I ran, hell for leather.

I ran first into the centre of the clearing. There I stopped, had second thoughts, wheeled around and dashed back for my hammock and mosquito net. I went right past Yepe and Pim. They were snoring like bellows. *Didn't* they care?

Then I was away, and into the black forest. At the river I heard a soft, sighing noise in the trees and knew it was approaching rain. The river water was warm against my legs, and the mud soothing on the mosquito bites. I coiled the mooring-rope and heaved the canoe clear of the bank. Then I leapt aboard, colliding with Cashoe. We spun around, while I fumbled for the paddle. No one would think of going upstream to find me, I thought, and it felt good fighting against the current, so that was the direction I took.

I looked over my shoulder and saw, fading into the distance, a pale crocodile. It was Edwardio's canoe. I watched until it was lost in the darkness.

I was alone.

Rocks and branches were snared in the water, but I steered clear of them by listening to the ripples in the water flow ahead. It was a trick Yepe had taught me. The rain came, tearing at the leaves, and dancing on the water. The frogs splashed and frolicked along the riverbank, popping and grunting. The river was swelling. Making headway was hard. I began to long for the chatter of the Indians. The canoe was so empty without them. My paddle made the only sound; a lonely *slop, slop, slop* in the water.

The sky cleared; the breeze stung my wet face. A silver crescent moon shone on the water and turned it the colour of milk. Then the river narrowed. The trees were shipping across the canoe, and I tasted blood on my lips.

Three days later I was still on the run. I lived on fish baited with palm berries, and nuts scavenged from the floor or thrown down by monkeys. At dusk I assembled a camp – just a hammock, mosquito net and canvas-sheeting roof. I tucked it in the trees a few dozen paces from the riverside. Each morning I woke in the cool mist when it was so quiet you could hear the dew dripping, and wondered if this was a dream. But the clammy earth smell was real enough and so were the canopies of leaves, matted yellow orchids and moss-smothered branches. The red leaves of creepers were heaped like fishing nets over everything else.

Dog-tired, I was looking for the track from the river to the east, the one Mendez had told me led out of the forest. 'Who knows?' I said aloud. 'If we find it we might yet reach the mouth of the Amazon!' This thought kept my spirits up. It was my hope; and as long as I knew I had some, that was just fine. With my stores I could make the jungle a comfortable enough home for a week or so. I kept a vision of the Amazon mouth – a sunset view of water-like, ripple-less golden glass – in the forefront of my mind. This image helped me to forget everything else that might go wrong. *No one escapes without a taste of malaria*, a goldminer had said.

– 16 –

The eternal prison?

The third day on my own, the water ruffled and whitened. The weed didn't spiral up from the depths any more, it streamed from the lee of rocks, trailing in the current. My hands became red, flayed from hauling the canoe by rope. I missed Pim and Yepe more than ever.

'You can start bailing out the water if you want to feel useful, Cashoe!'

The dog was my companion and long-standing friend. He had been through thick and thin with me since the Wai-wais, about 600 miles over to the west. Others – Wai-wais, Tiriós, Wayanas, goldminers – had come and gone, but he had stayed. He was a symbol of stability and, just now, someone I could talk to.

'It looks to me as if I'm going to have to catch a monkey and train it to do the bailing, Cashoe. You're useless!' He would cock his head and wag his tail, although he could not understand a word. He was not a dog in my mind, but a member of the expedition team – the one that guarded the stores at night. He had been painted red with the rest of us at the Indians' party. Tautau had said of him, 'He good friend.'

So what he did now seemed like a betrayal.

Just out of the jaws of the rapids, beyond the spray but before we were safe, I jumped into the canoe and took up the paddle again. Cashoe knew how unstable the canoe was. Maybe he was thinking soon we would be off hunting and was over-excited. Nevertheless, he should have known better. He bit into a rice sack, and began to tussle with it.

'Not now, Cashoe! Lie *down*!' It was already too late. The rice sack spilled, two other sacks tipped over, and everything else happened so quickly the whole incident must have been over in a few seconds.

As the rice sacks shifted, giving the canoe a left-hand list, I stuck my paddle out to the right to balance it. Even then I had a feeling of inevitable disaster, like in a nightmare when you are trying to escape from a tidal wave across endless sticky mud. After the canoe's lurch, there was the slipping back into the teeth of the rapids, the tug of the white water behind, the canoe shipping water, taking it on board in gulps, drinking it down.

There was the sight of the receding calmness of dark russet water ahead; my panicky wild strokes with a paddle; gravel whisking up from the river bed and clattering on the canoe underside. All the time I knew what lay behind, cataract after cataract, because I had spent the whole morning towing the canoe up through them. Back and back we jogged, Cashoe yelping. The twisting white foam streaked past under my nose as I dug and dug the water; the dull throbbing ache in my shoulders; the bucking worse and worse; the despair; and at last – a relief now – the canoe splintering against a tree trunk.

The dugout crumpled as easily as a matchbox, and the baby screams of Cashoe suddenly stopped.

Later, I caught my breath on the riverbank. My hands were coated in a green jelly which was algal slime from the river boulders. I had bashed my head on a rock as I was being flushed downstream, and one of my fingernails had been split as I clawed at the shingle for a hold. The cut was painting circles of blood on my knees. I had just seen Cashoe choke to death in the surf. I was stuck in the jungle and I had lost almost everything.

I wanted to close my eyes and shrivel up in the bleaching sun.

The air was grey, dusty and hot. It buzzed gently on my face. A parrot fluttered down to the far bank and dabbled in the fingery black tree roots. The bird was a type I had rarely seen. Its head was black, its wings chalky green and yellow, and its beak like a black can-opener. Another bigger version hurtled down from a cloud of leaves and bickered with it until the smaller bird ducked its head, shrieked and flew off.

No help was going to come my way, so that was straightforward enough. I had to help myself. But how should I start?

Thinking of the Indians left a bad taste in my mouth. Pim and Yepe had betrayed me, the Wai-wai dog had let me down, and Tautau had commended both Pim and Cashoe to me. My thoughts

went all the way back to 'Jungle Eddie' McGee, and the advice he
had dished out in London at the Royal Geographical Society. Just
like that, I forgot everything the jungle had taught me, and went
back to first principles.

I did what Eddie McGee would have instructed. I trampled out a
clearing in the reeds and laid out everything I had salvaged. Then I
began to take stock.

Survival belt kit:

1 large compass
1 spare compass
Waterproof (lifeboat) matches, 1 pack
Fishing hooks, all sizes (approx. 50)
Fishing line, 10 metres each of heavy,
    medium and light (breaking strain)
Explosive flares (defensive firearms), 3
Pens (2) and paper
Water sterilizing tablets (for 100 litres)
Razor blades, 1 packet
Dried soup, 4 packets
Glucose tablets, 12 packets
A whistle
Aspirins, 20
Anti-malaria tablets, for four weeks
(All other antibiotics, etc., too sodden to use)
One polythene bag containing the above, as water container
Money belt, with passport, airticket and dollars

With the clothes I was standing in was a leg-knife with a
sharpening blade, my machete and my hat (found snagged in some
waterside weed). I had also rescued a cooking pan, water bottle,
empty rucksack, a small strip of orange polythene, and my pipe
and tobacco. Here too, mocking me, was Pablo's jaguar tail, the
armadillo tail and the monkey's paw. It all seemed so unjust. Why
had these survived? Where were my medicine, hammock,
mosquito net, shelter and food? Even Jorge's dagger had slipped
out of my boot. Instead I had three macaw feathers which had
come all the way from Fritz, and two picture postcards of London.
There was nothing else of use, but a notebook, in which I sketched
a map. I drew it to the same scale as the one I had memorized,

This book
Postcards — He Majesty!
Trafalgar Sq.!
Piccadilly!
"Greetings from London!"

* Survival Kit
* Strips Polythene (with holes)
* Rucksac
* ~~Hammock~~ NOT HERE!
* Machete (+ holder)
* Knife + Sharpener (+ sheaf)

Trousers
Shirt
Pants
Watch
* Boots
2 pairs socks (thick)
Tobacco — USE AS REPELLANT

● Pipe
* Matches (1 pocket)
* Hat
* Money Belt
* 1 Pen
* Wine bottle
* Mess Tins
$70 Notes

worn at moment
20 Aspirins
Have various pieces of bark
Skulls for fever
+ 2 waterproof packets found

poly bag FOOD
£100 Cruzeros
Air tube
Passport
$ Traveler Cheque

● USELESS
* Thank God

Hooks assorted
Line assorted
Malaria tablets
Compass 20 Aspirins
Blade
Poly bag (small)
Toilet Paper & Biro
4 Packets soup
12 bars Cheese
Post-card
Matches
Stereo tablets

NO HAMMOCK
MOSQUITO NET
WATERPROOF SHEET
MEDICINE
FOOD
TORCH
CHANGE OF CLOTHES
WARMTH (NIGHT)
REPELLANT

$10 Note
2 gram gold
Fishing Line
Razor Blades
2 Large Hooks

Chuck Out!

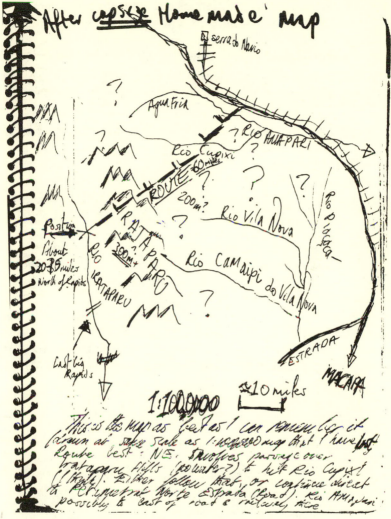

1:100,000, and filled up all the blank spaces – jungle either un-
charted or not remembered – with question marks.

According to my calculations, the edge of the forest was at worst
seventy to eighty miles, as the crow flies, to the north-east. *As the
vulture flies, you mean*, Pinkerton-Smithe had said.

I wrote a few words down:

That damn dog. What the hell made me feel compassionate towards it? I
should have left it to die like the Indians were going to. Now it might be
the death of me.

Then I wrote out some instructions and made myself swear never to contradict them. I wondered how you could tell when your brain began to soften in the heat; whether you knew when it was time to stop trusting your own judgement.

Route best: NE. Involves passage over Irat, paru hills (no water) to hit Rio Cupixi (I think). Either follow that river or continue direct to Perimetral Norte (road).

I thought I might manage two miles a day; half a dozen miles a day perhaps while I had the strength. The true distance to the road would be double my estimate, avoiding gullies and cliffs. It would be triple this if I caught a fever.

If I caught malaria I might as well sit down and wait for a jaguar.

The evening clouds were painted a crimson red from the dying sun, which was bleeding, as if torn by the trees on its way down. The dusk gnats were already flitting in my hair. I closed my eyes tight, and once again it was a winter's day. There I was, standing on the soft turf of an English lawn. My hands were dug into the pockets of my dufflecoat. The city-stained red bricks of the Royal Geographical Society stood behind and 'Jungle Eddie' McGee was squatting at my feet. He had his black polished boots on. And there was the snowflake which still had not melted on his toe. My ears were numb from the cold wind.

And if you remember only one thing today, it must be this: your will to survive counts more than anything else – OK? His precise military tone was so positive and confident.

Now on to building the shelter.

If you watch carefully now, you'll never be without a home. It'll be good enough not only for the tropical rains, but for winter snow as well. He was going to make it from leaves. *Leaves?* Yes, leaves; no branches, no tarpaulins.

I had forgotten the jungle; I was at 1 Kensington Gore, London SW7. I didn't know anything about my capsize, or that I had lost even my last friend. I had not set eyes on Mendez, the frog-faced *garimpeiro*, or any of my Indians – the enchantress Yimshi with her sharp teeth and breath smelling of honey. That was all to come. Now I was watching a man drawing a long thread of fishing line from his loose green canvas smock. He swept up leaves in handfuls from around his feet and stitched them one at a time on to that line. He laid the string of leaves across a frame of twigs and began another. An instant later – who would have believed it? – in front of us on the grass, he had pitched a tent of leaves. They shone the colour of brass in the low sun. A muffled voice came from inside the shelter. *'Much easier in the jungle!'* it said.

I wrote in my notebook:

6.30 p.m. Almost dark. I have caught no fish. I made a makeshift camp. Eddie McGee would burst into fits of laughter over it. I have decided to set out tomorrow on a north-east bearing, to get as much distance behind me as possible, before I am weak with hunger and disease. The prospect of what is ahead is ghastly.

The night was hot. My scalp was prickly with sweat, and I lay wide awake on the ground listening to the sawing and munching of insects for hours. The damp, rotting odour was of death and decay. I rolled about in my tent sponging up cold water from the flannel-like leaf mould. If it wasn't the ants trekking across my chest, it was mosquitoes circling above my eyes, or centipedes burying into the small of my back.

In a sleepy, tortuous way, my brain shuffled through what I must do the next day. I'd list down on paper every item I had salvaged. *Everything has its use in survival,* said Eddie McGee. I'd smear tobacco over my skin as a mosquito repellent. And I'd use the dollar notes I had hidden in my waist belt by making a shelter out of them. They were more flexible than leaves and didn't wither. I tried to make myself laugh by picturing what Mendez's fat face would look like if he saw me sheltering under all that cash.

The chill of dawn was already lifting when I woke. The leaves of my shelter had shrivelled over and hung like walnuts. Others were stuck fast to my face like leeches. But that morning, in the dewy dampness, I was stronger. I wanted to prove to Pablo that this wasn't an eternal prison.

I disentangled the knots of fishing line, slung my rucksack over my shoulder, took hold of my machete in my right hand, placed the compass in the palm of my left, and marched off in a north-easterly direction, counting every single pace.

1 . . . 2 . . . 3 . . . 4 . . . .

– 17 –

Armed neutrality

1st July. I have walked and walked and walked all day. Ate half a packet of dextrose tablets. This will be my ration each day (= 24 days' ration). Had a shock when I opened the packet. The tablets were all mottled: white/artificial raspberry. Make the water taste foul. Don't seem to offer much energy. The first of my four packets of soup – 'Onion' – is on the boil now. I can scarcely wait. I licked the packet out for its salt.

Dinner.

Watching it boil I try to think of the Indians who have always shared meals with me. But I can't picture them. I have not been able to, since the capsize. I will fight on without them. Such a betraal.

2nd July. a.m. Have a slight fever. Don't think it's malaria, but must wait and see if it gets worse. My rule is to move camp every day, whatever my health. I must keep going, keep putting a good distance behind me. Continuing on a north-east bearing. It is

simplest. I am still convinced that my memory of the maps is good.
Approx. 10 miles done *total*. Eddie McGee would be impressed. I
count each one of my paces. Every single step in a north-easterly
direction, through the bars of vines, leaf plates, snaking roots. I
notch every hundred paces up on a stick. The numbers tick
through my mind. My head works like a clock, measuring time. I
tick along. 97 . . . 98 . . . 99 . . . 100 . . . 1 . . . 2 . . . 3 . . . .

6 p.m. Fever worse. Chances of malaria also worse. Don't feel
like eating – lucky I haven't any food! Did approx. 1 mile today. 65
approx. to do. Slept 4–5 hours. Made myself sit in a small cool
stream, forcing myself to submerge in the water every hour. My
skin tingles in the water unbearably, but I'm better after.

3rd July. 9.45 a.m. Fever about the same. I have only just got up.
Cold damp ground at night must be making it worse. However
deep I make my leaf bed, I can always feel the roots grinding into
my back. My skin is softening with the wet air. Trying to think of
ways of making a hammock. 1 . . . 2 . . . 3 . . . 4 . . . . At least the
continual pace-counting blocks out one thought: how long to go – a
month or two more of this darkness?

4 p.m. Half a mile done and with considerable effort. Going to
'bed'.

4th July. 9.30 a.m. Feel better, but fever still could be malaria.
That disease haunts people like this. It hangs over you, coming
and going in spells as it pleases. Since the capsize I have eaten only
the soup, glucose tablets (six a day!), a handful of berries, the pith
of a palm (you peel back the bark like a banana skin), and a few fat
roots. I have some medicinal barks and andiroba nuts, which Pim

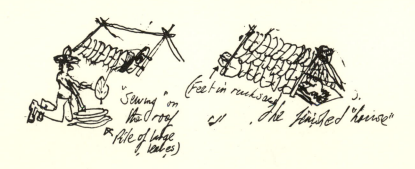

taught me to find. Saving those till I'm on my last legs. Alone and vulnerable.

p.m. Slight fever. Feel *very* weak. ½ mile done.

5th July. 8 a.m. Feel: what was all the fuss about?

5 p.m. Depressed. Keep making mistakes. One day I'm going to stumble into a wasps' nest, and that will be the end. The 'accident' happened on 30th June. So I have been going five days. Feels like a month. 14 miles done of approx. 75 (?) total, i.e. only a fifth the way. The thought is unbearable – it is such an effort to do just two miles in an exact straight bearing (NE). My pen looks as if it's giving up the struggle. Why don't I? I think I have a month to go at this rate. Can you imagine how enthralling that thought is? I must do more miles, fever or not, each day.

The worst thing is not the gloom, the reeking moss, the ants in my eyes at night, monkeys taunting me, chucking sticks down, it is noise: the scraping and whistling of all the insects. I cannot escape from it. It's as if I've got earwigs in my ears.

Worse are the memories churning in my head. It is a battle between the weaker and stronger sides of my will. The stronger urges me on with sarcasm, 'A fool, a fool, I met a fool in the forest.' The weaker side tells me to give up this struggle: 'Out of the wood do not desire to go.' I need something to let my mind feed on. To keep my sanity, I'm going to concentrate on building a castle in my mind. The strongest, most splendid castle the world has seen.

Later. The other pen has given up. I have shaved today for the first time since the accident. It gave me a sense of triumph, that I was on top of things. I took one razor blade, and strapped it with fishing line to a strong thin twig (the sort Maipuri's boy Ak-ak lashed me with that day I was bathing, as 'a joke'). It also makes an effective knife, and a better one than the survival knife in my leg sheaf. Who the hell designed it? It was meant for crashed aircraft pilots: a survival tool. Humph! I wonder how many poor pilots survive?

I designed the castle today; drew up the plans. I'm going to create something wonderful. It will have a moat with crocodiles, a drawbridge, portcullis, walls as thick as whole houses. And arrow slits, of course. Hopefully a damsel in distress in one of the towers, waiting to be rescued!

Sometimes, crouching around my camp fire, drying the fungi and slime off my skin in the sparks, I wonder if I should hang around, make a bow and arrow as Tautau taught me. Or snares, traps and spears. But: 'No one escapes without catching malaria,' the goldminer said. I'm not trying to make this forest a home. I need to get out! (And before I catch a disease or am too weak to think clearly. But let's face it. Really it's just a matter of time.)

The seven glucose tablets a day are almost worse than nothing. I have promised myself to stop and catch some fish at the next decent stream, however long it takes. I have the armadillo tail, the monkey paw and Pablo's jaguar tail. I keep them but don't know why.

6th July. 5 p.m. Crossed a 'decent stream'. Lost two (medium) hooks and didn't catch a thing. I imagine my stomach looks like a prune, shrunken, withered and black. That's what it feels like. I laid the foundation stone of the castle today. Then started laying the bricks one by one with each step I took. Heavy granite boulders from Aberdeen. I do 1700 paces in each mile. Did five miles. That's 8500 bricks. 97 . . . 98 . . . 99 . . . 100 . . . 1 . . . 2 . . . .

When I try to picture home, all I see are the postcards I brought with me to distribute as gifts. I still have a couple: the Houses of Parliament and Piccadilly Circus. Look at Big Ben. If only I was there! But how does the clock strike? Ah, yes, I remember it from the BBC World Service. Fritz made me listen to it on his stupid immaculate German transistor – 'Best in ze whole vide vorld.' Sometimes during the day as I walk, I think of him, and look to him for strength, his long gangly strides, just like mine. I look to him for strength, yet *he told me he could teach me nothing more*.

I should be well over the Iratapuru ridge by now. But it is still just exhausting up and down. The hills were only 300m. Must be over that height now.

7th July. 6 p.m. 4½ miles done. Camped by stream with a surface like green glass. Badly stung by wasps today. Bumped into a small nest suspended from a palm, and they tipped out and poured over me like treacle. The wasps are only small yellow/orange things, but painful enough, and I walk like a hunchback – like Yakka-yakka with bee stings. Brazil-nut oil would be a balm. I have none.

Today, thought I had hit a human path. Certainly wasn't one (unless the human in question lives in a burrow, which is where it led). Toyed with catching whatever it was, then carried on. 1 . . . 2 . . . 3 . . . 4 . . . 5 . . . . Even at night I hear myself counting. 1 . . . 2 . . . 3 . . . 4 . . . . Through my dreams, as I kick away a prickly spider, or lie awake sweating. 2 . . . 3 . . . 4 . . . 5 . . . .

Sometimes it is just my mind. Sometimes I wake and find it is my wristwatch near my ear. Yes, the Timex is still ticking. The flimsy red watch that Fritz sneered at, the one that the *garimpeiros* offered 12 grams of gold for, is still ticking along as it always has done. My only companion.

Last night I dreamt I had accepted the can of baked beans of the missionary and sucked an icecube from his fridge.

8th July. 6.00 p.m. Fruit, fruit, fruit! Plenty of it. Marajá berries. I'm camping by a small icy water brook in the mosquito clouds, mashing up those juicy, purple berries, each one like a grape. My neck must be crimson from the wasp bites of yesterday, but for the first time my stomach is full and bloated.

Why did Tautau tell me to bring that dog along with me? Why? Everything might have been fine. I was so near to success. Haven't I got the right to feel angry? Maybe the dog lived. Maybe it is trotting downriver to Mendez, and will live happily ever after.

I will take enough berries for many days. 4½ miles done today.

9th July. My stomach cannot take the diet. The stronger half of me shouts in my ear: 'Don't be so damn soft!' But have crippling stomach pains. These helped by chewing charcoal from my camp fire, an Eddie McGee and SAS trick. He would be pleased with me, and I can see him now, grinning. 2½ miles completed today, 35 miles total. Must be almost half-way, but my pace is slower today. *Poco a poco* I will get there, Peña said. But now I know *poco a poco* I am packing up.

10th July. 5.00 p.m. Stomach pains continuing as I walk. Today I felt weak and light headed. Is it alcohol in the marajá berries, or am I fading away through lack of sugar in my blood? Today I came across a splash of daylight on the forest floor. Yes, it's that rare. A capybara had spotted it as well, and was dozing on some bark chippings. I stalked it clumsily and wanted to cry when it bolted off into the forest. The jungle is my larder. I see it as an Indian does now. Not for its majesty, or beauty, but for its food. Strange that it has taken deprivation by force to bring me close to them spiritually. And though I am not well enough to think clearly, I sense the spirits they talked of. Whatever God is, he is here, and he is not the person that Jorge, and the other Godmen, are worshipping.

Sometimes, even under this hardship, I have moments of utter inner peace. With no company or possessions I am close to God. The Indians had a better idea all along! God is not manlike. He is everything: the stones, the water, the brazil nuts, the parrots. If you have to picture him as a human, see him as a woman. Maternal. God is Mother Nature.

Collected some andiroba nuts, much like brazil nuts, crunched them for my stomach ache, just as Tautau showed me.

3 miles done. 38 total. No water near camp today and passed only two (pathetic) streams. You should see the castle now. The walls are soaring up! The moat is being dug. I'm almost up to the battlements. Stone by stone it's coming along. 2 . . . 3 . . . 4 . . . 5 . . . .

11th July. Noon. Not at all well. Slept in. Just cannot make myself move camp. I've therefore broken a resolution. I know I will regret the weakness. It just cannot be helped. It is stupid to try and move. Slight fever. Headache. Thoroughly tired. Just unwell. *Can you imagine what it feels like to be slowly winding down like this? To know you are petering out?* My life seems like the flame of a candle. The wind is growing stronger. Now I am flickering. Soon I'm going to be snuffed out. I cannot see my castle, or hear the scrape of the bricks slotting into place today. The forest is silent. Every now and again in that deep silence I hear the dull wine of bluebottle flies – 'zzzzzzzzzz' – droning in my ears. They are swarming in the trees. The leaves are heavy with them. If only I could run away from the flies. To stop them jumping over my face I have to bury my face in the earth. No miles done.

Made tea from *quina-quina* bark to lessen the fever. Took two aspirin. Feel so weak.

12th July. 6.30. Help in the form of Cashoe! He's with me again. Is it a dream? No, he really is warm in my arms.

Last night, I knew I was being tracked by an animal. I thought I was going to come face to face with a jaguar, and with only a machete. Never mind Maipuri's pig! A jaguar, with claws and teeth! In the darkness, I slid from my shelter, crouched in its entrance with my boots covering my face and fired off two of my three explosive flares into the bushes. Pow! Pow! I blasted away the bush ahead of me. The air clouded with a grey sulphur. The forest burned yellow. Then silence, and nothing but jabbering monkeys, which were grabbing at branches and rolling through the branch limbs, making a run for it.

I stoked the fire, waited five minutes, and then heard a whimper. An emaciated Cashoe, with his white tail high but his ribs jutting out so far they cast shadows in the fire-glow. Twelve days after the capsize he has found me. How? I don't know.

He ate a little of the cooked marajá, but not much. I think he thinks I have more decent food. His poor condition makes me feel strong. But 'tomorrow and tomorrow and tomorrow' I creep on with my petty pace. Will I be stronger with the dog? He knows the jungle like an Indian.

Once, Pim told me *I* did. 'I have learnt more since.'

5 p.m. I'm up and about again, back in the race. Did three miles. Cashoe following. Clearly he isn't the world's greatest hunting dog, to my disappointment. He is slow and easily exhausted. I refuse to wait for him. 'Be bloody bold and resolute.' The stronger half of me is in the ascendant, I almost march through the greenery now, 1 . . . 2 . . . 3 . . . 4 . . . whisking my boots through the ground creepers, kicking off those that try and hold me back, tinging my machete through the lianas, carving the jungle up. For the first time I'm convinced I'm coming out of the

hill range. But today I had not a dribble of water since this morning's camp. Yet I'm sweating gallons of it. I suck pebbles to keep saliva in my mouth. I lick my arms for salt. I no longer wash my exposed skin. I cannot afford to wipe off the stinking tobacco. I have to fend off those mosquitoes somehow. That, and sleeping in the woodsmoke, is the only way.

So my shirt and trousers are greasy and squidge against my skin because of the algae, but with the dog to chat to I am happier than ever. We both hope for water tomorrow.

Cashoe, as I write this, looks into my eyes and pleads with me for water. He pleads with the same face as the convicts by the roadside in El Callao, wagging their tongues in the dust of my car, as I passed. I know now how they suffered, and wish I had stopped for them.

13th July. My tongue swelled up in the night, and almost choked me. But later the rain came in torrents, and I laid my head out from my shelter and let it splash in my eyes. Then I lapped it up from puddles like Cashoe.

5 p.m. Only about two miles done. Wallowed in the forest stream. That water tasted so sweet. Cashoe drank furiously. But he can't keep up. He is dying. I'm sure of that now. He came to me as a last hope. The stronger half of me, still strong, whispered in my ear, 'Of course he's a walking refrigerator.' A thought I cannot dismiss. The meat on him could make all the difference. . . . If I spend a while smoking it on the fire, I could have perhaps four days' good supply. I have had no decent protein for two weeks. I am wasting away. I cooked up my last packeted soup, I did not share it. I must be firm about this. Have I the right to do this? Is it

so inhumane? I'm not going to weaken my resolve. We would both die. He caused the whole mess. Yet I feel a traitor writing this.

Did only two miles again. Yes, if things don't get dramatically better, he is for the chop. Wonder if he is waiting for me to die? He looks at me, and his look is so hurtful. I saved him from agony once – saved his life – now he looks to me for further help. I'm trying not to become a friend again. It will only make it harder. 43 miles done total.

14th July. 5.30 p.m. Continuing without deviation on a NE bearing. I'm sure this obstinacy will pay off. My rhythm is strong. 1 . . . 2 . . . 3 . . . 4 . . . . I can last two hundred paces now, before notching them up on my stick. And the notches are not gashes any more, they are neat nicks. The castle is coming along well. The moat complete, crocodiles installed, and underfed so as to appreciate trespassers. The arrow slits are there; the battlements. I am working on the tower for the damsel in distress. I think I will choose a girl like Yimshi with long straight Indian hair, as thick as thread; but a girl less like a jaguar – she wouldn't surrender herself to imprisonment anyway – though with the same satiny skin. Maybe Zorola of the Orinoco delta, with the long nimble fingers. I wonder if she has been married off yet? 1 . . . 2 . . . 3 . . . .

Today I came across a clearing. Daylight! The sun. A burning sphere, instead of putrid stuffy air. It is so good to feel my clothes baking, the water percolating away in steam. To smell the jungle burning to a frazzle, the leaves suffering under the sun's rays.

This is a small patch of neck-high grassland only the size of a tree crown. I can't think why it's here. Not man-made. No tree stumps, burnt-out settlements, or scruffy man-spoilt vegetation. The greatest excitement is that there are locusts here. Big juicy fat things. Tomorrow I may have the strength to go after them.

Four miles done, and for long stretches Cashoe was out of sight. He still manages to smell me out, and now limps in pursuit of the locusts.

15th July. 6.00. The locusts are massive and slow. Forefinger length, vivid green jobs, with red/orange-tinged bellies. They flash as bright as beetroot when they fly, and edge round the other side of branches when you approach. Clobbered 15 with a stick. Netted 16 more with my shirt. I packed mud on my shoulders the way that Narru and Camahu showed me that day we spent hunting in the grey mud delta. But my back is still cracking open, red and blistered with the sun. The oil of my andiroba nuts should help smooth them. This evening I fried the last of the locusts on a stick. For the first time I shared food with Cashoe. I gave him the three biggest ones. I value his company so much. Why didn't I listen to the Sicilian in El Callao? Why did I ever come through the gold zone? I think it couldn't have been avoided. That is my comfort, but I broke my promise.

I ought to have a celebration. 50 miles done! Three today. I'm in better-than-should-be-for-circumstances spirits. But why, oh why, didn't I hang around the clearing? I could have scrounged

some more food. Now it's back in the darkness, with the cobwebs in my eyes and skin raw with fungi. 1 . . . 2 . . . 3 . . . 4 . . . .

16th July. 5.00 p.m. The dog seems to have picked up in spirits. I have a sneaking feeling he found some food today. Maybe a rat. I feel weak again. My lips are puffed out and chafed. They feel like tyre treads.

My cheeks have been slashed with a poisonous spiky palm. The dog licked the cuts clean. The only water nearby was black and stagnant. It smelt of tarmac. I filtered it with a trouser pocket, and boiled it. I shared some boiled palm stems with the dog. We are companions again. I share my food with him nowadays. Having him here is uplifting. This jungle is his home. He knows the ropes.

I tapped a banana tree for water today, and remembered Fritz doing the same. Chico, *his* dog, was a source of strength to him, as Cashoe is to me. But Cashoe as well reminds me of the times when I was with the Indians. In those days I could live off the jungle. *That* is why having him here makes me feel stronger.

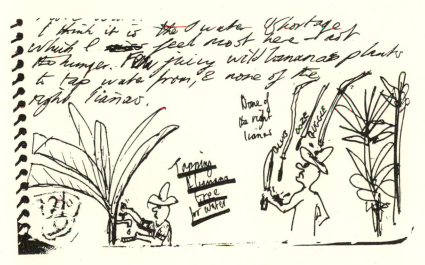

17th July. 5 p.m. Did three miles (58 total). Something sad: today I resorted to another non-Indian survival trick: the edibility test. I feel I am letting the Indians down.

To test if a root was poisonous, I mashed a piece up, stuck out my tongue, plonked a piece on it. Waited ten minutes. No acid taste and it wasn't dissolving away on my tongue, so I gulped a speck down. Waited half an hour, no ill effects, so took a bit more. Then more. . . . Eventually gobbled down the whole lot. I wonder how many explorers have 'kicked the bucket' through losing patience. Later I was trying mashed termite grubs. I've also eaten bigger white grubs which look like baby's fingers. I eat them in the Indian manner, plucking off the heads first, frying them if I can be bothered. I found 11 today peeling back bark of trees.

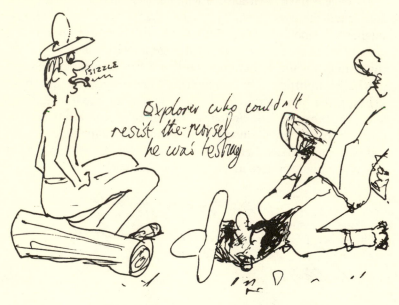

Explorer who couldn't resist the morsel he was testing

I'm losing interest in the struggle. I must keep the fight up, even if it's only to raise the flag of the castle, on its completion day. The weaker side of me is taking over. I am hardly stirred by the thought: 'To die, and go we know not where.' Such words don't even scare me any more.

18th July. 4.30 p.m. Gathered up fifty orange nuts – can't think of their name, but Pim and Yepe used to say they were good. Cast away the nuts, and kept the orange sticky fruit coating. Saving a quarter as a reward for when I've made my jungle tent.

The dog is still following. Now he whimpers if he falls far behind. What am I to do? Brutal as it might be I almost ignore him. He must speed up. Otherwise chance his luck. Did three and a half miles. That's about what non-Indians do when they are fresh. I have done 61½ miles. Can I congratulate myself? No, because the

Indians would have laughed at that. Some days the jungle is like beechwood, crinkly metallic leaves underfoot, empty spaces, like a park. Other days it is knotted and tangled like an old spider's web, gathering dust.

19th July. Violently sick. Do I eat the rest of the orange fruit or not? Stomach ache and dysentery as normal. My stomach feels explosive. I'm chewing a charcoal stick as I write. The grit of the carbon on my teeth is good. My skin is red, and bleeds where the layers have been sponged away by the wetness. I am working on the interior of the castle, filling rooms with four-poster beds, chambermaids and bedpans, and hanging tapestries in the corridors to warm the narrow stone passages. The berries don't affect Cashoe. He can have the lot for all I care.

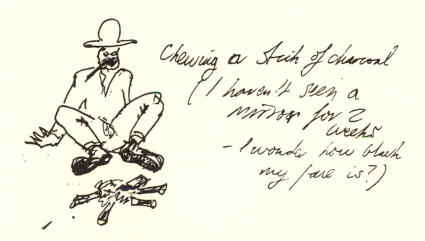

Chewing a stick of charcoal
(I haven't seen a
mirror for 2
weeks
– I wonder how black
my face is?)

20th July. 6 p.m. 3 miles, after my greatest of struggles of will. Just wanted to carry on lying in my tent this morning. Just a bit longer than usual. Cashoe came and licked my face till it was dripping. I think he thought I had died. I really would have just lain there and lain there. I almost had given up the struggle. His continual nagging forced me to my feet. That was 11.30 a.m. Together, we managed those three miles. Some of the time as we walked I was dizzy. My eyeballs sank to the back of the sockets – they felt right up against my brain. The trees looked black. The rivers the colour of Coca-cola. But the companionship of the dog made the walk beautiful at moments and the rain, when it came in the afternoon,

came in crystalline pearly drops. I wanted to tell someone how beautiful it was.

Cashoe is becoming less and less doggy, and more and more human. It makes the decision about what to do with him harder. I haven't even reached the Cupixi river yet and I have done 64½ miles. It makes no sense. How I long to see that river and its fish. Perhaps I am almost there. I don't want to have to do it, Cashoe.

21st July. 4.30 p.m. Suddenly I'm struck down by bad fever. Did 3 miles. Made camp. Found two different edible fruit palms. Ate the fruit raw. I had no stream to cool in. Running water would make all the difference. Going to sleep. The dog is somewhere around. Gave him a munch of my berries, but don't think my stomach can take any more.

6.30 p.m. Slept almost two hours. Struggled awake. Fever better in cool of the evening. Boiling up the *quina-quina* bark I've been saving. If it's malaria, a sip of that tea should give it something to think about.

Cashoe has eaten all the berries. I shouted at him: '*Go! Go* while you have the chance. If you want to live, leave!' He's cowering in the distance behind some palms. 'Take a chance and go. Please!' I half want him as company, but deep down I know I need that meat as well.

22nd July. 8.00 a.m. Fever better, but it is the dewy coolness of dawn now and so would be. Going to move on to water. Chewing raw palm fruit. I have no inclination to keep writing this diary. I cannot see a use for it. I hardly have enough energy to move the pen.

5 p.m. Did 1 mile. With great effort. Shivering wildly. I really feel like I've had it. Please, God, let there be a road, just ahead. But why am I praying? Tautau said that God held no use for prayer. That the world is neutral, and man no more important than a lizard. If I could conjure spirits, like a witchdoctor, perhaps then I could gain external strength.

Alone for three weeks I know that this must be close to the truth. No, I won't pray. I write that; yet I know that if I don't get out of here I will be eaten up by one of the other animals. I can hear them competing around me. An ocelot. The shriek of a rat in the talons of an owl. Today I almost trod on a snake: a brown ropy creature. Who will God let live? Him or me? The answer is it is up to *us*. I can see why the forest people believe that now. 'The jungle is neutral.' At least where no sorcerer has been at play. So I won't pray.

My feet are rotting. My toes are cold and white. They cannot feel the forest floor.

I'm brewing up bark for fever, after crushing it with my knife, but Cashoe is whimpering – I suppose he wants food. Earlier he was chewing a bone – a bird's, as it was hollow.

Later. My *quina-quina* tea is ready. So the *garimpeiro* was right, no one does escape without malaria. My palms are sweaty, heavily creased and bright yellow, like French golden delicious apples. Medicine first, then sleep. I must keep dunking myself in the stream.

23rd July. 10 a.m. The fever is bad. If only I could have ventilation. The jungle isn't like a cathedral, as some romantic said, it is like a stuffy room with everything in it – chairs, desks, etc. – sodden. All windows closed.

'The jungle will be your glory, the jungle will be your downfall.' The weaker side of me is winning.

Found some snails in the stream, while cooling off. Will boil them. There are 25 of them, but only an inch long and looking like this:

Can hardly think. Has taken me half an hour to write today's passage. I'm not able to walk far. Just ten paces down to the stream. Shivering. Getting out of tent major effort. Again the dog roused me – just before 10 a.m. So I lay there for *15 hours* (since six o'clock yesterday). Taken two aspirin. I NEED VITAMINS AND PROTEIN.

4 p.m. Fever same or worse. It is so long since I have felt well that I find it hard to tell what condition my body is in.

Ate the snails. Gave half-dozen to dog. Also a mash of palm stems. Sometimes I want to use him as a taster, to sift out the poisonous foods. But this I haven't stooped to.

I want only to close my eyes, but I've got to collect firewood. It is damp. I need medicine.

24th July. 11'ish a.m. Cashoe has eaten the last of my glucose tablets. I am racked by fever. Squalid dysentery. Last night dreamt of Zorola. Stumbled across her crying alone in the forest where she was being kept away from me. We kissed each other in secret. She mopped our tears with her thick coal-black hair. Then I walked off into the forest. If, as Tautau said, dreams are spirits returned to earth, why can't they help me?

I cannot make a fire. I hoped Tautau would come and show how you do it when the wood is wringing wet. I half waited for him. No one came. Eddie McGee said you can use the tree bark. Can't remember what else.

Keep bathing, but just feel like curling up and dropping into a long delicious sleep. Found a large white grub in a fallen tree. Ate it alive, still wriggling.

I just cannot make that fire I need. Perhaps later.

Tautau, Yepe, Pim, where are you?

4.00 p.m. I cannot last with much more of this. My castle is crumbling away, brick by brick. Being laid to siege by my weakness. Perhaps the fever will just go away. But I know deep inside that unless someone comes for me or I move now and fight, I am *finished*. A painful word to write.

Pull yourself together. JUMP INTO THAT STREAM. Only one thing remains for me to write today. I am resolved. Fritz pulled himself out of a fever by killing a deer which 'miraculously' appeared for him. He ate the liver and kidneys. Parts 'viz all ze gootness unt vitamins'. I have been presented with an animal also. He is scratching at a burrow now. I will make a fire if I can. It doesn't matter too much.

I don't feel squeamish.

25th July. 8.00 a.m. Yesterday I killed my companion. Sharp blow with the machete butt to the back of skull. Then slit the throat; just as I did to the Wai-wai pig.

I waited till he wasn't looking. Afterwards, all bloody. I *did* make the fire. My adrenalin carried me through. Ate both kidneys and liver. Then bound body up again with fishing line and palm leaves around his belly. I want to be away before the vultures arrive.

Still keep bathing, the stream is just bath-sized. Mosquitoes ghastly because I'm clean. Flies play over Cashoe's body. I feel like a murderer. How silent it is without him.

3.00. First vulture has turned up. It is coughing and breathless for the feast. There is so much meat. And it will be fresh for only four days.

6.00. I stoked up the fire and smoked the legs as well as I could. Forced a broth of the meat down, though I had no hunger.

26th July. 10 a.m. All night I tossed and turned with the sound of scavengers. Heard the patter and breathing of predators around the camp. Blasted them away once with a distress flare, my last. Waited all night with my machete in my hands, in case the smell drew jaguars near. The carcass was stuffed up a tree, and protected from the vultures with prickly palms. That didn't stop them squabbling over it. This morning I found his skin stripped and his eyes pecked out. I'm marginally stronger than yesterday. I'm going to have another broth from the bones of the dog, and taking

on with me flesh for fishing bait and the remaining ribs for this
evening's meal. I buried his heart in a deep pit. Why should the
vultures have it?

5.45 p.m. 5 hellish miles. Lonely, feverish, and have all the
usual stomach problems. To be expected after the dogmeat.

But for the moment the castle is *no longer tumbling down.*

I plunge my hat into streams and let water dribble down from
my hair when I put it on. My only luxury. Walked naked in the
forest but for my boots all those five miles, to let my skin breathe.
Now I have no company my mind flits away on the slightest
impulse. Today Pim stole my clothes again. He was testing me,
seeing if I would last long or not. Seeing if I was as good as an
Indian. And the leaves were drawing blood like razor blades today,
just as they did the other time when I was tracking him down with
Cashoe. This time I never found Pim.

Now I am by my fire. The wood is wet, and smoke blue and
thick. I have to put my head in it to drive parasites from my hair.
Then I will put my feet in the smoke to do the same. I am alone.
Very tired. Tomorrow I must make a giant push.

27th July. 5.30 p.m. The great breakthrough. Today I restored the castle. The crocodiles were back in the moat, snapping away, the tapestries are back on the walls. The tower for the maiden is finished. The stronger part of me is fighting back. Did 7 miles (79½ total) and camping by a river. Can only be *the* river. The Cupixi. A silver band of water as smooth as a mirror. My liver aches, it doubles me up, but my feet are in the water, and I am in gentle evening sunlight. A milky haze kisses the trees on the far bank, and I must be nearly out.

Have eaten all but two front limbs of Cashoe.

The vultures were hopping after me as I stumbled along. They speeded me up. I almost sprinted. They looked like undertakers in their heavy black coats. I despise their hissings and wheezings.

28th July. 7.30 a.m. Have caught three piranha (in only 25 minutes), with the last of Cashoe. Spent all but a minute of that time putting on new hooks. Sacrificed all but a couple. They bit straight through the line, without even jerking it.

29th July. 6.00 p.m. My calculations say I have done 85 miles total. What has gone wrong? Where is the road? Where is daylight? I'm still on a north-east bearing, and fought oh so hard today. Over six miles. Six miles through trees with snaky creepers up their trunks and bristly lianas.

I kept going only because the others – all my friends – were chanting for me. Calling me onward. Is it really true that they aren't here? The Italian brothers of the Orinoco, with their Warao Indians; the chief with pigtails tied with green polythene, Narru,

Camahu, Zorola. The Sicilian with his Winchester rifle, the *padre* of El Dorado, Peña: 'You will make it *poco a poco*. Don't look back and you will find your pot of gold on the horizon.' Even Fritz barking at me to keep walking. Even Jorge the missionary, Pablo with his silver spurs clinking just a few steps behind. Maipuri, Tautau. Ak-ak skipping, holding my left hand. Yimshi tugging me with the other. And Haimarha who still couldn't tell his left from his right. Toeleu, Yepe, Pim, and Cashoe. They were all walking with me.

But now the day is ending, and here I am still in the jungle. I have one more dried piranha for today. I am not moving.

I cannot write more. I have a bad fever.

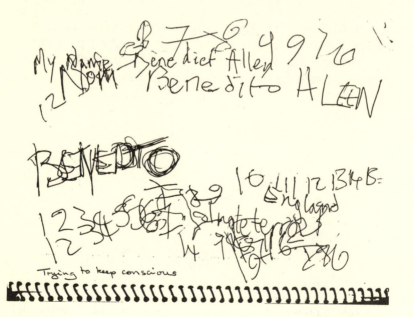

30th July. Didn't move camp today. This is my second night here. Sometimes I just sit and swat mosquitoes for hours on end. Today, put soldiers in the battlements of the castle, and poor Zorola in the tower.

What else is there to do? The castle seems complete. No, it can't be. I must keep my mind working on it. Keep strengthening it. I know once I give up on it, it will all come to pieces. Every one of those Aberdeen granite stones fall out of place. Tomorrow I must make another big push. All my strength has gone. Now I have only the strength of my friends who keep begging me not to let them down.

– 18 –

A good Indian

I walked like clockwork, tick-tocking along in the way I had become accustomed to: 5 . . . 6 . . . 7 . . . 8 . . . 9 . . . . It was no use trying to keep my mind on the jungle any more. Being able to escape from the trees in my thoughts was what kept me alive. Tomorrow I would have been going a month. My loneliness was mixed with confusion. What had gone wrong? Why had I not reached the outside world yet?

It just didn't make sense. Too weak even to cry, I walked on and let my thoughts gently lift out of the forest and drift away.

Vy are you not valking faster zan zis? It was Fritz's voice. *Get your lousy bum movings. You are ass lazy ass von off zose dirty Indians. Unt ze Indians, zey are no better zan ze animals.*

Joshua said, *Dat's true, man. Dem Injuns is like animals. I seen dem wid my own eyes. Dem's got monkey tails. Dem's got skin as white as bone.*

What about Louco Benedito? Maipuri's voice said. *He got skin more white than Wai-wai. But he as good as Wai-wai. Mmmmmmmmmm. Where you going, Louco Benedito? Why you not walking dis way, back to decent Wai-wai forest?*

'Can you tell me the way out of here, someone?'

The jungle is an eternal prison.

'Pablo! Where did you come from?'

Thought I'd come and see how you were getting along. You want a way out of the jungle?

'Yes. You know I do. It isn't an eternal prison, is it? I've been walking for a month, you know. But I've kept your jaguar's tail. And the monkey's paw, and armadillo tail. They helped me along, I think. Does that please you?'

Louco Benedito, said Maipuri. He was walking beside me. *If you want leave jungle, you marry Yimshi first.*

'Yimshi? Is she here as well?'

We are all here, said Pablo. *We've all come to see you off.*

'But where am I going? That's what I want to know.'

So do we, a chorus said. *So do we.* I looked and saw dozens of familiar faces, marching by my side. Someone muttered that he thought I was going to the Creator.

He not die. He my son, said Tautau. I searched for him in the crowd, but Yimshi was in the way.

'Yimshi, I haven't seen you for ages. Did Maipuri treat you badly after I left without accepting you that night? You are quite a jaguar, you know.'

And you are. . . .

'What am I?'

You are . . . Mad White Giant. Mad White Giant. Mad White Giant. Mad White Giant.

'What's going on? I'm feeling weak. Why aren't any of you helping me?'

We want see if you are good Indian.

'Pim! You are here as well!'

Why you wearing clothes?

'Did you really betray me that night? Did you and Yepe really not care if Mendez and Edwardio killed me? My God! Those two creeps aren't here, are they?'

No. Just your friends, said Pablo. *And I've come to see if the jungle really is an eternal prison, prison, prison.*

And I come see if jungle is your home, Mad White Benedito Giant. That was Tautau, but his image was a blur, and his voice fading.

'Why aren't any of you lot helping me? You all helped me in the past. Please, Tautau, you'll help, won't you? I'm beginning to feel dizzy.'

Ze jungle is your glory unt grave. Is funny, ja? Glory unt grave!

We want to see if you survive, Louco Giant Benedito.

I want to see if you giant all over, whispered Yimshi.

Maybe you not strong enough to be good Indian, said Pim.

'Where are my clothes?' I said. But all my friends were running off into the trees shrieking. 'Oi! Come back!'

I was alone again. I tried to track them, but there was no sign of bruised leaves or snapped twigs. No one had ever set foot here. I was on my knees, naked. But now in the Orinoco delta, on the mud flats. My skin was slashed by sea shells. I had a pelican tied around my waist with a cord of reed. Then the dizziness was too much for me.

5.00 p.m. Collapsed today at about 11.30. Just felt faint, and blood draining from my head. Blackness. Next I knew I was face down in the leaves.

Fever is very severe, though better now. I feel weak and have more difficulty in moving my pen than ever before. Did only 1½ miles. Dizzy again. The trees are all black above my head.

Later. Barely able to make a shelter. I will sleep. Ants everywhere. Hate them. Nasty orange almost invisible brutes that bite for no reason.

Later still. Putting the milky sap disinfectant of a tree, which Pablo told me about, on my cuts. Must rest. *I can hardly see straight.*

1st August. I've done it. Please don't take success away from me now. It would be too cruel. Dabbling in a brook this morning, my mind suddenly cleared. I saw a cut branch. Not a torn one, a ripped one, but a cut one. A beautiful, crisp, clean slice of a machete. And other cut branches are all around me. I want to remember them. Every one. And the purring of the mosquitoes, and the fragrance of the sprays of orchids which are clutching branches way up above. I want to remember the leaves shivering in the canopy breeze, and this little stream which woke me to it all.

Paths criss-cross around me. I will choose one leading northeast. I must have done it. . . . Success and a bed.

– 19 –

Daylight

Felled tree trunks were littered all the way along the track, but above their stumps the remaining forest canopy was as tightly shut as ever. The trees had closed ranks. Not a single rod of light shone through. But I half-skipped along, and giggled when I took a tumble over a stack of freshly cut branches.

Now the forest's stale larder reek was giving way to a dry earthy smell: that of a newly ploughed field. I stepped in the direction of the smell, to my right, knowing I had lost the path, but not caring. I was stopped by a thicket of grey and black bamboo shoots, laced together by a strangling creeper, and stretching way up above my hat. I slid my machete into my waist band, dropped to my knees, and cleaved the vegetation apart with my elbows. The creeper strings were sticky with sap as they broke.

The light, I had thought, would come all of a sudden. I would peel away a sheet of the creepers, and there I would be, standing in it, blinking, with my clothes already beginning to stiffen in the sun; and I would be laughing out loud.

But the light came at first in specks through the thicket, like stars in a clear night sky. The stars grew and grew, until they were touching each other. Then they coalesced into larger, irregular forms – triangles, diamonds and spheres – all just in front of my eyes in this dark thicket, as I pulled more and more of it away. The quality of the light was improving too, increasing in brilliance and purity each second. When it was the most stunning of whites, and the leaves and barks under my knees were crackling, not squelching, I knew the forest was behind me.

After the darkness, the light – too much of it; all this space; and everything so quiet; and dead.

I was on the verge of a cassava field. The spindly, shrubby plants looked meagre sitting there under the sun, bedded in an orange soil, which seemed to me as sterile as rock. Strangest of all, they were in orderly rows, ranks of them that continued right to the horizon, which was so low and even. On the horizon was a primitive square hut. The squareness of the hut seemed as odd as the straightness of the lines of cassava. It was all so unnatural, ridiculous after the ill discipline of the forest.

A person came out of the square hut; a man, with a back curved from too much field work. He stared at me. I stared at him. I scuffed and tripped through the cassava crop in his direction. My feet felt less heavy than for a long time, and for a second I managed a run. I slowed again; not out of tiredness, but because the man wasn't waiting with outstretched hands to welcome me back to the outside world. I'd somehow expected that he would. But no, he was just staring; more in horror than curiosity.

An arm's length away, I flipped off my hat and tried out a smile. He raised his eyebrows and his mouth fell wide open.

Along with my euphoria, my strength was going. I would fall soon. But I didn't want this man for support. He was regarding me as if I were an ogre. So instead I leant on the wooden palings of his hut wall.

I opened my mouth to speak, but the effort of explaining everything to this gaping farmer was going to be too much, and I looked away, down at my boots and the mud flaking off them as it dried. The selfish pride of the man! I thought. How could he leave me teetering like this on his doorstep?

A shaft of light flashed into my eyes from the glass face of my watch. The watch was still ticking: 10.30 a.m. My wrist was scarlet from where the watch strap had chafed it. Sheafs of translucent skin flapped loose like lace cuffs. I wondered what my face looked like.

The man confronting me must have been fifty years old. On his chin grew a rough grey bed of stubble, and he smelt of dry clay. I saw he had his hand out. I wondered just how long it had been there. I shook it, but the grip of this weak man was so tight on my twig fingers, I grimaced.

The man was going to speak. A word of warm welcome? He said, 'The *senhor* has been out walking a long way today?' My heart fell.

'Yes,' I managed slowly, 'a long way.'

'Will the *senhor* stop for a second to have a coffee?'

Good grief! I thought. Can't you see I'm at death's door? 'Yes, *senhor*. I would appreciate a coffee very much,' I said.

'You wait here, *senhor*. You sit and rest awhile.'

I was unconscious when he pottered back out of the hut, and the next thing I remember was lying in a hammock, gazing at the splinters of daylight that showed through the wooden tiles of the roof.

The man's name was José, and though I shared his rich coffee for three days, and he brewed me a dozen of his family herbal remedies, he never did ask where I had come from, or how I came to stagger into his field from the jungle that morning. As for myself, I had no desire to speak at all – conversation was something I had grown to be wary of, while alone – but I owed this man much, and so several times I tried to explain. José, however, was content to perch on a stool by my hammock-side, holding a warm cup of coffee ready to press to my lips. If I told him of the jungle and the Indians, he would listen out of politeness for a minute, then make an excuse and slip outside to his field with an axe or hoe. It was enough for him to know that I needed rest.

My skin was flayed, and hideously yellow, but his own was stretched as tight around his stomach as anyone's I'd seen. Starvation, it seemed, was normal on the jungle frontier land dished out by the government. After another day spent scratching in the field, José confided that he was just one of hundreds of thousands who knew what the government didn't. The jungle could not sustain a decent crop for more than a year or two. He was bitter about it. The government was crazy to send people here, he said. '*Louco.*'

I was happy to be alive, as I dozed in my hammock, but the happiness was mixed with uncertainty. I felt I didn't belong to this outside world to the extent that I used to. There was a feeling of loss, of bereavement. I had entered the forest where the road had faded, and had crawled out where the same road had been abandoned five years before by construction workers beginning on it from this end. Somewhere in the 700-mile gap in the road, I had left part of myself behind.

On the third day out of the forest, I was on my feet again. A yellow government jeep came up the track to José's plantation, where the road stopped. The four surveyors pondered awhile, frowned at the forest barrier, and explained that they were wondering whether it was worth starting work on the road project again, to open the forest right up.

I said that from what I'd seen of the forest, I wouldn't bother.

'Hah!' the men laughed. 'From what the *foreigner* has seen of the forest we shouldn't bother!' They said they appreciated the joke very much, and that as I was looking pretty rough they'd give me a lift back to wherever I'd come from. *I* laughed this time, far louder than the others had.

It took no time at all to pack. I had only to stoop for my belongings: a hat, jaguar's tail, monkey's paw, armadillo's tail, machete and little else. José saluted me, smiled fractionally and, as I was hauled aboard the jeep, bent down to carry on wrenching a cassava tuber from the soil.

I took up the journey again, just like that. I was on the road to Macapá, and the mouth of the Amazon, feeling over the moon. Though weak, I was strong enough to ride high on my seat, as we sped closer and closer to the river. But it wasn't the delta I was longing for any more; it was the stench of car exhaust fumes, the lick of new paint, the blare of transistors, and the smooth concrete walls. Quite suddenly they had become beautiful, after the jungle. Though I wasn't sure why, I was yearning for these things – just as Narru and Camahu had yearned for them, bright eyed and in their spanking new suits, only a few moons ago in the Orinoco delta, on the day my journey first began.

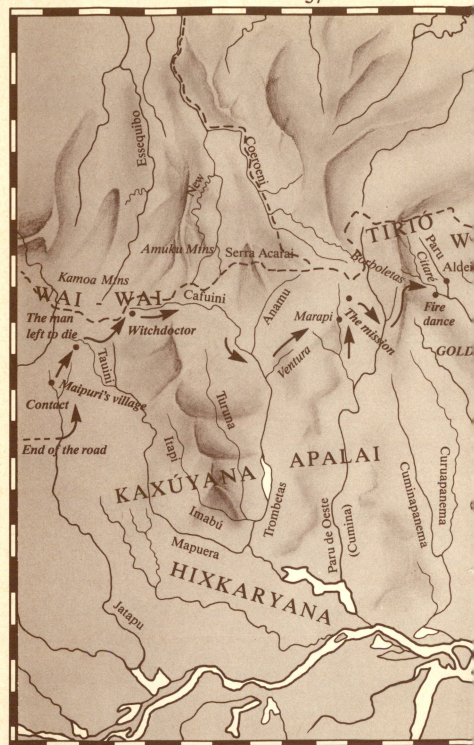

Essequibo

New

Coeroeni

TIRTÓ W

Paru

Citaré

Alde

Amuku Mtns   Serra Acarai

Botboletas

Kamoa Mtns

WAI - WAI   Cafuini

Anamu   *Marapi*   *The mission*   *Fire dance*

The man left to die   *Witchdoctor*

GOLD

Ventura

Tauini

Maipuri's village

Contact   Turuna

End of the road

Itapi

KAXÚYANA   APALAI

Trombetas

Paru de Oeste

(Cumina)

Cuminapanema

Curuapanema

Imabú

Mapuera

HIXKARYANA

Jatapu

The North-ea